全球核态势评估报告

Global Nuclear Posture Review:2014/2015

(2014/2015)

中国国际问题研究院军控与国际安全研究中心
The Centre of Arms Control and International Security Research China Institute of International Studies

时 事 出 版 社

图书在版编目（CIP）数据

全球核态势评估报告（2014/2015）/中国国际问题研究院军控与国际安全研究中心编．—北京：时事出版社，2015. 12

ISBN 978-7-80232-908-9

Ⅰ. ①全…　Ⅱ. ①中…　Ⅲ. ①核武器问题-研究报告-世界-2014~2015　Ⅳ. ①D815. 2

中国版本图书馆 CIP 数据核字（2015）第 259905 号

出 版 发 行：时事出版社
地　　址：北京市海淀区万寿寺甲 2 号
邮　　编：100081
发 行 热 线：（010）88547590　88547591
读者服务部：（010）88547595
传　　真：（010）88547592
电 子 邮 箱：shishichubanshe@ sina. com
网　　址：www. shishishe. com
印　　刷：北京市昌平百善印刷厂

开本：787×1092　1/16　印张：17. 25　字数：200 千字
2015 年 12 月第 1 版　2015 年 12 月第 1 次印刷
定价：65. 00 元

主　　编： 滕建群

主要撰稿人：（按章节出现顺序）

滕建群　王　正　余小玲　李　毅　葛爱东

刘丽军　孙同辉　戴艳丽　刘　敏　孙爱平

谭　奕　王　飞　刘俊波　宫旭平　高　原

李文盛　张艳苹　刘　放

出版说明

由中国国际问题研究院军控与国际安全研究中心编辑出版的《全球核态势评估报告（2014/2015）》，在全体作者和编辑人员的共同努力下得以付梓。本版报告延续了往年的模式，就过去一年全球核领域里相关事件做了综述和评估，对有关国家的核战略力量建设、地区核问题、战术核武器等问题进行了探讨，反映出当前国内研究此领域专家的前沿水平。

在编辑本年度报告过程中，我们得到国防科技信息中心、中国国际问题研究院、空军指挥学院、空军航空大学等单位的鼎力相助和支持。美国 William and Flora Hewlett Foundation 基金会提供了出版经费。时事出版社的同仁为保证报告能够及时出版和发行，相关编辑人员付出了重要贡献。在此谨代表军控与国际安全研究中心对上述单位和个人表示衷心的感谢。

由于时间仓促，本版报告可能会有不少缺陷，恳请广大读者进行批评指正。

2015 年 10 月于北京

目　录

综述

核力量

核武装

地区核问题

战术核武器

Content

Summary

Nuclear Forces

Nuclear Armed State

Regional Nuclear Issues

Tactical Nuclear Weapons

综　述
Summary

2014年国际核军控与裁军综述

滕建群

〔内容提要〕2014年，国际军控与裁军形势延续上年基本走势：国际组织积极推进军控与裁军进程；美俄核大国如期履约，但均未放慢核武器现代化计划，美国在导弹防御计划上大举推进，令俄罗斯和中国等国对此表现出极大关注；尽管作出努力，但由于美国和朝鲜缺乏积极互动，朝核问题一筹莫展；伊核谈判继续，但成果不多，11月有关各方不得不再次推迟最终协议签署时间；核安全成为年度亮点，核安全峰会上中国国家主席习近平提出有中国特色的核安全观。

主题词：国际军备控制　裁军　形势　综述

作者单位：中国国际问题研究院军控与国际安全研究中心

一、国际组织推进军控与裁军进程

（一）《不扩散核武器条约》会议

《条约》第九次审议大会三次筹委会于4月28日—5月9日在纽约召开，146个国家参会，大会分成两大阵营：无核国家要求有核国家不迟疑、不可逆、可核查地开展新一轮军控谈判，其他拥核国家适当时也要参加。此前，各国承诺不增加、不改进、不研发核武器。无核国家要求《全面禁止核试验条约》尽早生效，并禁止临界核试验，早日启动《禁产条约》谈判。美国等国强调防止核扩散，提出在退约问题上增加难度，以防诸如朝鲜退约后研发核武情况再次发生。按 2010 年《行动纲领》，5 个有核国家提交了核裁军国家报告。

（二）联合国

安理会和第一委员会就军控与裁军问题进行探讨。截至 2014 年 11 月末，安理会共通过 55 个决议，只有第 2141 号决议直接涉及军控与裁军。决议“认定核武器、化学武器和生物武器及其运载工具的扩散继续威胁国际和平与安全”，敦促所有国家及其他方面与朝核问题委员会和专家小组充分合作。[①] 针对国际原子能机构提供的伊朗核问题报告，安理会发表多个主席声明，就伊核问题作出规定。

12 月 2 日，联合国大会以 170 票赞成、1 票反对、14 票弃权的结果通过要求“国际社会为全面废除核武器，决心共同采取行动”的核裁军决议案。这是联大连续第 21 年通过废核武议案。决议对核武器的“破坏性且非人道的结果”表示担忧，强调召开防核扩散条约会议，各国为实现核裁军采取行动。朝鲜投了唯一反对票，中国和俄罗斯等国弃权。

（三）日内瓦裁军谈判会议

裁谈会于 1—3 月、5—6 月和 7—9 月举行会议，共举行了

① 联合国安理会第 2141 号决议，2014 年 3 月 5 日通过。见联合国网站：http：//www. un. org/zh/documents/view_ doc. asp？ symbol = S. RES/2141 （2014）。

28 次全体会议、29 次非正式全体会议，65 个成员国出席会议。议题如下：停止核军备竞赛和加紧核裁军、防止核战争、保证不对无核武器国家使用和威胁使用核武器的国际安排、限制新型大规模杀伤性武器，如放射性武器、综合裁军方案、军事透明等。①

（四）国际原子能机构

国际原子能机构加强与有关方合作。2 月和 6 月，总干事长向联大提交伊朗核能力报告，指出伊朗已执行其与国际原子能机构在 2013 年 11 月和 2014 年 2 月达成的合作框架措施，并就浓缩铀数量及相关设施做了报告。

二、美俄核裁军继续，但核力量现代化均未停止

世界核武器数量下降，但削减速度放缓。截至 2014 年初，世界有约 4000 件战略武器处于部署状态，搭载 16300 枚核弹头，与 2013 年比减少 930 枚。②

（一）美俄裁军谈判前景渺茫

2010 年的美俄条约将于 2018 年到期。俄部署的战略武器及运载工具已低于条约规定数量。③ 美国总统奥巴马称，美国可在

---

① “裁军谈判会议提交联合国大会的报告”，2014 年 9 月 10 日。

② ［瑞典］“斯德哥尔摩国际和平研究所报告”，载法国航宇网，2014 年 6 月 16 日报道。

③ 参见由美、俄、德三国专家组成的深度裁军委员会发表的《为深度裁减做准备：增进欧洲—大西洋及国际安全的举措》报告，2014 年 4 月 28 日。

《战略武器条约》基础上把规模再裁三分之一。俄罗斯则认为，在未来核裁军对话前，两国需解决战略关切，包括弹道导弹防御系统、常规精确打击武器、外空武器化。俄罗斯还坚持，拥核国家都应参与下阶段的核裁军谈判。

美俄未就下阶段核裁军达成一致：美国希望立即谈判，俄罗斯希望在条约到期后再续谈，但可各自采取行动，朝进一步核裁军努力。美国核武器现代化面临压力，希望进一步裁减核武器数量。美国拥有约 500 枚战术核武器，俄罗斯则拥有约 2000 枚。美国希望战术核武器得到削减，但俄罗斯坚持，战术核武器谈判的前提是美国从欧洲撤出全部该型武器及拆除相应设施。美国国会则关注美俄战术核武器的数量差异。

（二）美国核力量现代化重在延寿

2014 年 1 月，美国公布《战略武器运用指南》，指出核武器作用是威慑对手，使美国及盟国免于核攻击。美国只在极端情况下才使用核武器，不会对遵守《不扩散核武器条约》的国家使用和威胁使用核武器，不会把核武器瞄准平民或民用设施。奥巴马正计划对现有核武器进行全面升级，用时将持续 30 年，仅头 10 年就将耗费 2000 亿美元。

核武器现代化重点在于战略武器投送系统和核弹头，包括：（1）陆基。“民兵 – 3”导弹 450 枚，重点在于快速反应、弹头再入大气层、推进系统更换、制导系统、推进发动机。（2）海基。12 艘“俄亥俄”级弹道导弹潜艇部署 288 枚三叉戟 – 2D5 导弹。海军计划 2031 年前后让新型潜艇服役。（3）空基。空军保留 18 架 B – 2 轰炸机和 76 架 B – 52H。远程轰炸机预计 2018 年入役，每架造价 5.5 亿美元。未来 10 年，空军将为新型战略轰炸机投资 321 亿美元。[①]

（三）俄罗斯重点入役新系统

（1）陆基。46 枚 SS－18 重型弹道导弹（携带 460 个核弹头）2020 年全部退役。SS－19 弹道导弹计划 2019 年全部退役。SS－25“白杨”弹道导弹预计到 2021 年退役。2014 年，俄罗斯开始“萨尔玛特”液体燃料导弹的研制，以替代 SS－18 导弹。该导弹 2020 年开始部署。2022 年，俄罗斯洲际弹道导弹数量将减少到 200—250 枚，可携带多弹头的导弹比例由目前的 35% 提升到 70%。[②]（2）海基。第三艘“北风之神”战略核潜艇 2014 年 12 月入役，计划到 2020 年海军拥有 8 艘该型艇，分别部署在北方舰队和太平洋舰队。（3）空基。俄罗斯装备战略轰炸机图－160 和图－95MS 飞机 70 架。2013 年 11 月，俄罗斯批准新型战略轰炸机的概念设计，计划 2020 年用新型轰炸机替代图－160 和图－95MS 轰炸机。

（四）英国和法国继续核威慑能力建设

法国大约有 290 件部署的战略核武器，英国部署了 160 枚核弹。[③] 4 艘“凯旋”级弹道导弹核潜艇是法国战略威慑力量的主体。现代化主要是用 M51.1 潜射弹道弹头替代现役的 M45 导弹，此现代化计划拟于 2018 年完成。从 2015 年开始，M51.2

---

① 汤姆·科里：“美国核现代化计划”，载美国军控协会网站，2014 年 1 月。

② 汉斯·克里斯滕森和罗伯特·诺瑞斯：“2014 年俄罗斯核力量”，载［美］《原子科学家公报》2014 年第 3 期。

③ ［瑞典］斯德哥尔摩国际和平研究所：《SIPRI 年鉴 2014——军备·裁军与国际安全》，第 6 章：“世界核力量”，http：//www.sipri.org/yearbook/2014/06。

核弹将开始服役。[①] 2013 年底，英国公布“继承者”级弹道导弹核潜艇，它将替代现役“前卫”级弹道导弹核潜艇。“继承者”潜艇实现了创新，达到1.7 万吨排水量，高于现有“前卫”级的排水量。“继承者”级正处在5 年设计开发计划的第三年，最终方案将在2016 年提出。7 月，英国“三叉戟”委员会发表英国核武器政策评估报告，认为全球核裁军对国家安全具有极其重要的意义，英国可减少核弹头数量，但为保障国家安全及与盟国关系，英国必须保留“三叉戟”核导弹武器平台，确保拥有可信的核武器系统和核态势。

（五）中国核能力受到质疑

国际社会对中国核力量的猜测有二：一是认为中国核力量正向更高层发展，陆基和海基导弹系统有了长足发展。俄罗斯专家指出，中国正在努力建设符合“三位一体”的核力量。中国“东风—31”导弹表明中国拥有制造陆基和海基统一通用弹道导弹的能力。[②] 美国专家认为，中国还在“东风—31”导弹基础上制造出公路机动导弹，配装新型战略导弹核潜艇的出现将强化核力量的稳定性，意味着中国核反击能力进一步增强。二是认为中国核力量难以对有关国家构成威胁。俄罗斯专家认为，中国战略核力量无法威慑美国，一旦发生核战争，面对美国打击，中国坚持不了1 个小时。[③] 理由如下：中国具有核威慑能力的只有“东风—31A 型”导弹，但数量有限，而美国拥有此类

---

① ［瑞典］斯德哥尔摩国际和平研究所：《SIPRI 年鉴 2014——军备·裁军和国际安全》，第6 章：“世界核力量”，http://www.sipri.org/yearbook/2014/06。

② ［俄］军工综合体新闻网站，2014 年12 月11 日。

③ ［俄］《专家》杂志，2014 年1 月19 日。

导弹近 2000 枚。

三、朝核、伊核冰火两重天

（一）朝核问题停滞不前

就朝鲜核武器的数量和质量，美国洛斯阿拉莫斯国家实验室前主任、斯坦福大学教授赫克担心，“朝鲜具有每年生产大约 4 枚核弹的能力。到 2016 年，朝鲜将拥有约 20 枚核弹。”[①] 2014 年初，国际社会对朝鲜是否进行新的核试验而感到不安。3 月 30 日，朝鲜外务省声明称，为提高核威慑力，朝鲜不排除进行新型核试验的可能。此前两天，安理会应美国要求召开非正式特别会议，对朝鲜发射导弹事件给予口头警告，表示将继续协商采取适当对策。朝鲜外务省发言人指责美国盗用联合国安理会名义对朝鲜进行孤立，称朝鲜发射火箭是为保卫国家和人民安全、为守护和平使命进行的“防御性军事训练”。

7 月，习近平主席访问韩国。两国指出：“实现半岛无核化，保持半岛和平稳定，符合六方会谈成员国的共同利益，有关各方应通过对话协商解决以上重大问题。”双方一致同意，六方会谈是推进实现半岛无核化的重要渠道，有必要推动六方会谈的恢复。在半岛核问题上，中国国家领导人强调不允许在家门口生事。中国把朝鲜“弃核”放在了对朝三项原则首要位置上。[②]

---

① 英国《每日电讯报》网站，2014 年 12 月 11 日。

② 长期以来，中国对朝鲜政策更多地采取宽容的态度，把稳定放在三项原则之前。如今“弃核”问题放在了首要位置上，这是中国对朝鲜半岛政策的调整的具体表现。

尽管中国、美国、俄罗斯、韩国、日本频繁沟通，但“六方会谈”恢复前景渺茫。原因包括：一是朝鲜继续推进其核武器现代化计划，尽管下半年朝鲜展开“魅力”外交，但国际社会对朝鲜核政策仍将信将疑。二是美国政府继续推行所谓“战略忍耐”政策，中期选举使民主党失去国会多数，美国不可能腾出手来应对朝鲜核问题。

（二）伊朗核谈判得以延续

2013 年 11 月，美、英、法、俄、中、德和伊朗达成“共同行动计划”，伊朗将停止 5% 浓度以上铀浓缩活动，将现有 200 千克 20% 高浓缩铀稀释并转化为核燃料，不再增加离心机。美国等国家放松对伊经济制裁，暂停限制伊朗石化产品出口及放松伊朗对汽车与黄金等贵金属的进口等。计划规定，2014 年 7 月 20 日前，伊朗与六国应达成全面解决伊核问题的最终协议。

协议于 2014 年 1 月 20 日生效。至 7 月，伊朗和伊核问题六国在维也纳进行近三周谈判。各方没能在协议到期前达成全面协议，谈判最终延期至 11 月 24 日。全面协议期限一再延后，从 7 月延至 11 月，又从 11 月延至 2015 年 7 月前。分歧有二：一是如何限制伊朗铀浓缩的规模和能力，二是怎样制定解除对伊制裁的时间表。美国承认，伊朗已具备制造核武器的能力，但必须坚决阻止伊朗拥核，并把具体指标定为将伊朗生产 1 枚核弹所需高浓缩铀的时间控制在一年以上。美国将谈判重点放在压缩进行铀浓缩活动的关键设备——离心机的数量上，要求伊朗将离心机从当前 1.9 万台的水平削减至数千台，而伊朗则希望保持当前离心机数量基本不变。

在取消制裁问题上，双方立场相去甚远。美国认为，始于2012 年的制裁是将伊朗拉回谈判的关键，美国需要尽可能维持制裁。尽管伊朗在制裁上获得少许松动，但对其整体经济帮助非常有限。伊朗要求美国取消对其石油出口、金融转账、能源投资等关键领域的制裁。

2014 年，六国和伊朗进行了十轮磋商，避免谈判破裂已成为各方共识。延期表明各方不只是制订时间表，还规划出具体路线图：六国和伊朗将开始新一轮会谈；2015 年 3 月，争取达成政治性框架；6 月底，完成所有技术细节和草案。

四、亚太地区导弹防御部署速度加快

和欧洲相比，亚太地区导弹防御系统建设出现新的发展趋势。美国参联会副主席詹姆斯·温尼菲尔德在大西洋理事会上指出，美国鼓励亚太地区的盟友和伙伴国发展自己的导弹防御能力，但加强地区导弹防御合作比一国单独发展导弹防御更好。美国将继续推进亚太地区的导弹防御。美国提出改进“地基中段防御”系统的计划，研究增强杀伤能力以替换 CE－1，2017 年使其具备作战能力。美国正在阿拉斯加增加部署 14 枚地基拦截弹，耗资 10 亿美元，使该基地的拦截弹总数达到 44 枚，同时还决定在美国东部海岸建设第三个导弹拦截基地，已经确定 5 个备选地点。

日本导弹防御系统是美国亚太反导计划的重要组成部分。8 月，日本发表《防卫白皮书》，强调发展导弹防御系统的重要性。当月下旬，日本防卫省申请将 2015 财年的预算增加 2.4%，所增费用主要用于提高日本情报、监视和侦察能力，重点是应对海上和弹道导弹威胁等能力。[①] 目前，日本导弹防御系统建设已初具规模：一是建立起陆海空三位一体的预警探测系统。陆基由 4 部 FPS－5 远程预警雷达和 7 部改进型 FPS－3 雷达组成。美国已在日本青森县部署一部 X 波段雷达，同时达成协议，将在日本京都府部署第二部 X 波段雷达，并计划于 2020 年左右在亚太地区部署新型远程雷达。二是海基系统由 6 艘“宙斯盾”驱逐舰组成，该型驱逐舰装备 S 波段雷达。三是空基预警系统，由从美国引进的 13 架 E—2C 空中预警机和 4 架 E－767 空中预警机组成。未来，日本在导弹防御领域将发展“完善、自主和有效”的体系。

韩国计划耗资 2—3 万亿韩元于 2015 年完成本国研发的导弹防御系统。韩国称，朝鲜拥有 800—1000 枚中短程弹道导弹，导弹威胁日趋严重。长期以来，美国一直要求韩国加入其导弹防御系统，但韩国均以自发研制而拒绝。从技术角度看，韩国导弹防御系统与美国导弹防御系统有较大区别。美国系统是针对朝鲜、伊朗、中国和俄罗斯的射程在 5000 千米以上的导弹威胁，保护美国本土，而韩国的导弹防御系统则是拦截朝鲜的 1000 千米左右的中短程导弹。

5 月，美国众议院批准 2015 财年国防预算，指出国防部要探索与日韩加强导弹防御合作的方式，明确美、日、韩加强导弹防御合作的可能，内容包括三国在哪些领域强化信息共享、系统融合与合作行动。美国强力推荐在韩国部署一套“未端高空区域防御系统”。此举引发中国高度关注。中国指出部署反导系统不利于地区稳定和战略平衡，中国驻韩国大使邱国洪表示：

① 美国防务新闻网：“日本防卫省申请将 2015 财年军费预算增加 2.4%”，2014 年 9 月 15 日。

"我们坚决反对。这将严重损坏韩中关系。"①

五、核安全峰会达成共识，确保安全任重道远

3 月 24—25 日，第三届核安全峰会在海牙召开，会议达成三项成果。在减少高浓铀和钚等危险核材料的使用上，各国领导人达成如下共识。一是减少危险核材料数量。2009 年以来，全球已有 12 个国家和地区移除境内所有高浓缩铀；15 个国家完成和正在完成高浓缩铀或钚的移交。二是降低对高浓铀的依赖。有关国家大幅度降低对高浓缩铀的依赖，拥有 1 千克以上高浓缩铀的 28 个国家中有 26 个减少了危险核材料数量。海牙会议期间，13 个国家签署了"无高浓缩铀联合声明"。

在确保核和其他放射性材料的安全保障上，与会各方承诺：一是加强实物保护和敏感信息保密并重。这将降低不法分子在第一现场窃取放射性材料的可能。二是完善符合国际法准则的立法。各国已经或者正在审查、更新立法，使其符合国际标准和最佳实践活动。30 多个国家支持制定"与核安全有关的国家核安全法规实施办法"。三是打击核走私。与会各国均表示，自 2010 年以来各国在港口和边境检查站加装了放射性检测系统；21 个国家签署了"打击核走私"互助协议；14 个国家承诺到 2016 年前使可用资源和培训课程到位；27 个国家支持在核取证方面提供相互帮助。四是积极开展核安全培训。12 个国家成立核安全培训中心，还有 8 个在建中心；34 个国家承诺保护敏感核信息。

---

① "韩媒称中国大使罕见回应韩部署 THAAD：坚决反对"，参见《参考消息》网站，2014 年 11 月 27 日，http：//china. cankaoxiaoxi. com/2014/1127/578654. shtml。

在增进国际合作上，与会者一致同意强化国际原子能机构的作用。随着《核材料实物保护公约》即将生效，许多国家正在积极地调整相关立法并批准必要的修订。一是逐渐完善国际核安框架。自2010年核安全峰会以来，19个国家已经批准了该修正案；33个国家承诺全面落实联合国安理会第1540号决议。二是发挥国际原子能机构的作用。自2010年峰会以来，11个与会国家接受了由原子能机构提供的实物保护咨询服务，还有10个峰会国家已经邀请了机构提供此项服务。

峰会期间，美日达成一致，日本向美国退回300多千克武器级钚核材料，这些材料是冷战期间美国以研究名义提供给日本的。日本承诺，把日本原子能研究开发机构的临界实验装置中的全部高浓缩铀和分离钚“移除和处理”。“这些材料在被安全运至美国后将被送往一个安全设施，全部转化成不敏感材料，其中的分离钚将进行最终处置，而高浓缩铀则被稀释成供民用的低浓缩铀。”日本储存大量超出其需要的核材料引发国际社会的关注。据报道，日本已囤积1.2吨高浓缩铀以及约44吨钚，其中包括200千克武器级铀和300多千克武器级钚，这些材料足以让日本生产上千枚核弹。[①]

习近平主席在峰会上提出“发展和安全并重、权利和义务并重、自主和协作并重、治标和治本并重”的核安全观，呼吁国际社会携手合作，实现核能持久安全和发展。从国内看，中国国家安全委员会首次会议提出了11项安全领域，其中就包括了核安全。

① “日本将向美国移交敏感核材料”，新华社—华盛顿，2014年3月24日消息。

六、结语

总体上看，2014 年国际核军控与裁军趋势基本与当前国际关系和国际安全形势的演变相吻合。由于美国和俄罗斯之间关系趋紧以及各国国内政治的影响，双边根本无精力探讨进一步的核裁军安排。地区核问题与地区安全形势也密不可分，朝鲜和伊朗核问题已不单单是核技术的去留问题，而是演变成有关国家角力的政治游戏。各国在核安全上的努力取得了一定的成果，但要实现最终目标，各国仍有很长的路要走。

The International Nuclear Arms Control and Disarmament: 2014

*Teng Jianqun*①

In 2014, international arms control and disarmament followed the previous year's basic trend: international organizations actively promoted arms control, while nuclear powers including the United States and the Russian Federation honored their commitments yet did not slow down their nuclear weapons modernization scheme. In particular, the U. S. pressed ahead with its missile defense plan, drawing great attention from Russia, China, and other countries. Despite endeavors on the North Korea nuclear issue, little headway was made due to a lack of active cooperation between Russia and the US. Iranian nuclear negotiations continued, yet with few results. In November, related parties had to delay signing the final agreement again. Nuclear security became a focus of the year. At the Nuclear Security Summit, Chinese President Xi Jinping put forward a nuclear security concept with Chinese characteristics. By the end of the year, *Arms Trade Treaty* came into effect, while the export and transfer of

① Teng Jianqun is the Director of the Centre for Arms Control and International Security Studies and also the Director of the Department of American Studies at China Institute of International Studies.

conventional weapons remained a concern.

I. International Organizations Push for Arms Control

1. Nuclear Non-Proliferation Treaty Conference

The third preparatory committee of the ninth review conference on nuclear non – proliferation was convened from April 28 to May 9, 2014. The 146 countries were divided into two camps: nuclear – free states demanded nuclear states carry out a new round of arms control negotiations in a readily verifiable and irreversible manner, with the proper participation of other nuclear states. Prior to the conference, nations pledged not to increase, upgrade or develop nuclear weapons. Nuclear – free states demanded that the Comprehensive Nuclear Test Ban Treaty (CTBT) take effect as soon as possible, critical nuclear tests be banned, and negotiations on Fissile Material Cut – off Treaty (FMCT) start at an early date. Nuclear states, including the U. S. emphasized the need to prevent nuclear proliferation and proposed making exiting the treaty more difficult to prevent nations from developing nuclear programs after exiting the treaty, much as what North Korea did. According to the 2010 *Action Plan*, five nuclear states should provide national reports on nuclear disarmament.

2. The United Nations

The UN Security Council and the Disarmament and International Security Committee conducted discussions on arms control and disarmament. By the end of November, the Security Council had passed

55 resolutions, yet only Resolution 2141 is directly concerned with arms control and disarmament. According to the resolution, the proliferation of nuclear, chemical, and biological weapons remain a threat to international security. It urged all nations to fully cooperate on theNorth Korea nuclear issue. ①In response to the report prepared by the International Atomic Energy Agency (IAEA) on the Iranian nuclear issue, the Security Council issued several Presidential Statements making rules concerning the issue.

On December 2, 2014, the UN General Assembly passed the nuclear disarmament resolution by a vote of 170 to 1 with 14 abstentions, which demands "the international society should jointly take actions for the comprehensive abolition of nuclear arms". This marks the 21st consecutive year the General Assembly passed a resolution on the abolition of nuclear arms. The resolution expressed concern on the "destructive and inhumane consequences" of nuclear weapons, emphasized holding a nuclear non – proliferation treaty conference, and urged all nations to take actions to realize nuclear disarmament. North Korea casted the only negative vote. China and Russia abstained from voting.

3. Conference on Disarmament (CD) in Geneva

The CD was held three times from January to March, from May to June, and from July to September, with 28 plenary sessions and 29 informal plenary sessions attended by 65 member states. Topics discussed included: ceasing the nuclear arms race, accelerating nu-

① *UN Security Council No. 2141 Resolution*, passed in March 5th, 2014. Website: http: //www. un. org/zh/documents/view_ doc. asp? symbol = S. RES/2141 (2014).

clear disarmament, preventing nuclear war, pledging to never use or threaten the use of nuclear weapons, controlling new types of weapons of mass destruction, formulating a comprehensive disarmament plan, and promoting military transparency. ①

4. **The International Atomic Energy Agency**

The IAEA should strengthen cooperation with related parties. In February and June, the Director General of IAEA submitted the Iranian nuclear capacity report to the UN General Assembly, which pointed out thatIran reached cooperation framework measures with the IAEA in November 2013 and February 2014, and had reported on the number of uranium enrichment facilities.

Ⅱ. U. S. and Russian Disarmament Continues

The number of nuclear weapons in the world declined, but the pace of that decline has slowed. By the start of 2014, 4000 strategic weapons were ready for deployment, carrying 16300 warheads, a decrease of 930 compared with 2013. ②

1. **Gloomy Prospects for U. S. – Russia Disarmament Talks**

The Strategic Arms Reduction Treaty (START) between the U. S. and Russia will expire in 2018. The strategic weapons deployed

① Conference on Disarmament (CD), report by CD to the UN General Assembly, Sep. 10th, 2014.

② [Sweden] *Report by Stockholm International Peace Research Institute*, published on France Aerospace Website, reported on June 6th, 2014.

by Russia have fallen below the specified number in the treaty.[①] President Barack Obama said the U. S. could further reduce its arsenal by one – third of the scale on the basis of START. Russia said that before the disarmament dialogue could continue, the two countries should settle strategic concerns including missile defense systems, traditional precision – strike weapons, and outer – space weaponization. Russia also insisted that all nuclear states should participate in the next stage of disarmament talks. Ⅳ

The U. S. and Russia have failed to reach agreement on the next stage of disarmament. The U. S. wants immediate negotiations, while Russia wants to resume negotiations when the treaty expires, suggesting that the two countries can take actions respecively to move toward further nuclear disarmament. Under pressure from nuclear modernization, the U. S. hopes to further reduce the number of nuclear weapons. The U. S. has 500 tactical nuclear weapons, while Russia has around 2000. The U. S. wants the number of tactical nuclear weapons reduced, while Russia insisted that the prerequisite for negotiation on tactical nuclear weapons is that the U. S. must withdraw all tactical nuclear weapons and demolish corresponding facilities in Europe. The U. S. Congress, meanwhile, focuses on the difference in the number of tactical nuclear weapons between the U. S. and Russia.

2. The Key to U. S. Nuclear Modernization

In January, the U. S. released a *Strategic Weapons Application*

---

① *Prepare for in – depth disarmament: measures for enhancing Europe – Atlantic and international peace*, published by the in – depth Disarmament Commission on April 28th, 2014.

Guide, pointing out that the significance of nuclear weapons is to deter adversaries and protect the U. S. and its allies from nuclear attacks. The U. S. will use nuclear weapons only in extreme cases. It will not use or threaten to use nuclear weapons against nations abiding by the Nuclear Non – Proliferation Treaty, nor will it target nuclear weapons against civilians or facilities for civil use. President Obama is planning a comprehensive upgrade of existing nuclear weapons, which will take 30 years, with $200 billion to be spent in the first decade.

The key to nuclear modernization lays in strategic weapons deployment system and nuclear warheads, which include land – based, with 450 LGM – 30G Minuteman – Ⅲ. The key components lie in quick response, warhead re – entry into the atmosphere, and changes to the guidance and propulsion systems. Second, there are sea – based weapons with 288 Trident – 2D5 deployed on twelve Ohio – class ballistic missile submarines. The Navy plans to put the new submarine design in service in 2031. Third, there are air – based weapons, with eighteen B – 2 stealth bombers and 76 Boeing B – 52H strategic bombers. Long – range bombers are expected to be into service in 2018. Each costs $550 million. In the next decade, the Navy will invest $32. 1 billion on the new type of strategic bombers.[①]

3. **Russia's New Systems to Enter Service**

First, Russia possesses new land – based weapons. 46 SS – 18 heavy ballistic missiles (carrying 460 nuclear warheads) will be de-

① Tom Korina, "U. S. nuclear modernization plan", published on the website of the U. S. arms control association, January 2014.

commissioned by 2021. SS – 19 ballistic missiles will be decommissioned by 2019. The SS – 25 Aspen ballistic missile is expected to be decommissioned by 2021. In 2014, Russia started to develop liquid fuel missiles to replace the SS – 18. The new missiles will be deployed in 2020. By 2022, Russia will cut the number of intercontinental ballistic missiles to 200 – 250, with the share of missiles capable of carrying multiple warheads rising from the current 35% to 70%.[①] Secondly, there are sea – based delivery systems. The third Borei class strategic submarine entered into service in December. By 2020, the Navy is expected to have eight submarines of this type, deployed respectively to the Northern Fleet and the Pacific Fleet. For air – based delivery systems, Russia is equipped with 70 Tu – 160 and Tu – 95MS. In November 2013, Russia approved the conceptual design of a new strategic bomber, which is planned to replace Tu – 160 and Tu – 95MS.

4. **Britain and France Continue Building Nuclear Deterrent Capacity**

France has around 290 deployed strategic nuclear weapons. Britain has deployed 160 nuclear warheads. The four Triumphant[②] class strategic submarines constitute the main body of France's strategic deterrence. The modernization, which mainly uses M51. 1 submarine – launched ballistic missile warheads to replace the M45

① Hans Kristensen and Robert Noris, "2014Russia's nuclear strength", published at the *Bulletin of the Atomic Scientists* (U. S.), the third issue of 2014.

② [Sweden] Stockholm International Peace Research Institute year book, *Armament, disarmament and international security* (2014), Chapter six: World Nuclear Forces. http://www. sipri. org/yearbook/2014/06.

missiles in service, to be completed by 2018. From 2015 on, M51.2 N – bomb will enter into service.[①] At the end of 2013, Britain released the Successor – class SSBNs, which will replace the Vanguard – class SSBNs. The Successor made some innovation with its displacement up to 17, 000 tons, larger than the Vanguard. The Successor – class is in the third year of the five – year design and development plan. The final plan will be unveiled in 2016. In July, Britain's Trident Committee released the assessment report on Britain's nuclear policy, believing that global nuclear disarmament is of great significance for national security. According to the report, Britain can cut the number of nuclear warheads, but to safeguard national security and ties with its allies, Britain must maintain the "Trident" nuclear missile weapons platform.

5. **China's Nuclear Capacity Comes under Question**

The international community makes two guesses. First, China's nuclear capacity has been developing to a higher level, with significant developments achieved in land – based and sea – based missile systems. Russian experts pointed out that China has been working to build a triad nuclear capacity. China's DF – 31 missile proves that China is capable of building a unified ballistic missile for land – based and sea – based use.[②] U. S. experts believed that China has built highway mobile missiles based on the DF – 31. The emergence of

① [Sweden] Stockholm International Peace Research Institute year book, *Armament, disarmament and international security* (2014), Chapter six: World Nuclear Forces. http://www.sipri.org/yearbook/2014/06.

② [Russia] Military and Industry complex news website, reported on December. 11, 2014.

the new type of SSBN will enhance the stability of nuclear capacity, which means China's nuclear counterattack capacity will be further strengthened. The second estimate about China is that its nuclear capacity cannot pose a threat to countries concerned. Russian experts believed that China's nuclear capacity is not able to deter the United States. If a nuclear war breakout, China can resist no more than one hour against U. S. attack. ①The reason is that China's only missile for nuclear deterrence, the DF – 31 missile, is of limited number, while the U. S. possesses near 2, 000 of this type of missile.

Ⅲ. North Korean and Iranian Nuclear Issues in Contrast

1. North Korea Nuclear Issue Stalemated

In terms of the number and quality of North Korea's nuclear weapons, Siegfried S. Hecker, professor at Stanford University and the former Director of Los Alamos National Laboratory, expressed his concern: "North Korea is capable of producing around four nuclear bombs a year. By 2016, North Korea will have around 20 N – bombs."② At the beginning of the year, the international community was worried whether North Korea was conducting new nuclear tests. On March 20, 2014, the North Korean Foreign Ministry said that the country would not rule out the possibility of carrying out new nuclear tests to improve its nuclear deterrence. Two days before, the

---

① [Russia] *Experts*, January 19, 2014.

② On Britain Daily Telegraph website, December. 11th, 2014.

UN Security Council convened a special meeting at the request of the U. S. and issued a verbal warning against North Korea's launch tests, saying it would continue consultation about appropriate measures. A North Korean Foreign Ministry spokesman accused the U. S. of isolating North Korea. He stated that North Korea's rocket launch was a defensive military drill to fulfill the mission of safeguarding the security of the nation and its people.

In July, President Xi Jinping visited South Korea. The two countries pointed out that, "to realize denuclearization on the Korean Peninsula and maintain regional peace and stability serves the common interests of members of the Six Party Talks. Related parties should settle dwon the major issues through dialogue and consultation." The two agreed that the Six Party Talks would be an important channel to push for denuclearization and it is necessary to restore the talks. On the Korean Peninsula nuclear issue, Chinese state leaders emphasized not allowing troubles at their doorstep. China has put denuclearization at the top of the three principles in its relations with North Korea.[①]

Despite frequent communications among the U. S., Russia, ROK, and Japan, the prospects of restoring the Six Party Talks are gloomy. The reasons are as follows. One is that the DPRK proceeds with its nuclear weapons modernization plan. Despite its charming diplomacy in the second half of the year, its policies are still suspected

① For a long time, China had more adopted a tolerant stance on policies on DPRK, putting stability at the top of the three principles. Now denuclearization is at the top. This is a concrete reflection of China's adjustment in policy on the peninsular governments.

by the international community. The second reason is that the U. S. continues its "strategic patience" policy. With the Democratic Party losing the majority in Congress, the U. S. is unlikely to spare extra efforts in handling the North Korea nuclear issue.

2. **Iranian Nuclear Talks Continued**

In November 2013, the U. S. , Britain, France, Russia, Germany, China, and Iran reached a "joint plan of action" . Iran will suspend 5% or above uranium enrichment activities and dilute and turn the existing 200g of 20% enriched uranium into nuclear fuel without adding more centrifuges. The U. S. and other countries lifted economic sanctions against Iran and suspended import restrictions on Iranian petrochemicals and export restrictions on automobiles, gold, and other rare metals. According to the plan, Iran would reach a final stage on resolving the nuclear issue by July 20, 2014.

The divergences are as follows. One is how to restrict Iranian uranium enrichment scale and capacity. Second is how to make a timetable for lifting sanctions against Iran. The U. S. admitted that Iran was capable of developing nuclear weapons, but insisted on preventing Iran from owning nuclear weapons. It has set specific targets of making the time needed to produce an N – bomb by Iran to over a year. The U. S. gives priority to reducing the number of centrifuges, which are the key facility of high – enriched uranium. It requires Iran to cut the number of centrifuges from the existing 19000 to several thousand, while Iran wants to maintain the existing number of centrifuges. The plan took effect on January 20, 2014. By July 2014, Iran conducted negotiations with the six countries in Vienna, which lasted three weeks. Related parties failed to reach a final agreement by the deadline and the negotiation was postponed to November 24, 2014. The deadline for a final agreement was repeatedly postponed, first from July to November, then from November to July 2015.

The United States and Iranian stances on the issue of lifting sanctions differ greatly. The U. S. believes that the sanctions starting from 2012 are the key to bringing Iran back to the negotiating table, so it wants to maintain the sanctions as long as possible. The limited relaxation of sanctions is of little help to the overall economy of Iran. Iran requires that the U. S. lift sanctions against it in key areas including oil exports, financial transfers, and energy investment.

In 2014, the six countries conducted ten rounds of consultations withIran. Avoiding a breakdown in the negotiations has become the consensus of all parties. Postponing the final agreement shows that related parties not only make the timetable, but also plan for a specific roadmap: the six countries would start a new round of meetings with Iran, they would strive to reach a political framework by March 2015, and they would complete all technical details and drafts by the end of June 2015.

Ⅳ. Deployment of Missile Defense in the Asia – Pacific Region

The construction of missile defense system in the Asia – Pacific region has shown a developing trend different from that in Europe. The U. S. Vice Chairman of the Joint Chiefs of Staff James Winnefeld said at the Atlantic Council that the United States has been encouraging its allies and partners in the Asia – Pacific region to acquire their own missile defense capabilities. But he also said that strengthening regional missile defense cooperation would result in better performance than individual countries acting alone. The U. S. will continue to boost missile defense in the region. It has proposed a plan to enhance ground – based mid – course defense systems, while researching enhanced kill vehicles as a substitute to the CE – 1, making it operationally capable by 2017. It is deploying fourteen additional ground – based interceptor missiles to Alaska at a cost of $1billion, bringing the total number of interceptors in that base to 44. In addition, it has decided to build a third ground – based interceptor site along the east coast. Five alternative locations have already been identified.

The missile defense system inJapan is a key component of the U. S. anti – missile plans for the Asia – Pacific. Japan's Defense White Paper, published in August, emphasized the importance of developing a missile defense system. Later in that month, Japan's Ministry of Defense requested a 2.4% budget hike for the 2015 – 2016 fiscal year. Most of the additional funds would be devoted to enhancing intelligence, surveillance, and reconnaissance capabilities, with a view to better responding to maritime and ballistic missile threats.[①]The missile defense system in Japan is already quite robust. First, sea – and land – based systems and airborne early warning and detection systems have been established. The land – based system includes four FPS – 5 long – range early warning radars and seven improved FPS – 3 radars. The U. S. has already deployed X

① Defense News. com, Japanese Defense Ministry Requests 2.4% Budget Hike, Sep. 15, 2014.

– band radar in Tsugaru City and, according to agreement, will deploy another one in Kyoto Prefecture. Moreover, it plans to deploy new long – range radars in the Asia – Pacific region by 2020. Second, the sea – based system includes six Aegis destroyers equipped with S – band radar. Third, the airborne system includes thirteen E – 2C and four E – 767 early warning aircraft imported from the U. S. . In the future, Japan will develop a complete, autonomous, and effective system in the area of missile defense.

The ROK plans to spend 2 – 3 trillion Won to complete a self – developed missile defense system in 2015. It claims that the DPRK has 800 to 1000 medium – and short – range ballistic missiles, posing an increasingly severe threat. For a long time, the U. S. has demanded the ROK join its missile defense system. But the ROK refused to do so. Technically, the ROK and U. S. missile defense systems are quite different. The U. S. system is directed against those 5000 – plus kilometer long – range missiles launched from the DPRK, Iran, China, and Russia to protect its homeland, while the ROK system aims at intercepting 1000 kilometer or so medium – and short – range missiles launched from the DPRK.

In May, the U. S. House of Representatives approved the 2015 – 2016 defense budget. This points out that the Department of Defense should explore ways to strengthen missile defense cooperation with Japan and the ROK, and identifies possibilities for enhanced missile defense cooperation among the U. S. , Japan, and ROK, including where the three countries could strengthen information sharing, system integration, and cooperative actions. The U. S. strongly recommends the deployment of Terminal High Altitude Area Defense in the ROK. This has raised serious concerns in China, which points out that the deployment of anti – missile systems would do no good to regional stability and strategic balance. Chinese Ambassador to the ROK Qiu Guohong said that "we strongly oppose it. It will seriously harm China – ROK relations".

V. The Nuclear Security Summit Reached Consensus

The third Nuclear Security Summit was held in The Hague on March 24—25, 2014. The conference achieved three outcomes. On the issue of reducing the age of dangerous nuclear materials, such as highly enriched uranium (HEU) and plutonium, the participating leaders agreed to two points. First, reduce the amount of dangerous nuclear materials. Since 2009, twelve countries and regions around the world have removed all the HEU within their respective borders. Fifteen countries have completed or are on course to complete turning over HEU and plutonium. Second, lessen the dependency on HEU. Related countries have significantly lessened their dependencies on HEU. Among the twenty eight countries that own more than one kilogram of HEU, twenty six have reduced the amount of dangerous nuclear materials. During The Hague Conference, thirteen countries signed the *Joint Statement on Countries Free of Highly Enriched Uranium*.

On the issue of improving the security of all nuclear and radioactive materials, the participants made four commitments. First, put the same emphasis on keeping sensitive information secret as on improving the protection of materials, so as to reduce the possibility of radioactive materials being stolen on – site by criminals. Second, enhance legislation in line with international law. All participating countries have, or are reviewing and renewing, national legislation bringing them in accordance with international standards and best practices. Over thirty countries support drafting nuclear security – related implementation guidelines for national nuclear security regulations. Third, according to the participating countries, since 2010 radioactive detection systems have been added to ports and border inspection stations in their countries. Twenty one countries have signed anti – nuclear trafficking mutual assistance agreements. Fourteen countries promise to put resources and training courses in place by 2016. Twenty seven countries support mutual assistance in nuclear forensics. Fourth, nuclear security training centers have been set up in twelve countries and eight more are under construction. Thirty four countries promise to protect sensitive nuclear information.

On the issue of deepening international cooperation, the participants all agreed to strengthen the role of the IAEA. As the Convention on the Physical Protection of Nuclear Material will soon enter into effect, many countries have been actively adjusting related legislation and approving necessary amendments. After the 2010 Nuclear Security Summit, nineteen countries approved this amendment. Thirty – three countries have promised full implementation of UN Security Council Resolution 1540. Second, after the 2010 Nuclear Security Summit, eleven participating countries have accepted IAEA physical protection advisory service. Another ten NSS countries have invited IAEA to provide this service.

According to the agreement reached by the U. S. and Japan during the summit, Japan will return to the U. S. more than 300 kg of weapons – grade plutonium which had been provided to Japan by the U. S. in the name of research during the Cold War era. Japan promises that all HEU and separated plutonium would be removed and disposed from the Fast Critical Assembly at the Japan Atomic Energy Agency. "This material, once securely transported to the United States, will be sent to a secure facility and fully converted into less sensitive forms. The plutonium will be prepared for final deployment. The HEU will be downblended to low enriched uranium (LEU) and utilized for civilian purposes." Japan has been stockpiling large amount of nuclear material, which is far more beyond its need and raised concerns from the international community. According to reports, Japan has a stockpile of 1. 2 tons of HEU and around 44 tons of plutonium, including 200 kg of weapons – grade uranium and over 300 kg of weapons – grade plutonium. These materials are sufficient to produce thousands of nuclear bombs if Japan wishes to do so.①

During the summit, President Xi Jinping put forward an approach to nuclear security that places equal emphasis on development and security, rights and obligations, independent and collaborative efforts. He called on the international community to work together for lasting nuclear security and development. Domestically, the China National Security Commissionhas identified eleven security fields during its first meeting early in 2014, including nuclear security.

---

① *Japan to turn over sensitive nuclear materials to the U. S.*, Xinhua – Washington, March 24, 2014.

当前亚太地区核态势评估

王　正　余小玲

〔内容提要〕当前亚太地区核态势存在一个平衡点、一个碰撞点、一个僵持点、一个隐患点、一个争议点和一个合作点。具体来看，美俄就下一阶段核裁军存在诸多分歧，南亚次大陆战略对峙仍然激烈，朝核问题的僵持局面难以打破，日本政坛对核武器的态度值得揣摩，导弹防御问题成为亚太地区大国战略博弈的重要舞台，核安全、核安保问题有赖各国广泛参与。为此，有关各国应进一步推动核裁军，努力完善防扩散体制，加强核安全、核安保合作，并通过建立安全机制等措施，改善地区安全环境，维护亚太核态势的安全与稳定。

主题词：亚太地区　核态势

作者单位：中国国防科技信息中心

本文所指的亚太地区，是太平洋地区周边区域的总称。本文试图对当前亚太地区的核态势进行初步评估，就其对地区安全形势的影响及挑战进行分析，并对维护亚太地区核态势的安全与稳定提出思考。

一、当前亚太地区核态势的主要特点

（一）一个平衡点：美俄核博弈

奥巴马政府上台后，提出建立“无核武器世界”的倡议，与俄罗斯通过近一年多达 10 轮的谈判，在 2010 年 4 月签署了《关于进一步削减和限制进攻性战略武器措施的条约》（即新战略武器条约）。协定至 2018 年将双方实战部署的战略核武器削减至 1550 枚。时至今日，新战略武器条约生效已有 4 年。目前，双方履约情况比较乐观，条约的执行也并没有因近期美俄关系恶化而受阻，并且在一定程度上维护了美俄的战略稳定。[①] 截至 2014 年 9 月，美国部署了 794 件核武器运载工具，共搭载 1642 枚核弹头；俄罗斯则部署了 528 件核武器，搭载 1643 枚核弹头。[②]

核战略方面，美俄两国均未作出重大调整，核武器仍是两国国家安全战略的基石。美国 2015 年出台的《国家安全战略》反映了奥巴马政府对核武器一贯的态度，即“只要核武器存在，美国就将投入必要的资源，维持安全、安保、有效的核威慑”。[③]

---

① Frank Rose, Four Years In, the New START Treaty Still Works, the U. S. Department of State Official Blog, February 5, 2015. 参见：http：//blogs. state. gov/stories/2015/02/05/four – years – new – start – treaty – still – works.

② Fact Sheet：New START Treaty Aggregate Numbers of Strategic Offensive Arms, Bureau of Arms Control, Verification, and Compliance, January 1, 2015. 参见：http：//www. state. gov/t/avc/rls/235606. htm.

③ Fact Sheet：The 2015 National Security Strategy, The White House Office of the Press Secretary, February 06, 2015. 参见：https：//www. whitehouse. gov/the – press – office/2015/02/06/fact – sheet – 2015 – national – security – strategy.

此外，奥巴马总统于2013年签署的《核力量运用指南》中，称“美国核武器的基本作用仍是遏止对美国及其盟友和伙伴国的核打击”，而且“只有在保护自身及盟友和伙伴国的核心利益的极端情况下才考虑使用核武器”，并承诺将“降低核武器在美国国家安全战略中的作用”。新指南看似对使用核武器的条件做了严格的限定，但并未对其中的“核心利益”和“极端情况”给出解释，因此其政策调整的空间还很大。[①] 对俄罗斯而言，核武器仍是其威慑核打击、遏止大规模军事冲突的重要工具。2014年底出台的《俄联邦军事学说》在使用核武器的条件方面与2010年的版本保持一致，即“使用核武器或其他大规模杀伤性武器袭击俄罗斯或其盟友”，以及“使用常规武器对俄罗斯实施侵略并使其生存受到威胁”。[②]

令人遗憾的是，美俄两国的核态势受“冷战思维”的影响依然严重。双方均保留了“三位一体”的核力量结构，坚持“打击军事目标”的作战策略，依然保持“预警即发射”（或称“遇袭即发射”）的高度警戒状态。继续这些“冷战态势”是在21世纪保持威慑所不必要的，也不利于进一步降低核武器的作用，还可能阻碍深度核裁军的开展。

另一方面，美俄在亚太地区的核力量对比也发生了微妙的变化。经过多年努力，美国基本上完成了潜艇部队主力由大西

① Fact Sheet: Nuclear Weapons Employment Strategy of the United States, The White House Office of the Press Secretary, June 19, 2013, 参见: http://www.whitehouse.gov/the-press-office/2013/06/19/fact-sheet-nuclear-weapons-employment-strategy-united-states.

② New version of the military doctrine, Russia strategic nuclear forces, December 26, 2014. 参见: http://russianforces.org/blog/2014/12/new_version_of_the_military_do.shtml.

洋向太平洋的战略转移，包括14艘“俄亥俄”级战略核潜艇中的8艘，以及55艘各级攻击型核潜艇中的29艘；此外，美国还将最新型的P-8A“海神”反潜机部署到日本嘉手纳基地，[①] 并笼络亚太多国联手构建多维反潜网。使得美国在亚太地区的战略威慑能力因反潜侦查和作战能力大大提升。俄罗斯一直视其战略力量为遏制威胁、支撑国家安全和对外政策的核心手段，自然也不甘示弱，并着手加强西伯利亚和远东的核力量建设。俄罗斯在2014年对驻扎在西伯利亚伊尔库斯克的战略导弹部队进行突击演练，以检验部队及武器装备的战备状态和作战效率。[②] 该导弹部队还将在2015年接受最新的RS-26“先锋”导弹。[③] 两艘最新的“北风之神”级战略核潜艇——“亚历山大·涅夫斯基”号和“弗拉基米尔·莫诺马赫”号——也将在2015年进驻维柳钦斯克，加入俄罗斯太平洋舰队。[④]

在下一阶段核裁军方面，奥巴马总统在2013年6月的柏林讲话中提出，美国可将部署的战略核武器数量在新战略武器条

---

① The U. S. sends new submarine - hunting jets to Japan amid East Asia tension, Reuters, December 2, 2013. 参见：http://www.reuters.com/article/2013/12/02/us-japan-china-planes-idUSBRE9B104220131202.

② Siberia's Irkutsk missile formation starts surprise military exercises, Sputnik News, July 8, 2014. 参见：http://in.sputniknews.com/indian.ruvr.ru/2014_07_08/274393309/.

③ First RS-26 to be deployed in Irkutsk in 2015, Russian strategic nuclear forces, July 1, 2014. 参见：http://russianforces.org/blog/2014/07/first_rs-26_to_be_deployed_in.shtml.

④ What to Expect From Russia's Pacific Fleet in 2015, The Diplomat, March 2, 2015. 参见：http://thediplomat.com/2015/03/what-to-expect-from-russias-pacific-fleet-in-2015/.

约的基础上再削减 1/3，即减至 1000 枚左右。[①] 美国不大可能单方面进行削减，而是会通过与俄罗斯谈判，寻求实现双边核裁军。美俄两国已就下一阶段核裁军开始接触，但目前双方已暴露出诸多分歧：一是导弹防御和非核战略武器问题，俄罗斯希望将下一阶段核裁军与导弹防御和非核战略武器等问题绑定，而美国并不乐意这样做。二是战术核武器问题，美国希望将战术核武器问题也纳入到下一轮核裁军谈判中，俄罗斯虽表示同意，但要求在谈判开始前将海外部署的战术核武器撤回本国。三是是否开启多边核裁军，美国认为在开启多边核裁军之前，美俄还需进行至少一轮双边核裁军，而俄罗斯则声称应将所有"拥有核武器"的国家都纳入到下一轮核裁军谈判当中。

2014 年乌克兰危机爆发后，美俄关系急剧降温，其影响也直接反映在美俄核领域的互动中。2014 年 7 月，美国国务院在其发布的军控履约报告中公开指责俄罗斯违反《中导条约》，[②] 俄罗斯对此予以坚决否认，并指责美方涉嫌违约。[③] 虽然双方退约的可能性微乎其微，但前前后后的争执使得双方的分歧更难以弥合，为下一阶段核裁军造成了不利局面。此外，美俄关系转冷也破坏了两国核安全、核安保方面的合作。俄罗斯于 2014

① Remarks by President Obama at the Brandenburg Gate – – Berlin, Germany, The White House Office of the Press Secretary, June 19, 2013，详见：http：//www. whitehouse. gov/the – press – office/2013/06/19/remarks – president – obama – brandenburg – gate – berlin – germany.

② 2014 Report on Adherence to and Compliance With Arms Control, Nonproliferation, and Disarmament Agreements and Commitments; Bureau of Arms Control, Verification and Compliance; Washington, DC, July 31, 2014. 参见：http：//www. state. gov/t/avc/rls/rpt/2014/230047. htm.

③ 【俄】米·维利达诺夫："华盛顿没有履行诺言"，《独立军事观察》2014 年 9 月 5 日。

年12月决定在保障本国核设施安全方面终止与美方合作，这也意味着取代“纳恩－卢格协定”的新的削减核威胁双边框架协定宣告结束。[①]

（二）一个碰撞点：印巴核竞赛

1998年，在冷战结束后美俄大幅裁减核武器的背景下，印度逆世界潮流而动，公然进行核爆炸试验，成为事实上的核国家。而巴基斯坦也不甘示弱，紧随其后进行了地下核试验。印巴之间就此开始了针锋相对的核军备竞赛。时至今日，印巴核军备竞赛的势头并未衰退。2015年1月31日，印度进行了“烈火－5”导弹的第三次试射；[②] 随后，巴基斯坦于3月9日试射了“沙欣－3”中程弹道导弹。[③]

核力量建设方面，印巴致力于建立各自的“三位一体”核力量体系。目前印度拥有90—100枚核武器，陆基导弹构成其战略核力量的主力，包括“大地”系列和“烈火”系列弹道导弹。空基核力量很可能由“幻影”2000H多用途战斗机构成，但印度还没有发展相应的空射核巡航导弹。印度还在加快海基核力量建设，正在发展“K－15”和“K－4”两款潜射弹道导

① Russia ends deal with the U. S. to protect nuclear material, The Telegraph, January 22, 2015. 参见：http：//www. telegraph. co. uk/news/worldnews/europe/russia/11363053/Russia－ends－deal－with－US－to－protect－nuclear－material. html.

② India test－fires canister－launched Agni 5 missile, IHS Jane's Defence Weekly, 01 February 2015, 参见：http：//www. janes. com/article/48504/india－test－fires－canister－launched－agni－5－missile.

③ Pakistan test fires Shaheen 3 MRBM, IHS Jane's Defence Weekly, 11 March 2015, 参见：http：//www. janes. com/article/49902/pakistan－test－fires－shaheen－3－mrbm.

弹，其战略核潜艇“歼敌者”号已于2012年开始海试。巴基斯坦拥核武库规模与印度相当，拥有100—120枚核武器。与印度类似，陆基导弹也是巴基斯坦核威慑的中坚力量，包括“阿布达里”、“加纳维”、“高里”和“沙欣”等弹道导弹。巴基斯坦正在发展“巴布尔”和“拉德”两款巡航导弹，“拉德”导弹将由“幻影”-3或“枭龙”战机搭载，成为巴空中核力量的重要组成部分；“巴布尔”有空基和海基两个版本，巴基斯坦很有可能在其基础上发展潜射巡航导弹。

核材料方面，印巴两国核材料的库存情况和生产能力使得它们可以进一步扩充核武库。据估计，印度核材料库存包括2.4±0.9吨高浓缩铀，以及0.54±0.18吨武器级钚；巴基斯坦则拥有3±1.2吨高浓缩铀，以及0.15±0.05吨武器级钚。目前，两国都在进一步扩建核设施，提升核材料生产能力。[①] 印度“奇特拉达加”铀浓缩设施正在建设，建成后既可以生产核电站使用的低浓缩铀，也可以生产核武器或核潜艇反应堆所需的高浓缩铀。巴基斯坦库沙布的第三和第四座反应堆一旦开始运行，将使巴基斯坦生产武器级钚的能力从每年12千克-24千克，提升至25千克-50千克。

印巴两国在激烈的核军备竞赛中，也互相发出危险的信号，局势令人担忧。一方面，巴基斯坦为了抵消印度常规军力优势，应对其“冷启动”作战策略，[②] 发展了射程为60千米的“纳赛

① International Panel on Fissile Materials, Global Fissile Material Report 2013: Increasing Transparency of Nuclear Warhead and Fissile Material Stocks as a Step toward Disarmament, October 2013，参见：http://fissilematerials.org/library/gfmr13.pdf.

② “冷启动”，是指通过一系列快速猛烈的进攻，歼灭敌方有生力量，在短时间内实现作战目的的作战理论。巴基斯坦担心印度通过“冷启动”的作战方式，决定性地打击巴基斯坦的军事潜力，使之不能跨越核门槛，利用常规军力优势快速达到作战目的，并且国际社会没有时间和机会进行干预。

尔”战术弹道导弹。这说明巴基斯坦的核战略不排除面对印度入侵时在其领土范围内使用核武器的可能。另一方面，印度核力量发展也表现出超越其“不首先使用”和“最低威慑”核政策的迹象。印度国防研究与发展组织主任阿维纳什·詹德还曾表示，“烈火”-6导弹将携带分导式多弹头，并将大幅减少反应时间。[①] 此外，印度正在研发更加精确的“普拉哈尔”战术导弹，将有可能为印度提供“第一次打击”的能力。[②] 这些都与印度所宣称的“最低威慑”和“不首先使用”的核政策相悖。

此外，印巴核能力的不平衡也在进一步加剧，可能导致南亚地区脆弱的战略安全环境进一步恶化。在核武器制造能力方面，巴基斯坦的导弹制造能力并不完整，外界估计巴可自行生产导弹单体、火箭发动机机体和喷嘴、固体推进剂药柱、以及弹头部分，但其他部件仍依赖进口，[③] 因此在与印度进行核军备竞赛的过程中可能出现脱节，严重影响战略稳定。另一方面，印巴民用核能力的差距也可能拉大。2008年《核供应国集团》解除了对印度的核禁运；2015年1月奥巴马总统访印，重启了此前冻结的《美印民用核能协议》。若该协议得以实施，印度可广泛从国际市场上获取核原料和技术。而受“卡迪尔·汗地下核网络”以及“苏丹·巴希卢丁·迈哈迈德事件”影响，美国对巴

① Hans M. Kristensen, “India's Missile Modernization Beyond Minimum Deterrence”. FAS Security Blog, Oct 04, 2013, http://blogs.fas.org/security/2013/10/indianmirv/#more-6160.

② Narang V. Five Myths about India's Nuclear Posture [J]. The Washington Quarterly, 2013, 36 (3): 143-157.

③ Michael Elleman and Mark Fitzpatrick, “Thrd-State Missile Theat Assessment,” in Missile Defense: Confrontation and Cooperation, eds. Alexei Arbatov, Vladimir Dvorkin, and Natalia Bubnova (Moscow: Carnegie Moscow Center, 2012), 98.

基斯坦核扩散问题表示担忧，因而拒绝与其签署任何一项核电站或民用核合作协议。印巴民用核领域发展的不平衡，也可能成为印巴之间潜在的不稳定因素，为印巴战略失衡埋下隐患。

（三）一个僵持点：朝鲜核问题

2013 年 2 月 12 日，朝鲜不顾国际社会的反对，悍然进行了第三次核试验。之后朝中社的新闻公报称，试验采用了“爆发力大、小型化、轻量化的原子弹”，并“在高度水平上安全而完美地进行”。朝鲜的举动使得半岛核危机重现，严重冲击了地区安全形势。时至今日，朝核问题仍未得到妥善解决，虽然当前局势有所缓和，但有关各方立场难以调和，减持局面仍无改观。

金正恩掌权以来，朝鲜拥核意志非常坚定。一方面，朝鲜不断发展核武器能力，试射“银河”3 号运载火箭，进行第三次地下核试验，对宁边核设施和西海发射场进行扩建，并进一步发展弹头小型化及远程投射能力。据美国核科学家齐格弗里德·赫克博士估计，朝鲜已有多至 12 枚核武器，并且这一数字可能在两年后达到 20 枚。[①] 朝鲜目前大约拥有不到 100 枚射程在 1000 千米以下的“飞毛腿”和 KN－02 短程弹道导弹，不到 50 枚射程 1250 千米的“劳动”中程弹道导弹，以及不到 50 枚射程 3000 千米的“大浦洞”－1 中程弹道导弹。[②] 此外，朝鲜

---

① Siegfried S. Hecker, The real threat from North Korea is the nuclear arsenal built over the last decade, Bulletin of the Atomic Scientists, January 7, 2015. 参见：http://thebulletin.org/real－threat－north－korea－nuclear－arsenal－built－over－last－decade7883.

② “Ballistic and Cruise Missile Threat,” National Air and Space Intelligence Center, Wright－Patterson AFB, 2013，详见：http://www.25af.af.mil/shared/media/document/AFD－130710－054.pdf.

还拥有数量不明的“舞水端”中程弹道导弹，并正在研制射程5500千米以上的“大浦洞”-2和KN-08[①]洲际弹道导弹。另一方面，朝鲜将拥核在政策上和法律上固定下来。2013年3月，朝鲜劳动党中央委员会制定了“并进”的新战略路线，即经济建设与核力量建设并进。同年4月，朝鲜召开最高人民会议，会议上通过了《关于进一步巩固自卫性的核拥有国地位》的法令。[②]

朝鲜在第三次核试验的紧张局势过后，开始主动缓和立场，表示愿意在不设先决条件的情况下重返六方会谈。然而奥巴马执政以来一直对朝鲜采取“战略忍耐”的政策，坚持将朝鲜以“可验证的、不可逆转的方式”放弃核武器计划作为与朝鲜实现关系正常化的前提。美国还与日韩一道设置恢复谈判的先决条件，即履行《2·29协议》的“无核化先决条件”，暂停核试验，暂停导弹试射，以及暂停宁边铀浓缩活动。2015年1月28日，美日韩六方会谈首席代表在东京举行会谈，就继续敦促朝鲜半岛无核化、推动重启六方会谈达成一致，认为有关各方遵守2005年达成的《9·19共同声明》是非常重要的，因此在六方会谈重启前，朝鲜应拿出具体表现，履行对无核化的承诺。但朝鲜始终宣称在任何情况下都不放弃核武器，与美、日、韩三国立场相距甚远。由此看来，六方会谈仍没有重启的基础。

---

① “舞水端”导弹也被称作“劳动”B型（Nodong-B）或“大浦洞”X型（Taepodong-X）导弹，在2010年阅兵中被首次展出。KN-08导弹也被称作“劳动”C型（Nodong-C）或“火星”-13（Hwasong-13）导弹，在2012年阅兵中被首次展出。目前这两款导弹尚未进行试射。有学者分析认为，出现在阅兵中的这两款导弹只是模型而已，并没有实战能力。

② “朝鲜决定进一步巩固自卫性的、核拥有国的地位”，新华网，2013年4月1日。

与此同时，美国为增进盟友的信心，采取了一系列强化东北亚军事同盟的举措。美国宣布与韩国共同执行针对朝鲜的“定制威慑”战略，并先后举办“关键决心”、“乙支自由卫士”等联合军演。作为回应，朝鲜频繁试射导弹，甚至威胁进行新形式的核试验。此外，美国还以朝核问题为借口，推进反导系统在亚太地区的部署，而日本也借机炒作，大力扩充军备，破坏了地区的和平与稳定。这些举动不仅没有缓和朝核问题，反而给朝鲜带来更大的军事压力，刺激朝鲜进一步发展核武器，与促使朝鲜放弃核武器的目标背道而驰。

朝核问题不仅仅是“核”的问题，它还牵涉到安全、经济、社会和人权等因素。2014 年 11 月 18 日，联合国大会第三委员会在纽约通过朝鲜人权决议案后，朝鲜不断对该决议案进行驳斥和谴责，朝鲜外务省发表声明，反对联合国在美国操控下通过该决议案，称美国的行为正在“逼迫朝鲜继续新一轮核试验”。此外，索尼影业由于拍摄制作了有关刺杀朝鲜领导人金正恩的喜剧电影《采访》，而遭受黑客组织“和平卫士”的网络攻击，美国指责朝鲜支持了这一行动，[①] 并对朝鲜进行了一系列制裁。随着人权、网络安全等问题持续发酵，朝核问题的形势将进一步复杂化。

（四）一个隐患点：日本核野心

日本自然资源匮乏，约有 84% 的能源依赖进口。因此，日本很早便开始重视核能发电等能源自给措施。2011 年福岛核事故之前，日本有 54 个商用核反应堆，其发电量占日本的近

---

① Weise, Elizabeth; Johnson, Kevin. FBI confirms North Korea behind Sony hack. U. S. A Today. December 19, 2014.

30%。福岛核事故之后，日本核电一度停摆，但由于采用化石燃料发电费用高昂，因而日本在2014年宣布支持“重启核电”的政策。

日本是《不扩散核武器条约》的缔约国，可在接受国际原子能机构监督的前提下，获得、生产、使用或运输钚和铀等核材料。日本一直致力于在国内建立一套核燃料循环体系，并制定了以钚后处理为基础的闭循环核燃料政策。经过多年建设的日本六所村钚后处理厂将于2015年3月正式投入使用，工厂建成后，日本将具备自行处理乏燃料的能力，这是日本实现国内完整闭合燃料循环的关键环节，将使日本成为签订《不扩散核武器条约》的无核国家中，唯一拥有包括浓缩铀和后处理钚的几乎完整核燃料生产能力的国家。今后六所村还将建造混合燃料工厂，最终形成核燃料再处理的联合工厂。根据国际原子能机构的报告，截至2012年底，日本拥有44.2吨分离钚，其中9.3吨存放于国内，其余34.9吨存放于法国和英国的后处理厂。[①] 美国军控专家西普尔分析认为，日本储藏的钚材料足够制造1000枚核弹头。[②] 此外，日本在处理敏感材料方面的表现也无法令人满意，不仅在向美国归还331千克武器级钚材料时屡拖不决，而且在2014年向国际原子能机构提交的钚持有量报告中，漏报了640千克钚材料，难免让外界对此中内幕产生怀疑。

① “The Current Situation of Plutonium Management in Japan,” Atomic Energy Commission of Japan, September 11, 2013, http://www.aec.go.jp/jicst/NC/sitemap/pdf/130911e.pdf.

② Frank von Hippel, “Should the U.S. Encourage South Korea and Japan to Make Plutonium-Based Nuclear Fuels?” presentation at a Nonproliferation Policy Education Center, Washington, D.C., April 4, 2013).

除了过剩的核材料储备之外，日本还通过太空项目获得了研制核武器运载系统所需的技术能力。日本于 20 世纪 90 年成功研制了固体推进、有效载荷 1.8 吨的 M－V 运载火箭，并在 2013 年首次试射了新一代运载火箭“艾普斯隆”－1。此外，日本太空发展署自 1994 年开始进行大气层再入试验，并于 2011 年成功实现了 H－2B 火箭最后一级的大气层再入。日本还通过与美国开展反导合作，进一步发展精确定位和轨道跟踪等技术。①

一份于 1994 年解密的文件显示，日本外务省曾于 1969 年提出一套核政策，即“暂时采取不拥有核武器的政策”，同时“保留制造核武器所需的经济和技术潜力”。② 这套政策也被称为“技术性威慑”政策。尽管日本声称这份文件仅仅是研究报告，但事实上日本一直沿着这条道路发展，目前日本过剩的核材料储备，以及通过太空项目获取的技术和能力，已经使其拥有研制核武器的潜力。

此外，日本政坛近年来对待核武器的态度也值得关注。尽管日本宣称坚持其“无核三原则”，但日本国内主张“拥核”的呼声不断涌出。2002 年，自由党党首小泽一郎曾公开表示，日本拥有足够的钚材料，可以“一夜之间拥有上千枚核弹头”。③

---

① Samuels, Richard J., and James L. Schoff. “Japan's Nuclear Hedge: Beyond ” Allergy “ and Breakout.” Strategic Asia 2013 – 14: Asa in the Second Nuclear Age. Eds. Tellis, Ashley J., Abraham M. Denmark, and Travis Tanner. Seattle: National Bureau of Asian Research, 2013.

② Norihiro Kato (Translated by Michael Emmerich), Ambiguities of Japan's Nuclear Policy, The International New York Times, APRIL 13, 2014.

③ 李春玲：“国际核不扩散机制与日本的‘核武装’问题”，《世界经济与政治论坛》2005 年第 4 期，第 48 页。

2006 年，时任外相麻生太郎在参议院安全事务会议上指出，拥有核武器并不违反和平宪法。2011 年，东京都知事石原慎太郎表示，日本应当发展核武器，以应对迅速崛起的中国构成的威胁。2014 年，日本外相岸田文雄在众议院预算委员会会议上称，发生紧急状况时，为保护国民安全，在不得已的情况下，不排除允许美军将核武器运进日本的可能性，这一表态明显违背了“无核三原则”不运进核武器的精神。从日本核材料生产、存储状况，制造核武器所需的工业能力和技术，以及经济实力等方面来看，只要拥有足够的政治动机，研制核武器并不会有很大障碍。特别是在日本政坛右倾化严重的今天，其核政策动向值得关注。

（五）一个争议点：导弹防御问题

导弹防御是美国“新三位一体”战略威慑体系的重要一环，美国自 2002 年退出《反导条约》以来，一直致力于建立全球一体的导弹防御体系。2013 年朝鲜进行了第三次核试验，半岛危机重现，美国借口“朝鲜导弹威胁”，进一步推动亚太地区导弹防御体系的部署。美国的做法引发了俄罗斯和中国的强烈关注，导弹防御问题也成为亚太地区大国战略博弈的重要舞台。

朝鲜第三次核试验后，美国在日本青森部署了一部前置 X 波段雷达，向台湾地区出售了“铺路爪”远程预警雷达，在太平洋阿达克岛附近部署了一部可移动的海基 X 波段雷达。2014 年 10 月，美国又在日本京都部署了第二部前置 X 波段雷达。目前，美国在关岛基地部署有“末段高空区域防御”（THAAD）系统，其阿拉斯加部署的地基拦截弹也将增至 44 枚。此外，美国在太平洋共有16艘“宙斯盾”战舰,[①] 估计约50枚以上的“标准”-3IA拦截弹，一旦需要可快速部署至西太平洋地区。

此外，美国还推动与盟友的反导合作。日本自20世纪90年代末开始与美国合作发展反导系统。目前，其由“宙斯盾”和“爱国者”-3组成的双层导弹防御系统已初步建成。美日两国还构建了联合预警和作战指挥机制，2011年横田基地设立了导弹防御联合作战指挥所，配备美国的“联合指挥系统”（JCMS），两国导弹防御体系进一步融合。美国还决定在2017年之前向日本增派2艘“宙斯盾”战舰，届时美国在日本的“宙斯盾”战舰数量将增至7艘。[②] 美国还希望与澳大利亚就导弹防御问题进行合作。2014年6月，美国总统奥巴马和国防部长哈格尔与访美的澳大利亚总理艾博特进行会谈，商讨了加强美澳导弹防御合作的有关事项。此外，美国也在一直努力将韩国纳入其反导体系。目前，韩国表示暂无意购买美国的THAAD系统，而希望独立打造自主的防空反导体系。但在美国的压力下，韩国已承诺将增强其与美国导弹防御系统间的互操作性。随着朝鲜半岛局势进一步紧张，不排除韩国加入美反导体系的可能性。

美国推动亚太导弹防御体系的部署，特别是试图将韩国纳入其反导体系的努力，遭到了朝鲜的强烈不满。2014年9月，朝中社发表评论文章，称美国捏造“朝鲜威胁论”，企图以朝鲜半岛为跳板，称霸亚太地区，这一举动将导致朝鲜半岛军事形势不稳，并引发军备竞赛。

---

① Fact Sheet: Aegis Ballistic Missile Defense, Missile Defense Agency, January 2015. 参见: http: //www. mda. mil/system/aegis_ bmd. html.

② Hagel: the U. S. to Send 2 More Aegis Ships to Japan, By Cheryl Pellerin, American Forces Press Service, TOKYO, April 6, 2014. 参见: http: //www. defense. gov/news/newsarticle. aspx? id = 121992.

美国的举动也引发了中国和俄罗斯的严重关切。由于“标准”－3IA和IB拦截尚不具备拦截洲际弹道导弹的能力，并且具备此拦截能力的“标准”－3ⅡB的研制计划被暂时搁置，因此目前美国的导弹防御系统还未对中国或俄罗斯的核威慑能力构成直接威胁。但有中国科学家认为，美国的反导雷达已部署在中国周边国家，随着未来“标准”－3ⅡA在亚太地区的部署，将有可能对中国的战略导弹进行上升段拦截，抵消中国有限的核报复能力。更重要的是，美国拒绝接受对其导弹防御系统的限制，随着技术的进一步提升，其威胁到中俄的核威慑力量似乎只是时间问题，这使得未来的形势更加复杂。因此，尽管美国一再表示亚太地区的导弹防御系统仅仅是为了应对朝鲜的导弹威胁，但仍然使中国和俄罗斯感到十分不安。

美国导弹防御在亚太地区的持续扩张，影响了中美的战略稳定，加重了双方的疑虑和猜忌，一定程度上影响了中美核对话的开启。导弹防御问题也阻碍了美俄双边核裁军的进程，俄罗斯要求下一阶段核裁军解决其在该问题上的安全关切，就此美俄两国存在很大分歧，将影响下一阶段核裁军谈判进程。此外，导弹防御领域还酝酿着新一轮的军备竞赛。事实上，俄罗斯在反对美国导弹防御扩张的同时，也高度重视空天防御体系的建设，致力于打造独立的导弹防御体系。2011年，俄罗斯成立了“空天防御部队”，负责保护俄罗斯领空、拦截弹道导弹和巡航导弹以及运作俄罗斯军事卫星。目前，俄罗斯在莫斯科周围部署了A－135战略导弹防御系统，其武装力量各军兵种部署的包括S－300、S－400、“布克”、“道尔”等在内的多种防空导弹，都具备较强的防空与反导能力。此外，俄罗斯还在研制新一代的A－235战略反导系统，以及新一代S－500防空和战术反导系统，并将进一步研发海基导弹防御系统。

（五）一个合作点：核安全、核安保问题

尽管2011年日本福岛第一核电站发生了严重的事故，亚太地区在核电领域依然保持着较高的发展速度。截至2013年底，东亚和南亚地区共有119座核电反应堆投入运作，另有49座正在建设之中，此外，根据各国核电发展计划，还将新建100座核电反应堆。① 随着核电计划的推进，各国核材料储量也逐步增长，亚太地区核安全、核安保问题也引发更多的关注。

总的来看，亚太地区核安全、核安保现状并不乐观，一些国家和地区对这些核材料与核设施缺乏有效的保护，核设施安全存在严重隐患，核材料与核技术存在扩散的风险。赫克博士曾表示出对朝鲜核设施安全状况的担忧，朝鲜宁边核设施一度面临导致日本福岛核电站重大核事故的冷却水供应故障。韩国总统朴槿惠也曾指出，一旦宁边核设施发生事故，其严重程度甚至会高于切尔诺贝利核电站事故。巴基斯坦核安全、核安保能力一直饱受质疑，历史上也曾有“汗博士核走私网络”的核扩散事件。巴国内局势动荡，恐怖势力活动猖獗，并且“基地”组织和“虔诚军”等恐怖组织都曾对掌握核武器表现出兴趣，一旦核材料甚至核武器落入恐怖分子之手，后果将不堪设想。日本违背1997年向国际原子能机构作出的“无过剩钚”承诺，拥有着可疑的过量钚库存。此前，日本被曝在2014年向国际原子能机构提交的钚持有量报告中，漏报了640千克钚材料，也暴露出其在核材料监督和管理方面存在严重漏洞。

目前，有关核安全、核安保的国际机制仍不完善，不仅缺

---

① WNA Reactor table, country papers, OECD/IEA World Energy Outlook.

少有约束力的国际标准，而且没有特定的申报和监察制度。尽管许多专家表示同行评审以及技术合作对提升核安全、核安保水平十分必要，但目前采取的措施还远远不够，且大都是自愿性的。更重要的是，核事故一旦发生，将可能危及周边国家；核材料一旦失窃，全世界都面临威胁。因此，核安全、核安保需要各国的共同努力。近些年来，亚太地区各国也进一步认识到核安全、核安保问题的重要性，围绕这一问题的合作也越来越广泛和深入。东盟十国逐步加强防扩散和打击核恐怖主义的合作，2012 年东盟原子能监管机构成立，为东南亚各国探讨核安全、核安保问题，分享有关信息创造了平台。东盟地区论坛也自 2009 年开始，主持军备控制与防扩散的闭会期间会议，旨在讨论打击核扩散、推动核裁军、促进和平利用核能的措施。国际原子能机构倡导的亚洲安全网络（ASNS）以及亚太区域核科技合作协定（RCA），也为亚太地区分享核安全相关知识、促进多边核合作等发挥了重要的作用。

中国在推动各国核安全、核安保合作方面也作出了卓著的贡献。中国不仅在发展核能的过程中严把核安全关，保持了良好的核安全记录；并且认识到实现普遍核安全的重要性，积极促成更多国家加入核安全进程。中国国家原子能机构与美国能源部共同建设的“中美核安保示范中心”也是亚太地区核安全、核安保合作的亮点之一，其主要功能是开展核安保、核材料管制、核进出口管理的国际交流与合作、教育与培训、分析与测试、先进技术展示等。预计在 2015 年底建成并投入使用，它将成为亚太地区乃至全球规模最大、设备最齐全、设施最先进的核安保交流、培训中心。

然而，亚太地区核安全、核安保领域的合作也存在着开倒车的现象。受乌克兰问题影响，美俄关系进一步恶化，俄罗斯终止了两国削减核威胁的双边框架协定。尽管俄罗斯表示有能力确保国内核材料和核设施的安全，但目前俄罗斯遭到西方国际多轮制裁，经济受到严重影响，外界担心俄罗斯无法为其核材料和核设施的保护提供足够的资金支持，因而存在核材料流失的隐患。此外，俄罗斯还表示将不参加 2016 年的芝加哥核安全峰会，[①] 这无疑严重打击了国际核安全、核安保合作的努力，使得核安全问题成为地缘政治的牺牲品。

二、亚太地区核态势对地区安全的影响与挑战

（一）诱发核军备竞赛，加大核扩散风险

目前，美国、俄罗斯、印度、巴基斯坦和朝鲜等国均在进行着各自的核力量现代化计划——美国将在 30 年内斥资数千亿美元，用于升级其核武器系统及核武器综合体；俄罗斯计划在 10 年内将苏联时期的洲际弹道导弹全部退役，“白杨” -M 及各改进型号将成为其战略导弹部队的主力；[②] 印巴两国致力于建立各自的“三位一体”核力量体系；朝鲜则在进一步提升洲际弹道导弹能力和弹头小型化技术。

亚太地区各国争相推进核力量现代化计划，诱发新一轮的

① Comment by the Information and Press Department on the U. S. media reports that Russia does not intend to take part in preparations for the 2016 Nuclear Security Summit, The Ministry of Foreign Affairs of the Russian Federation, November 5, 2014. 参见：http：//www. mid. ru/bdomp/brp _ 4. nsf/e78a48070f128a7b43256999005bcbb3/fdb1c2c6f7427fe4c3257d88004155b5！OpenDocument.

② Hans M. Kristensen, Russian ICBM Force Modernization：Arms Control Please!, May. 07, 2014. 参见：http：//fas. org/blogs/security/2014/05/russianmodernization/.

核军备竞赛，这无疑是对国际防扩散体系权威性的一种削弱，将打击无核国家参与防扩散合作的积极性，使得国际防扩散合作难以形成合力。与此同时，随着一些国家核力量的发展，核武器及其技术扩散的事件也时有发生——巴基斯坦“核武器之父”卡迪尔·汗博士曾将核技术和有关设备转让给朝鲜、伊朗和利比亚等国；朝鲜则采取“以弹养弹”的策略，将转让导弹及其技术作为进一步发展导弹技术的经济来源之一，据美国中央情报局分析，朝鲜曾向巴基斯坦、伊朗、伊拉克、叙利亚、也门、埃及和利比亚等国转让导弹或相关技术。

倘若亚太地区核军备竞赛激烈程度不减，将可能刺激更多国家诉诸核武，特别是在研制核武器方面具有很大潜力的日本，一旦掌握足够动机，将在较短时间内将“技术性威慑”的基础转化为“拥核”的资本。由此看来，亚太地区面临的核扩散风险将越来越严峻。

（二）毒化大国关系，影响核裁军进程

1998年，印巴两国先后进行核试验，成为事实上拥有核武器的国家。持乐观态度的学者认为，核武器的出现会使印巴两国领导人认识到冲突升级至核战争的恐怖后果，因而可以避免冲突的发生，使得两国像冷战时期的美苏一样，得以维持一种稳定的战略平衡关系。然而事实却恰恰相反，两国相继拥核后，仍然爆发了一次激烈的军事冲突，即1999年的卡吉尔冲突，以及一次严重的政治危机，即2001年的印度议会大厦遭袭事件。

总的来说，核武器的出现以及战略对峙态势的形成，增加了印巴关系的不确定因素。由于目前两国均未形成可靠的“第二次打击”能力，因此威慑的可信度有限，加之双方在核力量

和常规力量方面并不平衡，导致两国战略稳定关系十分脆弱。[①] 双方为了建立这种“第二次打击”能力而导致了针锋相对的军备竞赛，这也不利于为今后多边核裁军的开启创造条件。

此外，美俄两国当前的核态势仍未摆脱“冷战思维”。尽管双方都曾表示愿意改变以“相互确保摧毁”为基础的战略稳定关系，但目前来看在这方面并无太大改观。并且近期两国的核战略方面也没有重大调整，短期内不会摆脱“打击军事目标”、“预警即发射”等策略。这势必对未来核裁军造成负面的影响。近一段时间美俄关系的恶化也影响了两国的核关系，使得下一阶段核裁军谈判的形势更加不明朗。美俄围绕《中导条约》的争论又现，两国在防扩散及核安全方面的合作也遭受打击。

（三）引发核安全问题，增加核恐怖袭击风险

联合国秘书长潘基文曾指出，“核恐怖主义是这个时代最为严重的威胁之一”；美国总统奥巴马也对外宣称，“核恐怖主义是当今最紧迫和最极端的危险”。制造一个核爆炸装置最少只需获得 25 千克高浓缩铀或 8 千克钚，“基地”组织、“虔诚军”、“奥姆真理教”等恐怖组织都有获取核武器的意图，其中一些组织已经试图通过黑市获取核材料。此外，恐怖分子还可以通过袭击核设施，或者利用少量放射性材料制造脏弹等手段实施核恐怖袭击。

亚太地区核军备竞赛加剧，核扩散的形势越来越严峻，使得核恐怖主义获取核武器、开展核恐怖袭击的风险大大增加。并且

---

① “第二次打击”是核战略术语，也称为“核报复”，第二次打击能力指在遭到敌方首轮核打击后，可以保存足够的核报复力量并实施有效的核反击。从核威慑角度看，第二次打击能力愈强，威慑的可信度越高，两国的战略稳定性越强。

各国在核安全、核安保方面尚未形成可执行的、统一的“黄金标准”，各国核安全、核安保水平高低不一。一些国家和地区对这些核材料与核技术缺乏有效的保护，核材料与核技术存在扩散的隐患；一些国家局势动荡，国内恐怖势力活动频繁，核设施遭受袭击的风险很高。虽然目前尚未发生重大核恐怖事件，但鉴于复杂多变的国际安全形势，核恐怖主义的威胁不容忽视。

（四）恶化安全形势，损害地区和平与稳定

其一，朝鲜核问题已成为东北亚地区安全的焦点与核心，如不能妥善解决，将严重影响地区安全与稳定。美国对朝鲜的敌视政策是朝鲜拥核自保的重要因素，而美、日、韩强化军事同盟的做法，会造成东北亚地区安全结构的失衡，给朝鲜带来更大的军事压力，使得促其弃核难上加难。

目前围绕朝核问题的分歧依然严重，如果有关各国特别是美朝双方没有实质性的战略调整，即便恢复六方会谈也难以取得突破性进展。朝核问题若悬而不决，地区局势恶化的可能性将进一步上升，半岛和平更加遥遥无期。

其二，印巴战略对峙使得南亚次大陆安全形势恶化。印巴两国间的战略稳定十分脆弱，目前双方都在发展“可信的”的威慑能力，双方争先恐后地大搞核力量建设，军备竞赛的稳定性很差。印巴竞相发展当量小、射程短的战术核武器，使得冲突中的核门槛更低，导致两国的危机稳定性遭受极大挑战。印巴两国受宗教意识形态和领土争端影响，长期处于敌对状态，历史上曾多次爆发战争。并且宗教意识形态的差异将长期存在，而领土争端在短期内也无法妥善解决，很可能会成为冲突的直接导火索，一旦核武器在冲突中被使用，后果将不堪设想。

三、对维护亚太地区核态势安全与稳定的思考

维护亚太地区核态势的安全与稳定，既符合各国的共同利益，同时也是各国的共同责任。有关各方应积极寻求利益的最大公约数，开展良性互动，减少战略猜疑和误判，共同推进国际核裁军和防扩散进程，深入开展核安全、核安保合作，共同改善地区安全环境，促进亚太地区的和平、稳定和繁荣。

（一）进一步完善国际防扩散体系

国际防扩散体系在防止和延缓大规模杀伤性武器及其运载工具的扩散、维护世界和地区的和平与安全方面，发挥了积极的作用。然而，目前的防扩散体系仍存在一定的局限性。朝鲜曾利用《美朝核框架协议》的缺陷，限制国际原子能机构的检查监督权，并继续储存其所含有武器级钚的乏燃料。[①] 联合国安理会针对朝鲜的一系列制裁也未能有效遏制其拥核。此外，日本1997年向国际原子能机构承诺遵守“无过剩钚”原则，而目前却拥有着可疑的过量钚库存。这些都说明当前防扩散体系亟待加强，有关各国应不遗余力地贯彻和落实防扩散政策，推进相关法律法规建设，进一步完善国际防扩散体系。更重要的是，各国的防扩散努力不应仅限于防止大规模杀伤性武器本身，而需寻找和解决造成问题的根源。

---

① Goldschmidt P. The Urgent Need to Strengthen the Nuclear Non – Proliferation Regime ［J］. Policy Outlook，2006（25）：360.

（二）稳定推进核裁军进程

美俄两国应稳定推进核裁军进程，为最终全面、彻底核裁军创造必要条件。美俄两国需要彻底抛弃“冷战思维”，进一步降低核武器的作用，取消“一触即发”的高警戒状态，尽早就下一阶段核裁军展开谈判。美国还应努力推动国会批准《全面禁止核试验条约》，这将为国际不扩散体制带来积极的影响，有力地支持各国的防扩散努力。印巴两国也应尽快参与到国际防扩散的进程中，维护国际防扩散体系的有效性和权威性；同时两国还应避免进一步的核军备竞赛，为今后加入多边核裁军进程创造有利条件。

（三）深入开展核安全、核安保合作

加强核安全、核安保措施是防止核事故、降低和扩散风险的直接和有效途径。深入开展核安全、核安保合作符合各国共同利益。因此，各国应积极参与地区核安全、核安保合作，推动核能的和平利用。共同制定合理、有效的执行标准，建立合作示范中心，加强各国核材料和核设施的安全。

（四）改善地区安全环境，建立地区安全机制

和平与稳定的地区安全环境可以推动亚太核态势趋向平稳发展。建立地区安全机制，积极开展安全对话，有利于解决朝核问题，改善地区安全环境。美国通过加强地区军事存在的举措，非但不能有效解决朝核问题，反而会促使朝鲜加快拥核进程。因此有关各方应保持克制，避免对抗升级，积极为谈判的开启创造条件。此外，各国应积极推动印巴两国安全机制的建立，保持南亚地区的战略稳定，促进两国通过和平对话的方式化解矛盾。

Current Major Features of Nuclear Issue in Asia - Pacific

Wand Zheng and Yu Xiaoling[①]

Asia – Pacific here refers to the large area covering Asia and the Pacific. The nuclear status quo in the Asia – Pacific is characterized by one dilemma, one hot spot, one equilibrium and one hidden disaster.

I. One Dilemma: the Nuclear Issue in North Korea

In 2002, the nuclear crisis broke out after both North Korea and the United States tore up the *U. S. – North Korea Agreed Framework* (October 1994), and it has been on and off and has been escalating ever since then. After two tests of nuclear weapons in 2006 and 2009, North Korea conducted a third underground nuclear test on February 12, 2013, despite strong opposition from the international community, and claimed that the test had used a miniaturized nuclear device with greater explosive power. On April 4, North Korea held the 7th

① Yu Xiaoling and Wang Zheng are researchers at China Defense Science and Technology Center.

Session of the 12th Supreme People's Assembly (SPA) and adopted the ordinance *On Consolidating the Position of Nuclear Weapons State for Self - Defense*, legalizing the permanent possession of nuclear weapons for North Korea.

It is estimated that North Korea may possibly possess about 40 kilograms of weapons - grade plutonium materials, capable of producing 8 - 10 nuclear bombs. Moreover, North Korea is restarting the five - megawatt reactor and building experimental light water reactors, and thus more plutonium materials will be extracted. It is developing centrifuges, and carrying out uranium enrichment programs, but it is still uncertain whether the uranium enrichment plants have begun to produce weapons - grade uranium. It seeks to produce missiles capable of carrying nuclear warheads. According to the *2013 Ballistic and Cruise Missile Threat Assessment* produced by the National Air and Space Intelligence Center (NASIC) of the U. S. Department of Defense, North Korea now possesses fewer than 100 SCUD short - range ballistic missiles (SRBM) (maximum range of less than 1000 km), 50 No Dong medium - range ballistic missiles (MRBM) (maximum range of 1250 km), 50 Taepo Dong - 1 intercontinental ballistic missiles ICBM (maximum range of 3000 km), and it is continuing to develop Taepo Dong - 2 ICBM (maximum range of 5500 km) and has unveiled the new program to develop an intercontinental ballistic missile (ICBM).

At present, the North Korean nuclear weapons program is still in a stalemate. Though in the second half of 2013, it began to soften its stand and expressed willingness to reopen the 6 - party talk unconditionally, the Obama Administration has adhered to the strategic patience, demanding that North Korea should first of all change its attitude and express sincerity to give up its nuclear weapons and then resume their talks.

In the near future, neither side will give ground on its core position, and the future situation on the peninsular does not look optimistic. For a long time, North Korea has considered establishing relations with the United States as crucial to get out of the dilemma, and seeking to sign a bilateral agreement with the United States. Nuclear weapons are a tramp card to hold negotiations between North Korea and the U. S. and a powerful weapon to guarantee the survival of North Korean government, which North Korea will never give up easily. What worries the U. S. most in the near future is not whether North Korea possesses nuclear weapons but whether it spreads nuclear weapons. In the future, the U. S will make all possible efforts to halt the progress of North Korea developing nuclear armed missiles, especially intercontinental ballistic missiles that can reach the homeland U. S.

From the perspective of security in Northeast Asia, the North Korean nuclear weapons program is not only a problem of North Korea – U. S. relations, but also interwoven with the major powers seeking domination for security in Northeast Asia, touching upon some of the long – standing deep contradictions and security problems, on which rivalry for interests will never stop. The North Korean nuclear weapons program will be deadlock for a long time to come.

Ⅱ. One Hot Spot: India - Pakistan Nuclear Standoff

In 1998, against the background of U. S. – Russia significant disarmament after the end of the Cold War, India acted against the world trend, tested its first nuclear explosive device and became one of the countries that in fact possess nuclear weapons. India intended to add its weight in seeking the position of world political power by possession of nuclear weapons.

India never discloses the number of nuclear weapons it possesses, and it is estimated that it possesses 90 – 100 nuclear weapons. India possesses such delivery vehicles as the Prithvi and Agni series SRBM and IRBM (AgniⅣ is capable of 3500 – km range), and Dhanush (K – 15) submarine – launched ballistic missiles. India is now making all efforts to establish a "triad" of nuclear force system, and has accelerated its development of land – based ICBM and ship – based weapon systems, focusing on extending the missile range and the scope of strategic deterrence and improving nuclear counter – attack capability. In September 2013, India conducted the successful test launch of the Agni V ICBM with the largest range of over 5000 km, which will be deployed in 2015. An even longer ranged (6000 km) Agni VI is also in the design phase. In April 2013, India declared that it planned to deploy a suitable sea – based nuclear deterrent force in 2015 or 2016. In January 2013, the K – 15 submarine – launched ballistic missile was successfully test launched with a range of 700 km, which was the 14th test of the K – 15 missile and marks that India has achieved the limited capability of launching sea – based missiles. India is also planning to develop longer ranged submarine – launched missiles with greater destructive power.

After India conducted tests of nuclear weapons, Pakistan made successive tests of nuclear weapons, and in fact enters among the countries with nuclear weapons. Pakistan clearly takes India as the target of its nuclear deterrence, aimed at establishing a nuclear posture of reciprocal nuclear deterrence against India while it considers countering India's superior conventional military force. Pakistan develops its nuclear force against the reference of India, pursuing equilibrium with India. It is estimated that Pakistan possesses 90 – 110 nuclear weapons with fighter aircraft and ballistic missiles as means of delivery – F – 16s capable of carrying nuclear warheads, Mirage fighter aircraft, and the Ghauri and Shaheen SRBM and MRBM, and the Shaheen 2 is capable of a 2000 – km range.

Therefore, in terms of the nuclear posture, India and Pakistan face a relationship of nuclear competition and nuclear standoff.

Ⅲ. One Equilibrium: U. S. - Russia Nuclear Game

After the Obama Administration was established, it advocated establishing a "nuclear weapons free world" and negotiated and signed the new START with Russia, which stipulates that both sides will reduce the number of their nuclear warheads under deployment to 1550 by 2018. On this foundation, the U. S. pursues global cooperation efforts for stopping the spread of nuclear weapons and materials and countering nuclear terrorism, and reinforces the international nuclear non-proliferation system, including sponsoring the summit meeting for nuclear security, proposing measures to improve management of nuclear materials and weapon systems in the world, and preventing the spread of nuclear weapons. In June 2013, President Obama delivered a speech in Berlin, proposing that the United States seeks to negotiate with Russia, and conclude a joint effort to further reduce the number of deployed nuclear weapons by one-third on the basis of the New START treaty, that is, to around 1000 pieces. These measures improved the U. S. international image and gave the U. S. dominating power in international nuclear arms control and disarmament.

On the other hand, the U. S. continues its policy of nuclear deterrence and extended deterrence in order to ensure its nuclear superiority. In the President's new guidance of *Nuclear Weapons Employment Strategy of the United States* released on June 19, 2013, the U. S. emphasizes that "as long as nuclear weapons exist, the United States will maintain a safe, secure and effective arsenal that guarantees the defense of the U. S. and our allies and partners". By the beginning of 2014, according to the estimate of U. S. authoritative experts, the United States has approximately 4650 nuclear warheads in its stockpile plus 2700 warheads that are retired and awaiting dismantling, making up a total number of around 7400 warheads. As to the delivery vehicles, the U. S. possesses 450 Minuteman-Ⅲ land-based intercontinental ballistic missiles (ICBM); 14 *Ohio* class nuclear-powered submarines, armed with Trident Ⅱ D5 submarine-launched ballistic missiles (SLBM), with a total number of 239 submarine – launched ballistic missiles on the deployed submarines; and an estimated total number of 60 strategic bombers armed with nuclear weapons. At present, the U. S. is implementing a plan for modernization of nuclear weapons, and it will carry out all – round upgrading of the current nuclear weapons system (including missiles, bombers, submarines, fighters, warheads and integrated nuclear weapon systems). This plan will continue for 30 years and cost as high as several hundred billion dollars, and the first decade only will cost over 200 billion dollars.

Russia pursues its nuclear deterrent policy of "practical containment". Since the 1990's, Russia has increased its dependence on nuclear weapons because there exists an ever – widening gap in conventional armed forces between Russia and the United States. Russia holds that the only capability that can stand up to the U. S. is its powerful nuclear arsenal, and a strategic nuclear force is the core means to contain threat, and support national security and foreign policies, and therefore Russia will "maintain adequate strategic stability and nuclear deterrence capability". Since the Ukraine incident, the West has continued to impose all kinds of sanctions against Russia, which further stimulates Russia's determination to strengthen its nuclear force.

By March 2014, Russia possesses an estimated number of 4300 warheads (including around 1600 deployed strategic nuclear warheads, around 2000 tactical nuclear warheads and around 700 strategic nuclear warheads in reserve), and around 3500 retired nuclear warheads that are awaiting dismantling. Currently deployed are 313 land – based intercontinental ballistic missiles (ICBM); 4 Delta –

IV class and 3 Delta – Ⅲ class strategic nuclear powered submarines, each armed with 16 submarine – launched ballistic missiles (SLBM); and heavy strategic bombers of Tu – 160 Blackjacks and Tu – 95MS Bears. In recent years Russia takes modernization of strategic nuclear weapons as a key link on its military modernization plan. It plans to build 8 Borei – class nuclear – powered ballistic missile submarines, of which 2 submarines have completed construction and joined the Russian Navy. Now the new strategic nuclear weapon systems for key development include the sea – based submarine – launched ballistic missile (SLBM) SS – NX – 32 (the Bulava), new types of land – based intercontinental ballistic missiles (ICBM), the road – mobile RS – 26 Rubezh, the heavy silo – based liquid – fuel Sarmat and the rail – based Yar. A new subsonic bomber is under design and will be commissioned for active service in the next 10 years. A new long – range air – launched nuclear land – attack cruise missile (LACM) Kh – 102 is being developed by Russia.

On the one hand, Russia participates actively in the international cooperation for non – proliferation and countering nuclear terrorism, and seeks to play an important role in addressing a series of problems such as the regional nuclear issues and establishing the international nuclear fuel bank. On the other hand, Russia also takes an active part in nuclear arms control, seeking to maintain strategic equilibrium with the United States. After the New START Treaty was signed, Russia binds the next – stage nuclear disarmament and tactical nuclear weapons issues to the anti – ballistic missile deployment of the U. S. and NATO, the non – nuclear strategic weapons of the United States, and weaponization of the outer space and other issues, and asks the United States to address Russia's security concerns, pursuing maintaining strategic equilibrium with the United States. In addition, Russia insists that other nuclear countries including the United Kingdom, France and China should be included into the next stage of nuclear disarmament.

By 2018 when the New START Treatybeing completely implemented, the United States and Russia will still possess over 90 percent of the nuclear weapons in the world. In terms of comparison of nuclear forces, Russia will still be the only country that can threat U. S. existence, and both will maintain the posture of strategic equilibrium of "mutual assured destruction" .

Ⅳ. One Hidden Danger: Japan's Nuclear Ambition

Japan is a country with limited natural resources and 84 percent of its energy supplies depend on imports. Therefore Japan started early to attach great attention to self – supportive energy measures like nuclear power plants, and 57 nuclear reactors are now in operation for generating electricity within Japan, accounting for 30 percent of its total power supply, and it plans to increase to 40 percent by 2017. Japan is a state party to the *Treaty on the Non – Proliferation of Nuclear Weapons* (NPT) and it can acquire, produce, use and transport such nuclear materials as plutonium and uranium under the supervision of the International Atomic Energy Agency. Japan has been seeking to establish a complete set of nuclear fuel cycle system within Japan proper and has established the closed nuclear fuel cycle policy based on plutonium reprocessing. In the village of Rokkasho in Japan, the Rokkasho nuclear fuel (plutonium) reprocessing plant will begin operating in March 2015 after years of construction. After it is completed, Japan will possess the capability of processing spent nuclear fuel and therefore Japan considers it as the critical link for achieving the complete nuclear fuel cycle within Japan proper. The nuclear fuel reprocessing plant has a maximum annual capability of processing 800 metric tons of heavy metals, including plutonium, uranium and other actinides, with a maximum daily capability of processing 4.8 tons and storage capacity of 3000 tons of spent nuclear fuel. In addition, a uranium enrichment plant, a low – level radioactive waste landfill center, and a high – level radioactive waste storage control center are built in Rokkasho. In the future, a MOX (mixed oxide) fuel fabrication plant will be built and eventually the Rokkasho industrial complex will be completed for nuclear fuel reprocessing. Thus it enables Japan to become the only one of the non – nuclear weapon states that possesses the almost complete capability of nuclear fuel production including uranium enrichment and plutonium reprocessing.

The plutonium distilled in the fuel reprocessing can be used not only for providing fuel for nuclear power plants but also for producing nuclear weapons. By the end of 2011, Japan has a total of 44.3 metric tons of plutonium stockpile –9.3 tons stored at Rokkasho and nine other sites in the island nation, and the rest of around 35 tons of plutonium stored in France and the United Kingdom. According to the support and supervision criteria of the International Atomic Energy Agency, 8 kilograms of plutonium is adequate for making a nuclear weapon, and Japan's stockpile of plutonium is enough for making thousands of crude nuclear weapons. Moreover, the United States once gave Japan 331 kilograms of plutonium for research purposes during the Cold War, of which a large share was weapons – grade plutonium materials. The batch of plutonium is now used as fuel for the fast neutron reactors in Tokaimura, Ibaraki Prefecture, Japan.

There has been continuing support from within Japan for the development of nuclear weapons. In 2002, the then Chief Cabinet Secretary Yasuo Fukuda openly claimed that Japan could possess nuclear weapons so long as it adhered to the exclusively defense – oriented defense. Chairman of the Liberal Party Ichiro Ozawa once claimed that the nuclear power plants in Japan had enough amount of plutonium and it was very simple to produce nuclear weapons. Japanese right – wing activists such as Shinzo Abe and Shintaro Ishihara expressed their attitude to support the development of nuclear weapons on different occasions. At present, the tendency towards Right – deviation in Japanese politics becomes comparatively apparent, and the Japanese government has begun attempting to break up the "Three Non – Nuclear Principles". Judging from the production and storage of nuclear materials, the industrial capability and technology needed for producing nuclear weapons, and the economic strength, Japan has possessed the capability to develop nuclear weapons. As long as there is enough political motivation, insurmountable barriers do not exist for Japan to develop nuclear weapons.

核力量
Nuclear Forces

2014 年美国核力量综述

李　毅　葛爱东

〔内容提要〕2014 年，美国在强化核力量建设的同时不断推进军控与裁军进程，核弹数量有所下降。一方面，美国继续其核武器延寿计划；另一方面，美国还在加强核弹安全性与可靠性验证，论证研发新型投送平台。为了保证核力量的实战能力，美国还进行了系列发射试验和演习。在核安全领域，美国也提出了相关要求，并加以落实。

主题词： 美国　核力量　建设　评估

作者单位： 中国国际问题研究院军控与安全研究中心

一、强化国家战略核威慑，推进国际军控进程

2014 年，美国通过提出新的军事战略思想和调整国防预算，强化了对外核威慑，并通过对核力量的多方位评估，试图加快核力量发展规划。

（一）调整新型军事战略，强化核威慑的作用

美国在提出新军事战略的同时，讨论了战略核威慑在新世纪的地位和作用。2014 年 10 月，美国战略与预算评估中心（CSBA）公布了其首份有关美国国防部“对消战略”的研究报

告。该战略与美国在20世纪70年代的“对消战略”类似，旨在尽快达成核与常规力量的综合均势，以解决在财政紧缩情况下美国所面对的最紧迫军事挑战，即维持美军在全球的力量投送能力，慑止潜在对手，使美国的盟友及伙伴在A2/AD情况下仍具有自身安全保障。为此，美国在较大范围内对其核威慑作用进行了讨论，2014年8月，美国战略司令部召开了威慑专题研讨会，探讨21世纪广泛的威慑问题，美国能源部主管核安全的副部长兼核军工管理局局长克莰将军提出NNSA的作用包括：维持安全、安保和有效的核威慑；在全球范围防止核扩散和核恐怖主义；努力开发更加灵活的基础设施并保持一个强大的科研基础，以满足未来任务的需求和挑战。而在2014年，美国总统奥巴马多次强调，与俄罗斯在克里米亚问题上的举动相比，他本人更担心曼哈顿遭到核武袭击。以此表明了其对俄在乌克兰问题上提出核挑战的藐视，以及美国面临的现实核威胁的紧迫性。这些举措都强化了核威慑在确保美国未来核安全方面的独特作用。

此外，本年度内，美国还通过修订核作战计划保持对朝鲜等新兴对手的威慑。2014年4月，美国媒体透露，美军首次在其应急核作战计划中将朝鲜列为核对手。美在最新版本的“5029作战计划”中想定了朝鲜制造出简易核武器并通过船只或车辆运送的可能性。尽管美国及其盟国坚决拒绝将朝鲜视为核武器国家，但在核作战计划中还是将其作为核武器国家对待，以威慑其可能的核威胁。

（二）调整军事预算，突出核力量发展

2014年，美国在继续军事预算削减的同时，突出了核力量

的发展。奥巴马政府 2015 财年的国防预算申请在 5210 亿美元的基础上，又额外增加了 790 亿美元。通常，美国每年在核武器上的支出大致为 230 亿美元，最大一部分（42%）用在了制造和维护运载核弹头的导弹、发射井、潜艇和飞机上。另外的 36% 用于设计、制造和维护核武器，以及舰船和潜艇用的反应堆。剩余的 22% 用于预警、通信和控制系统。每年的核相关费用为 210 亿美元，其中 1/3 用于清理核武器开发与制造的陈旧设施；15% 用于军控；其余 50% 用于核武器防御，包括飞机和导弹防御系统。而现有核弹头的每年维护需要 10 亿多美元。2014 年 1 月，美国国会批准的 2014 财年支出法案把能源部核武器的资金增加了近 10 亿美元。其中，美核军工管理局核武器开发资金达到 78 亿美元，比 2013 财年增加了 8.74 亿美元。2014 年 11 月，美国国防部透露，依据 2016 财年国防预算草案，美国防预算申请可能会超出国会授权支出上限多达 600 亿美元。其还需要数十亿资金用于现代化核武器计划，预算限制使美国启动如远程轰炸机等新项目的空间越来越小。国防部长哈格尔告诉记者，美国需要数十亿美元的新投资来资助未来几年的关键核升级。詹姆斯·马丁不扩散核武器研究中心（CNS）在本年度发表的报告称，美国计划未来 30 年投入约 1 万亿美元，用于维护现有的武器库、采购替代系统以及升级现有的核弹及核弹头。可见，在国防预算持续紧缩的同时，美国仍保证了核武器发展的必要资金。

（三）积极推进国际军控进程，高度关注国际核安全

2014 年，美国不但积极维护了现行核军控体制，而且努力提高国际社会对核安全的高度关注。2014 年，美国在与俄罗斯

由于克里米亚问题关系紧张的情况下，仍在两国有效实施核裁军目标方面作出了努力。2014 年 10 月，美国务院军控事务负责人表示，“尽管存在紧张关系，在军控领域仍有摩擦，但美国和俄罗斯正继续以有效的方式执行条约”。2014 年 4 月，美国防部就美俄新《削减战略武器条约》（新 START）情况对外公布了履行计划，，提高了军控透明度。声明显示到 2018 年美军部署的陆基洲际弹道导弹预定减至 400 枚，将创 50 多年来的新低。这一举动显示，美俄因乌克兰问题交恶后，双方并未终止在裁军领域的合作。而在 2014 年 2 月举行的全球核安全峰会上，美国、荷兰等国积极推动了峰会参与者承诺将采纳和接受现有的核材料实物保护国际指南的约束。此举有效提高了国际社会对国际核安全的关注。

二、削减战略核武库，全面审查核力量

（一）实施新的退役措施，调整核削减计划

美国为淘汰陈旧武器，满足国际军控条约要求，在本年度内公布了一系列削减措施。2014 年 4 月，美国国务院公布了其核武器储备情况，称，截至 2013 年 9 月，美国核弹头储量为 4804 枚。比冷战结束的 1989 年的 22217 枚下降了 78%。而今后美国还将采取诸多措施支持核武器的削减计划。例如，美国将削减每艘“俄亥俄”级潜艇上的导弹发射管，将现有的 24 个发射管减少到 20 个，这将使美国在任何时候部署的潜射弹道导弹都不超过 240 枚。此外，美国为执行 2010 年核态势评估报告的要求，从 2014 年 6 月开始将“民兵” –3 导弹上的 3 枚弹头更改为 1 枚。同时，从 2014 年 1 月开始，美开始

启动对蒙大拿州第 564 导弹中队 50 个“民兵” -3 导弹发射井的摧毁工作；并在本年度内完成对沃伦基地内 50 个“民兵 3”发射设施的摧毁工作。在新《削减战略武器条约》要求下，美空军需要在 2018 年 2 月前销毁 103 套导弹发射设施和 10 套导弹预警设施。

但是由于核发展经费的削减，美国不得不部分调整现有削减计划。2014 年 3 月，美核军工管理局透露，经费削减可能迫使美国修改现有的拆除 2009 年之前退役核武器的计划。新的预算草案提出对主要承担退役核武器拆除的德克萨斯潘太克斯厂经费削减 40%，对田纳西州橡树岭国家实验室下一个年度的核弹头拆除经费削减 44%。这将使现行削减计划的 2022 年期限被推迟。

（二）进行核力量审查，讨论新的发展规划

鉴于美国战略核威慑力量出现的一系列问题，美国国防部于 2014 年 1 月下令对美战略核威慑任务及能力进行全面审查。目的是检查管理战略核威慑部队的基本领导和管理原则；制定战略核威慑部队人员管理方案等。美国防部哈格尔对此表示，美国核部队长期缺乏资金投入和相关支持；部队内部士气低落，人员短缺，管理不善，这危害到了国家核军事力量的安全、稳定和效率。因此美国防部根据审查结果于 2014 年 11 月启动全面改革计划，宣布国防部计划增强对核力量的关注，并增加经费以加强对核部队的管理、核基础设施的维护与现代化，确保美国核力量的安全、可靠和有效。同时，考虑投入 75 亿美元用以升级核武器并对核部队军纪进行整改。

在对核力量进行审查的同时，美国各方面开始考虑核力量

新的发展规划。2014 年 7 月，美国防部专家组在报告中表示，美核武库现代化计划在经济上是不可承受的，并且会对所需的常规兵力升级造成威胁，因此应重新评估这些计划。2014 年 10 月，美军控协会也发布报告认为，随着新一代武器预期成本的上涨，美国国防预算却在不断削减，“三位一体”核力量的现代化计划在预算紧缩时期根本无法维持，因此越来越高的核武器成本将使美国行政部门、国会和公众重新思考在未来几年内升级核力量的计划。实际上，此前在 2014 年 2 月，美国空军就在透露的“未来洲际弹道导弹维护与采办构想”（FISAC）文件中，提出新的导弹力量采办和部署模式，以适应新的国内外环境。

三、论证新型打击平台，保持核投送能力

（一）筹划战略导弹核潜艇发展

对新型战略导弹核潜艇的讨论仍是 2014 年美国战略核力量发展的重点。2014 年内，美国海军完成了“俄亥俄”级替代艇设计蓝图——潜艇技术规范书。新型弹道导弹核潜艇（SSBN）预计于 2031 年开始服役，服役周期将延续到 2085 年，首艇建造工作将从 2021 年开始。目前潜艇项目的需求设计、技术规范和早期试验原型等相关工作已经在通用动力电船公司开展了。新的潜艇总长 171 米，导弹发射管长 13. 4 米，可装 16 枚三叉戟 2D5 导弹。新型潜艇采用模块化建造，从而在“俄亥俄”级潜艇的基础上提高效率、降低成本。按照计划美国建造 12 艘；而英国建造 4 艘，每艘有 12 个导弹发射管。为确保新型潜艇的顺利发展，美国海军分别在 2014 年 1 月和 5 月与通用动力电船公

司和诺·格公司签订合同，制造新型潜艇使用的通用导弹舱和涡轮发动机。通用导弹舱也将适用于英国新一代导弹潜艇，而涡轮发动机将为潜艇提供推进和其他电力供应，以实现更为先进的电力驱动。

（二）论证新型战略轰炸机方案

美国新出台的“抵消战略”提出了发展远程、隐身飞机［包括远程打击轰炸机（LRS－B）和无人作战航空系统（UCAS）］的建议，这无疑加快了新型战略轰炸机的发展。美国空军新型轰炸机项目经历 2009 财年和 2010 财年的调整之后，从 2011 财年开始重新编列公开预算，其 2011－2014 财年每一年的预算申请均在该财年的《国防授权法》中获得全额批准。美国空军 2014 年 3 月公布的预算表明，空军在 2015 财年的该项目申请了 9.13728 亿美元，而 2015－2019 财年 5 年的计划预算总额达 114.18592 亿美元，首次突破 100 亿美元；2014 年 9 月，美空军表示，计划在 2015 年春天或夏季授权出台新型轰炸机的制造合同。在本年度内，美国空军明确了新型轰炸机初始型号的核打击能力。以前的计划只是要求新型轰炸机最初型号在设计上为某种后续型号增加核能力和实施核加固做好准备，但是美国空军在 2014 年 6 月表示基本型（baseline version）将从一开始就具备核能力。

（三）推进陆基战略威慑系统更替

近年来，美空军开始致力于陆基战略威慑系统更替计划。目前，美国陆基战略威慑系统以“民兵－3”导弹为主，在 2014 年内，美军完成了“民兵－3”导弹后续计划的“备选方案分析”（AOA）。2014 年 2 月，美空军司令部透露，美空军已经开始研究“民兵 - 3”导弹的后继系统，该系统在“备选方案分析”中被称为“陆基战略威慑”。未来的陆基战略威慑可能是“民兵 - 3”导弹的升级版，也可能是研发新的替代系统。目前空军正在考虑两种部署方式选项：改进固定系统及增加机动系统。固定系统在作战概念上与目前的“民兵 - 3”导弹具有可比性；机动系统采用机动平台发射，也可通过地下隧道系统将导弹在发射井之间机动部署。

（四）升级战术核打击系统

由于美军前沿空对地攻击系统全面换代，导致对其依赖的战术核打击系统也必须升级。2014 年 5 月，美空军开始与洛·马公司探讨由 F - 35 执行核打击任务的可能性，该机最早可能于2025 年具备这一能力。目前，美核军工管理局与洛·马公司、波音公司已经签订协议，以在风险较小的情况下发展 F - 35 核常兼备双用途战斗机（DCA）。美核军工管理局负责 B - 61 核钻地弹延寿项目，波音公司负责研制新型 B - 61 尾部套件，从目前计划看，核常兼备的 F - 35 战机要到 2026 年前具备实战能力。

四、改进现有作战系统，延长武器服役年限

2014 年，美国坚持对核作战系统进行升级改造，在延长其服役年限的同时，大力提高核作战能力。2014 年 1 月，美国防部长哈格尔在视察桑迪亚国家实验室和科特兰空军基地后表示，美国一直支持强大的核威慑，而且会继续这样做。此次视察表

明美国政府正在推进升级核武器系统的宏大计划。

（一）通过信息化改造，延长平台服役年限

在空基投送平台方面，美空军逐渐完成了老旧平台的信息化改造。2014 年 4 月，美空军完成首架 B－52H 轰炸机的“作战网络通信技术”（CONECT）升级。此次升级为 B－52H 加、换装了数字式显示器、计算机网络服务器和实时超视线通信链路，使该型机在执行任务的整个过程中可与外界保持通信联络，不断刷新的威胁和瞄准数据，不是仅依赖起飞前获得的信息，因而可利用机对机接口快速重新受领任务和重新瞄准，此次升级将使该型机可至少服役到 2040 年。此外，本年度内，美空军开始为 B－2 战略轰炸机研发了甚低频（VLF）无线电通信系统，使机组人员可在执行远程任务时与国家指挥当局保持通信。新系统弥补了先进极高频（AEHF）卫星通信系统在未来几年无法投入使用的空白。

在陆基投送工具方面，美空军仍致力于现有系统的改造。2014 年 12 月，美空军与波音公司签订合同，在 2015 年 9 月之后，继续供应和维修“民兵”－3 导弹制导系统，以保障该导弹拥有充足的备用制导系统的库存，并能保持长期的战斗警戒。

在海基投送平台方面，美国海军将提高核指挥控制作为发展重点。2014 年 8 月，美海军与通用动力公司签订合同，在 2015 年 7 月前升级美海军 AN/BYG－1 潜艇作战系统。通过该系统，作战人员可分析潜艇传感器获取的信息，跟踪深海和近海潜艇及水面舰艇，瞄准并发射多种武器。同时，美军还正在为“俄亥俄”级导弹核潜艇（SSBN）加装大型垂直阵列、特殊的艇身涂层材料，并对发动机进行特殊降噪处理。这些升级目

的是保持技术的先进性，确保美海军在水下领域的统治地位。

（二）升级现役核武器，提高核打击能力

对现有核武器进行升级，是美国保持核威慑水平，提高打击能力的重要途径。2014 年，美国继续升级现役核武器，完善作战能力。2014 年 1 月，美空军确认，已计划对 B61 – 12 核弹进行改进，该导弹将装备制导尾部套件，同时还将减少弹头的当量，以提高导弹的打击精度及减少产生放射性物质。2 月，美核军工管理局完成了 B61 – 12 型核武器的首次全系统机械环境测试，美核军工管理局表示，只要美国仍然拥有核武器，就必须在不通过地下核爆炸试验的前提下，确保其安全性、可靠性及有效性。此次测试是美国提高核炸弹安全性的一项重大进展。2014 年 4 月，美核军工管理局再次宣布完成了 B61 – 12 的首次风洞试验，并计划于 2015 年进行投弹试验。2014 年 6—7 月，美国能源部桑迪亚国家实验室对 W88 核弹头最新型号进行了两次飞行和坠落测试，并利用获得的数据开展设计验证、计算机模型改进和部件规格更新等工作。这些测试验证了雷达在核弹头再入大气层，穿过核弹头以远超超音速速度飞行产生的等离子体时的性能。此外，美海军在年度内继续推进了“三叉戟”2D5 导弹的升级计划。2014 年 4 月，海军与德雷珀实验室公司签订合同，用于升级“三叉戟”2D5 导弹的制导系统，调整导弹精度。这也属于美海军“三叉戟”2D5 导弹延寿计划的一部分。这些测试和改进对提高武器打击能力有重要意义。

（三）讨论通用核弹头发展，提高武器维护性

虽然美军希望提高海基和陆基导弹核弹头的通用性，但这

一计划仍存在较大争议。2014年6月，美国海军战略系统计划主管本尼迪克特表示：“过去海军设计潜射弹道导弹，空军设计洲际弹道导弹，从来没有交流。我正试图打破这些障碍”，海军应与空军合作开展战略导弹现代化工作，从而削减成本。而此前的2014年2月，美国核军工管理局宣称，计划推迟关于有争议的可互用弹头的工作。本尼迪克特表示，近期对替换两种核武器（用于陆基导弹的W78弹头和适用于潜基导弹的W88弹头）的计划评估显示，它们仍能够继续使用大约15年，因此没有必要开展新的通用弹头研制。实际上，新型通用弹头计划遭到了美国国会的很多议员的反对，他们担心这种通用弹头会比改造两种替换弹头的耗资更多。

五、开发核打击侦察技术，提高核作战指挥能力

（一）开发核爆探测技术，提高核作战感知能力

为了满足对地面机动核打击系统的侦察与监视能力，美军开始关注对公路机动导弹系统的侦察技术开发，以提高对敌地面机动核力量的先期打击能力。2014年11月，美国防部召集工业界会议提出发展“打击时敏目标的能力”的要求，以应对公路机动洲际导弹威胁。国防部要求新技术可对机动洲际导弹进行延迟、降级，摧毁其从部署到发射乃至飞行全过程的整条杀伤链上的后勤与指挥控制系统的武器系统，以应对机动洲际导弹威胁。虽然会议声明未明确对美产生此类威胁的国家或武器系统，但近年来俄罗斯公路机动导弹和朝鲜“火星13”、伊朗“泥石2”机动弹道导弹系统对美国的核威胁已经越来越大。

（二）发展新型核指挥系统，加强核力量指控能力

为提高美军核作战指挥能力，美国在本年度内加快了指挥控制系统的改造和技术开发。目前，美空军正在与波音公司合作研发 E－4B 空中指挥机的低频传输系统（LFTS），该系统将使美在核战或其他灾难中，维持军事紧急指挥机与水下潜艇的通信，合同计划于 2015 年 4 月前完成。该系统主要应用于美空军 E－4B 先进空中指挥机，E－4B 可通过低频传输系统维持对弹道导弹潜艇的控制，还可通过先进极高频（AEHF）卫星通信系统及其他保密通信系统，维持与其他核力量的通信。目前，E－4B 空中指挥机上的甚低频/低频（VLF/LF）传输系统使用年限已超过 35 年。此次项目旨在研发低频下传输强度达 100 千瓦信号的新型系统，可向水下导弹潜艇发送加密指令和信息。2014 年 12 月，美空军委托工业部门对其“战略自动化指挥控制系统”（SACCS）进行升级，在其中嵌入现代化数据存取技术。该系统是美国战略司令部的指挥与控制系统，用于协调美国核力量的作战使用，具备指令发布和密码认证的功能。新系统不但可检索和验证关键数据，还能降低发生人为差错的可能，此次升级的新系统将服役到 2030 年。

六、优化核力量部署，组织实弹发射与演习

（一）加快核部署调整，优化威慑态势

为了保证前沿核力量的高度战备和灵活性，美国在年度内加快了核武器部署的调整。美空军 2015 财年的预算显示，北约将在 2015 年开始为 F－16 和“龙卷风”战斗机装备 B61－12 核

弹，这将使美国在海外部署的核武器全面更新。同时，美在2014 年 6 月派遣 3 架 B－52 轰炸机前往欧洲进行飞行训练。此举旨在强化美国在欧洲的军力部署。美总统奥巴马在访问波兰时表示，美将在欧洲，特别是在东欧的“新盟国”领空加强 B－52 轰炸机的演习和训练。以此向俄罗斯施压，确保盟国安全。此外，美国国防部在 2014 年 12 月通告国会，正考虑在欧洲重新部署核巡航导弹，以回应俄罗斯违反 1987 年核条约部署新的巡航导弹。

（二）实施实弹发射，组织核力量演练

2014 年，美军进行了多次实弹发射，并组织了多次核力量参与的军事演习，在增强部队战备能力的同时，也对库存武器进行了检验。2014 年 6 月，美海军对现役的“三叉戟”2D5 导弹进行了第 149 和 150 次飞行测试，创造了大型弹道导弹新的可靠性记录。此次发射检验了导弹性能及核潜艇大修后部署的作战能力。本年度内，美军还进行了多次核力量参与的军事演习，以提高其战备和威慑能力。2014 年 2 月，美 B－52 轰炸机在朝鲜西海上空进行模拟轰炸训练；2014 年 5 月，美国战略司令部进行了大规模核武器演习，以“阻止和检测对美国及其盟国的战略攻击”，约 10 架 B－52 重型轰炸机和 6 架 B－2 轰炸机参加了此次核威慑演习。此外，本年度内，美海军也保持了较高的战备巡逻态势。2014 年 6 月，美“俄亥俄”级“宾夕法尼亚”号（SSBN 735）结束了为期 140 天的战略威慑巡航，这刷新了该级潜艇的最长巡航记录，并将美国海基威慑能力提高到了新的水平。

七、加强核基础技术开发，提高核安全水平

（一）加强核基础设施发展，保证核武器开发能力

美国能源部 2015 财年国防预算申请总额为 279.4 亿美元，比 2014 财年增加 2.6%。其中核军工管理局申请 116.58 亿美元，比 2014 年增加 4%。这些资金主要用于核设施的现代化和维持老化核武库及基础设施等。2014 年 7 月，美参议院通过法案要求国防部研究如何实现核弹头存储设施的现代化，并在 3 个月内制定出 5 个空军核弹头存储设施升级的计划。根据要求，原本存储常规军需物资的巴克斯代尔空军基地将升级为核武器存储基地，目前，在该基地部署的 B－52 轰炸机必须到其他地方才可挂载核弹头。此外，美国能源局为提高核禁试条件下的核开发能力，还积极发展了计算机模拟技术，以推动“库存管理计划”的任务。2014 年 7 月，美核军工管理局与克雷公司合作，开发称作“三位一体”的下一代超级计算机。该项目是 NNSA 先进模拟与计算（ASC）计划的一部分，主要用于规模最大和需求最强的库存管理模拟，在不进行地下核试验的前提下，确保美国核威慑的安全、安保和有效。新型计算机预计 2015 年年中交付，其性能至少是现有洛斯·阿拉莫斯“大提琴”超级计算机的 8 倍。2014 年 12 月，美国防部授出“高性能计算现代化计划”（HPCMP）的 2 份超级计算系统采办合同，以装备美国防部的 2 个超级计算资源中心，继续推进超级计算能力建设。新的技术手段将增强美国核武器维护与开发能力。

（二）开发新型核安全设备，提高核安保与检测能力

2014 年，美国继续加强了核安全设备的开发与研制，不断提高核安保与检测能力，以满足应对核反恐和军控检测的要求。2014 年 12 月，美国劳伦斯利弗莫尔国家实验室发明了新的密码生成法，该方法“是一种能够为核武器提供可量化的安全性和用户控制概念”。这种方法对每个核武器部件分发唯一的编号，利用核武器发射的不断涨落变化的辐射场来产生安全的随机数，这些随机数只有武器本身能确认。如果核武器部件被移除或替换，系统将不再识别该部件，其他保护性部件也将失效。2014 年 6 月，美国能源部宣布开发了可测试核弹头状态的新技术，这将成为核裁军调查人员的有用工具。该方法运用中子扫描仪确定核弹头状态而不泄露核弹头机密，该技术已获得美核军工管理局 350 万美元的资助。此外，为提高核应变能力，美核军工管理局在 2014 年 8 月参加了首届全美范围“辐射反应”演习，来自 38 个国家的 200 多人参与了演习，一天之内超过 2.1 万份环境辐射数据被成功搜集和处理。“辐射反应”网络是一个动态的、基于云层的辐射数据分析系统，可以为联邦、州及地区用户领导人提供标准化服务，以便对辐射数据进行管理、归档、分析和制图。该系统的建立源于福岛核事故，美国认识到在突发事件来临时，各级政府和相关方需要密切合作才能够更好地应对危机。此次演习的目的是在核事故及恐怖袭击后尽快让各级专家参与进来，快速搜集信息，为决策提供帮助。

A Review on U. S. Nuclear Forces: 2014

Li Yi and Ge Aidong[①]

In 2014, the United States continued to deepen its nuclear force reform under the guidance of new military strategy, adjust the size and structure of nuclear forces and accelerate improvement of nuclear weapons, nuclear safety and security measures. The U. S. nuclear forces presented a steady development in general.

I. Streng then Strategic Nuclear Deterrence

In 2014, through proposing new military strategy and adjusting-defense budget, the United States strengthened its nucleardeterrence. Meanwhile, through multi – purpose assessment on nuclear forces, the United States tried to acceleraten uclear forces development plan.

1. Adjust new military strategy, and strengthen the role of nuclear deterrence. While proposing a new military strategy, the United

① Li Yi and Ge Aidong are researchers of the Center of Arms Control and International Security Research at China Institute of International Studies.

States discussed the status and role of nuclear deterrence in the new century. In October 2014, U. S. Center for Strategic and Budgetary Assessments (CSBA) published its first research report on U. S. Department of Defense (DoD) Strategy. This strategy, similar to 1970s Strategy, aimed at obtaining a comprehensive balance of nuclear and conventional forces as soon as possible, in order to solve the most pressing military challenges in the case of fiscal austerity. That has maintained the U. S. army global delivery capabilities to deter potential adversaries and grant U. S. allies and partners security under Anti – Access and Area – Denial (A2/AD) cases. To this end, the United States conducted a wide range of discussion about its nuclear deterrence. In August 2014, U. S. Strategic Command held a symposium to discuss a wide range of deterrence issues in the 21st century. Under Secretary for Nuclear Security and Administrator for the National Nuclear Security Administration (NNSA) Frank G. Klotz proposed that the NNSA mission should include: maintaining a safe, secure and effective nuclear deterrence, preventing worldwide nuclear proliferation and nuclear terrorism, and making great effort to develop a more flexible in frastructure and maintaining a strong research in frastructure to meet the future challenges. In 2014, the U. S. President Obama repeatedly stressed he was more worried about a nuclear attack on Manhattan, compared to Russia's take over of Crimea. This indicated the United States defied Russia's nuclear challenge on Ukrainian issue, as well as the urgency of the U. S. real nuclear threat. These measuress trengthened the unique role of nucleardeterrence to ensure the U. S. nuclear safety and security in the future.

In addition, during 2014, the United States also maintained nuclear deterrence on North Korea and other emerging rivals by revising nuclear operation plans. In April 2014, U. S. media reported the U. S. troops rendered North Korea as a nuclear rival in its contingency nuclear operation plans for the first time. The United States supposed that North Korea created simple nuclear weapons and transported by vessel or vehicle in the latest version of 5029 Operation Plan. Although the United States and its allies firmly rejected to consider North Korea as nuclear – weapon state, they treated it as a nuclear – weapon state in the nuclear operation plan to deter possible nuclear threat.

2. Adjust military budget, and highlight nuclear force development. During 2014, while continuing to cut defense budget, the U. S. highlighted nuclear force development. At $521 billion basis, Obama's administration requested an additional $79 billion increase in fiscal year 2015 defense budget. Typically, the U. S. annual spending on nuclear weapons is roughly $23 billion. The largest part (42%) is used in the manufacture and maintenance of missiles, silos, submarines and aircrafts that carry nuclear warheads. Another 36% is used in design, manufacture and maintenance of nuclear weapons, as well asships and submarines reactors. The remaining 22% is used for early warning, communication and control systems. Annual nuclear – related spending is $21 billion, of which 1/3 is spent in cleaning obsolete facilities used in nuclear weapons development and manufacture; 15% for arms control; the remaining 50% for nuclear weapons defense, including aircraft and missile defense systems. The annual maintenance expenses of existing nuclear war-

heads need more than one billion dollars. In January, the fiscal year 2014 spending bill approved by the U. S. Congress made nearly $ 1 billion increase for Department of Energy nuclear weapons funding, of which NNSA nuclear weapons development funds reached $ 7. 8 billion, $ 874 million more than in fiscal year 2013.

In November 2014, Doe said, according to the fiscal year 2016 defense budget draft, the U. S. defense budget request may exceed the upper limit of Congress authorized spending $ 60 billion. The United States also will need billions of funding for its nuclear weapons modernization program, and budget constraints left less and less space for the United States to launch a newproject such as long - range bombers. Defense Secretary Hagel to ldreporters that the United States needto invest billions of dollars in key nuclear upgrading projects in the coming years. A report published by James Martin Center for Nonproliferation Studies of Nuclear Weapons (CNS) in 2014 said the United States planned to invest about $ 1 trillion for maintenance of existing arsenals, purchasing alternative systems and upgrading existing nuclear bombs and warheads in the next 30 years. It can be seen the United States will need necessary funding for nuclear weapons development with continued tightening defense budget.

3. Actively promote international arms control process, and pay a high attention to international nuclear security. The United States not only maintained the existing nuclear arms control system actively, but also made great efforts to improve international community's attentionto nuclear security in 2014. Due to tensions caused by Crimeanproblem between the two countries, the United States and Russia still made effort to implement nuclear disarmament goal effectively. In Oc-

tober 2014, U. S. Department of Statearms control chief said, "Despite of tension and friction in the field of arms control, the United States and Russia are continuing to implement the treaty in an effective manner." In April, Doe announced the execution plan of U. S. – Russia new Strategic Arms Reduction Treaty (New START), thus improving transparency of arms control. The statement showed deployed U. S. land – based intercontinental ballistic missiles would reduce to 400 as scheduled in 2018, the lowest of 50 years. This move showed that the United States and Russia did not terminate cooperation in the field of disarmament after Ukraine issues. During the Global Nuclear Security Summit held in February 2014, the United States, the Netherlands and other countries actively promoted participants to adopt and accept the existing physical protection of nuclear material bound by international guidelines. This would effectively improve international community's concern for international nuclear safety.

Ⅱ. Reduce Strategic Nuclear Arsenals

During 2014, the United States carried out nuclear weapon reduction according to plan and made efforts to maintain the existing international arms control mechanism.

1. Implement new disarmament measures, and adjust nuclear reduction plan. In order to phase out obsolete weapons to meet the requirements of international arms control treaty, the United States announced a series of reduction measures. In April, the U. S. Department of State released its nuclear weapons stockpile, saying the Unit-

ed States reserved 4804 nuclear warheads by September 2013, which was 78% less than 22217 in 1989 after the Cold War. In the future, the United States will take a lot of measures to support nuclear weapons reduction plan. For example, the United States will reduce missile tubes from 24 to 20 on each Ohio – class nuclear missile submarine, which will make the number of deployed ballistic missiles on U. S. submarine at any time no more than 240. In addition, in order to implement the requirements of 2010 Nuclear Posture Review Report, the United States began to download three warheads of Minuteman Ⅲ missile into one from June. At the same time, from the beginning of January, the United States started to eliminate 50 Minuteman Ⅲ missile silos of 564 Missile Squadron in Montana; and completed elimination of 50Minuteman Ⅲ missile silos at Warren Air Force Base within 2014. According to the new START, U. S. Air Force need eliminate 103missile launch facilities and 10 sets of missile warning facilities before February 2018.

However, due to reducing nuclear development funding, the United States had to adjust part of the existing reduction programs. In March, NNSA said funding reduction may force the United States to modify the program that dismantles nuclear weapons decommissioned-before 2009. The new budget draft presented cutting 40% funding of Pentax plant responsible for removal de commissioning nuclear weapons, and cutting 40% dismantled nuclear warheads funding of Oak Ridge National Laboratory in Tennessee. This will postpone 2022 deadline of the current reduction program.

2. Carry out a review on nuclear forces, and discuss new development plan. In view of a series of problems with the U. S. nuclear de-

terrence, DoD was ordered to conduct a comprehensive review of U. S. strategic nuclear deterrence mission and capability in January 2014. The purpose was to examine the basic leadership and management principles of managing strategic nuclear forces and to develop personnel management programs of strategic nuclear deterrence forces. DoD Secretary Hagel expressed that the U. S. nuclear forces were lack of funding and associated support; internal troops faced problems such as staff morale, staff shortages, poor management, which endangerd the security, stability and efficiency of national nuclear military forces. Therefore, DoD started a comprehensive reform program according to review results in November 2014. DoD announced that it planned to enhance focus on nuclear forces and increase funding to strengthen management of nuclear forces, nuclear infrastructure maintenance and modernization, so as to ensure safe, reliable and effective nuclear forces. Meanwhile, DoD considered to invest $7. 5 billion to upgrade nuclear weapons and rectificate nuclear forces discipline.

While reviewing nuclear forces, the United States began to consider a new nuclear force development plan. In July, DoD expert group said in a report that U. S. nuclear arsenal modernization plan was economically unsustainable, and would threat conventional forces upgrade. They thought those plans should be re – evaluated. In October, the U. S. Arms Control Association also released a report with a rising expected cost of the new generation weapons and reducing U. S. defense budget, triad nuclear forces modernization program simply cannot be maintained in the budget austerity. Therefore, increasingly higher cost of nuclear weapons would allow executive branches, Congress and the public to rethink upgrading nuclear forces in the coming years. In fact, earlier in February, U. S. Air Force proposed acquisition of new missile forces and deployment models in the revealed Future ICBM Sustainment & Acquisition Construct (FISAC) to adapt to the new environment at home and abroad.

Ⅲ. Demonstrate New Operation Platforms

With most active nuclear operation platforms close to the end of their service, the United States was planning to develop a new generation of strategic nuclear warfare system to maintain a lasting and reliable strategic deterrence.

1. Plan strategic submarine development. Discussion of new strategic submarines was still the focus of U. S. strategic nuclear forces development in 2014. In 2014, the U. S. Navy completed its blueprints of Ohio – class submarine alternative boat——submarine technical specification. The new ballistic missile submarine (SSBN) was expected to be in service in 2031 to 2085. Construction of the first boat would begin in 2021. Now General Dynamics Electric Boat Company has started demand design, technical specifications and early test prototypes of submarine project. The total length of new submarine is 171m. The length of missile launch tube which can be installed with 16 Trident Ⅱ D5 missiles. New submarine will use a modular – construction mode, thus improving efficiency and decreasing cost on the basis of Ohio – class submarine. The United States has planned to build 12 new submarines; and the British built 4, each ship will

have 12 missile tubes. In order to ensure smooth development of new submarines, Navy signed contracts with General Dynamics Electric Boat Company and Northrop Grumman in January and May respectively, to produce general missile compartments and turbine engines for new submarines. Common missile cabins will also apply to Britain's new missile submarines, and turbine engines will provide propulsion and other power supply for submarines to achieve more advanced electric drive.

2. Test new strategic bomber scheme. The new offset strategy proposed to develop long distance, stealthy aircraft (including Long – Range Strike Bomber (LRS – B) and Unmanned Operation Air Systems (UCAS)), which would undoubtedly accelerate the development of new strategic bomber. After going through a review in the fiscal year 2009 and 2010, the U. S. Air Force new bomber project started to restate public budget from fiscal year 2011. Annual budget request from fiscal year 2011 to 2014 obtained full approval in National Defense Authorization Act. The U. S. Air Force budget announced in March showed that Air Force applied 913. 728 million for this project in fiscal year 2015, while total planned budget for fiscal year 2015 – 2019 amounted to 11. 418592 billion, exceeded $10 billion for the first time. In September, the U. S. Air Force said it had planned to grant manufacturing contract of new bomber in 2015 spring or summer of 2015. During 2014, the Air Force made nuclear strike capability of new bomber initial type clearly. Previous program only required new bomber originally designed to get ready for a certain follow – up type to increase nuclear capacity and nuclear reinforcement, but the Air Force said the basic type (baseline version) would have nuclear ca-

pacity from the very beginning in June 2014.

3. Promote land – based strategic deterrent system replacement. In recent years, the U. S. Air Force has carried out land – based strategic deterrence system replacement program. Currently, U. S. land – based strategic deterrent system is mainly composed of Minuteman Ⅲ missiles. In 2014, the United States completed Analysis of Alternatives (AOA) of Minuteman Ⅲ missile follow – up plan. In February, the Air Force Command said the U. S. Air Force had begun to study Minuteman Ⅲ missile successor system, which was called Land – Based Strategic Deterrence in AOA. Future land – based strategic deterrence could be upgrade version of Minuteman Ⅲ, or it could be development of a new alternative system. U. S. Air Force was currently considering two kinds of deployment options: improving fixed systems and increasing mobile systems. Fixed systems were comparable to current Minuteman Ⅲ missile on operation concept; mobile system used mobile platform to launch, or deploy missile between silos through underground tunnel system.

4. Upgrade tactical nuclear strike systems. Due to a comprehensive updating of U. S. frontier ground attack systems, tactical nuclear strike systems depending on them must be upgraded. In May, the U. S. Air Force and Lockheed Martin began to explore the possibility of executing nuclear strike missions by F – 35 aircraft which may have this capability in 2025 at least. Currently, NNSA signed an agreement with Lockheed Martin and Boeing to develop F – 35 nuclear – conventional dual – purpose fighter in less risky situation. NNSA was responsible for B – 61 nuclear bomb life extension project, and Boeing was responsible for developing new B – 61 tail kits. According to

the current plan, F – 35 fighters with both nuclear and conventional strike ability would have operation capability before 2026.

Ⅳ. Improve the Existing Operational Systems

In 2014, the United States insisted on upgrading nuclear operation system, extended service life of weapons, while vigorously improved nuclear operation capability. In January, after inspecting Sandia National Laboratory and Kirtland Air Force Base, the U. S. Secretary of Defense Hagel said the United States had been supporting a strong nuclear deterrence, and would continue to do so. The inspection showed that the U. S. government was pushing an ambitious plan to upgrade nuclear weapons systems.

1. Extend service life of platform through information transformation. In recent years, extending service life of nuclear operation platform through information transformation has become the main way to maintain the U. S. nuclear forces operation capability.

For air – based delivery platform, the Air Force has completed information transformation of old platforms gradually. In April, the Air Force completed Operation Network Communication Technology (CONECT) upgrade of the first B – 52H bomber. B – 52H was added, and changed digital displays, computer network servers and real – time ultra – sight communication links, so that this type of machine can maintain communication with the outside world throughout executing task process, and constantly refresh threats and targeting data, rather than rely solely on the information obtained prior to departure, which can make use of machine – to – machine interface to quickly re – take task and re – target. This upgrade would allow this type of machine extend service life to 2040 at least. In addition, during 2014, the Air Force began to develop a strategic bomber Very Low Frequency (VLF) radio communication system for B – 2 that allowed the crew to maintain communication with national command authorities when implementing long – range tasks. The new system made up for bridging the gaps of Advanced Extremely High Frequency (AEHF) satellite communication system, which cannot be put into use in the next few years.

For land – based delivery systems, the U. S. Air Force committed to transformation of the existing system. In December, the Air Force and Boeing signed a contract to continue supply and maintenance of Minuteman Ⅲ guidance systems after September 2015, in order to ensure a sufficient stock of spare guidance systems, and to maintain long – term operation alert.

For sea – based delivery platform, the U. S. Navy would improve nuclear command and control as a development priority. In August 2014, Navy signed a contract with General Dynamics Company to upgrade Navy's AN/BYG – 1 submarine operation system before July 2015. Through this system, warfighters can analyze information obtained by submarine sensors, track deep – sea and offshore submarines and surface ships, aim and launch a variety of weapons. Meanwhile, U. S. military was installing large – scale vertical array, special hull coating materials for Ohio – class missile submarine (SSBN), and processing engines with special noise reduction technology. These upgrades aimed at maintaining advanced technology to ensure Navy's dominance in the underwater area.

2. Upgrade active nuclear weapons, and improve nuclear strike capability. Upgrading of existing nuclear weapons is an important way for the United States to maintain nuclear deterrence level and improve strike capability. In 2014, the United States continued to upgrade active nuclear weapons and improve operation capability. In January, the Air Force confirmed that the improvements of B61 – 12 nuclear bomb had been planned. This bomb would be equipped with guided tail kits, and would also reduce warheads equivalent to improve strike accuracy and reduce production of radioactive substances. In February, NNSA completed the first full system mechanical environment test of B61 – 12. NNSA said that if the United States still had nuclear weapons, they must ensure its safety, reliability and effectiveness without underground nuclear test. The test was a major step to improve the safety of nuclear bombs. In April, NNSA announced the completion of B61 – 12's first wind tunnel test and planned to carry out bomb test in 2015. In June and July, Sandia National Laboratory carried out two flight and fall tests with the latest W88 nuclear warheads, and used the data obtained to carry out design verification, computer model improvement and components specification updates and so on. These tests verified radar's performance when warheads re – entry in a far exceeding supersonic speed and generate plasma. In addition, the U. S. Navy continued to promote Trident Ⅱ D5 missile upgrade program. In April, the Navy signed a contract with Draper Laboratory, Inc. for upgrading Trident Ⅱ D5 missile guidance systems, and adjusting missile accuracy. This was also part of the U. S. Navy's Trident Ⅱ D5 missile life extension program. These tests

and improvements were of great importance to enhance strike capabilities of weapons.

3. Discuss the development of general nuclear warheads, and improve weapon maintenance. Although the U. S. military hoped to improve sea – based and land – based missile warheads versatility, this plan remained controversial. In June, Navy Strategic Systems program director Benedict said, "In the past Navy designed submarine – launched ballistic missiles and the Air Force designed ICBM. They never exchanged the design. I was trying to break those barriers. Navy should cooperate with the Air Force on strategic missile modernization to reduce costs." In February, NNSA declared to postpone work on controversial warheads. They said recent program evaluation on replacing two kinds of nuclear weapons (W78 warheads for land – based missiles and submarine – based missiles applied for W88 warhead) showed that they were still able to continue to use for about 15 years, so there was no need for developing new warheads. In fact, the new warhead plan was opposed by many members of Congress, who feared that new warheads would cost more than transformation of two kinds of warheads.

V. Develop Nuclear Strike Reconnaissance Technology

During 2014, the United States improved nuclear operation situational awareness and command and control capabilities as a development priority, in order to strengthen its strategic deterrence credibility.

1. Develop nuclear detection technology, and improve nuclear operation perception ability. In order to meet reconnaissance and surveillance on ground mobile nuclear strike system, the U. S. military began to address technology development for reconnaissance of road mobile missile system to improve advanced strike capability towards enemy's ground mobile nuclear forces. In November, the U. S. DoD convened an industrial meeting and proposed request of developing the ability to strike time – sensitive targets, in order to deal with road – mobile ICBM threat. The DoD required new technology could make mobile ICBM delay, downgrade and destroy logistical, command and control systems of the entire kill chain from deployment to launch and on the whole process of flight to cope with mobile ICBM threat. Although the meeting did not explicitly declare nations or weapons systems which produced such a threat to U. S., Russian road – mobile missiles, North Korean Mars 13, Iranian mobile ballistic missile systems had a greater nuclear threat to the U. S. in recent years.

2. Develop new nuclear command system, and strengthen nuclear force command and control capacity. To improve the U. S. nuclear operational command ability, the U. S. sped up transformation and technology development of command and control system. Currently, the U. S. Air Force was cooperating with Boeing to develop Low Frequency Transmission System (LFTS) of E – 4B airborne command aircraft. The system would enable the forces maintain communication between military emergency command aircrafts and submarines in a nuclear war or other disasters. The contract was to be completed before April 2015. This system was mainly used in the Air Force E – 4B

advanced airborne command aircraft. E – 4B could not only maintain control of ballistic missile submarines by low – frequency transmission system, but also maintain communication with other nuclear forces through Advanced Extremely High Frequency (AEHF) satellite communication system and other secure communication system. Currently, VLF/LF transmission system on E – 4B airborne command had been used for over 35 years. This project aimed to develop a new system with 100 kilowatts transmission strength under low frequency that could send encrypted instructions and information to underwater missile submarines. In December, the U. S. Air Force asked industrial sector to upgrade its Strategic Automated Command and Control System (SACCS), which to be embedded with modern data access technology. This system was the U. S. Strategic Command's command and control system for coordinating operational use of nuclear forces, with instruction issue and password authentication function. The new system can not only retrieve and validate critical data, but also reduce the possibility of human error. The new upgraded system would be in service until 2030.

Ⅵ. Optimize Nuclear Forces Deployment

In recent years, the U. S. has gradually adjusted nuclear forces deployment, and organized several live exercises to test military training and weapons readiness level, thus effectively improving nuclear forces deterrent ability.

1. Acceleratethe adjustment of nuclear deployment, and opti-

mize deterrent posture. In order to ensure a high degree of readiness and flexibility of forefront nuclear forces, the United State sped up the adjustment of nuclear weapons deployment. The Air Force budget in fiscal year 2015 showed that NATO would begin to equip F – 16 and Tornado fighter with B61 – 12 nuclear bomb in 2015, which would update U. S. nuclear weapons deployed overseas comprehensively. Meanwhile, the U. S. sent three B – 52 bombers to Europe to conduct flight training in June. This move was aimed at strengthening the U. S. military deployment in Europe. The U. S. President Obama said the United States would strengthen B – 52 bomber exercises and training in Europe, especially new allies airspace in Eastern Europe during his visit to Poland, so as to put pressure on Russia security to ensure allies' safety. In addition, the U. S. DoD notified Congress in December it was considering to re – deploy nuclear cruise missiles in Europe, in response to Russia's violation of 1987 nuclear treaty to deploy new nuclear cruise missiles.

2. Implement live nuclear force drills. In 2014, the U. S. military conducted a number of live firings, and organized a number of exercises with nuclear forces participated in. While enhancing operation readiness of the troops, stocks weapons were tested. In June, the Navy conducted active Trident Ⅱ D5 missile's 149th and 150th flight test, creating a new reliability record of large – scale ballistic missile. This missile launch tested the performance and operational capability of deployment after nuclear submarines on overhaul. During 2014, the U. S. military conducted a number of exercises with nuclear forces participated in, so as to improve operation readiness and deterrence capabilities. In February, B – 52 bombers

simulated bombing training over the West Sea of Korea; In May, the U. S. Strategic Command conducted a large – scale exercise with nuclear weapons to "prevent and detect attacks on U. S. and its strategic allies". About ten B – 52 heavy bombers and six B – 2 bombers took part in nuclear deterrence exercise. In addition, the U. S. Navy maintained a high readiness patrol posture. In June, Ohio – class Pennsylvania (SSBN 735) ended a period of 140 days strategic deterrent cruising, which set a longest cruising record of this class. This would take the U. S. sea – based deterrent capability to a new level.

Ⅶ. Strengthen Nuclear Infrastructure Technology Development

During 2014, in the context of slashed funding, the U. S. still adhered to developing nuclear weapons technology, and made efforts to improve nuclear security capability.

1. Strengthen nuclear infrastructure development, and ensure the ability of developing nuclear weapons. The DoD requested for $27. 94 billion in fiscal year 2015 budget, an increase of 2. 6% than fiscal year 2014. Among this, NNSA applied $11. 658 billion, a 4% increase over 2014. The funding was mainly used for modernization of nuclear facilities and maintenance of aging nuclear arsenal and infrastructures. In July, the U. S. Senate Act required DoD to study on how to modernize nuclear warhead storage facilities, and to develop five plans of the Air Force nuclear warhead storage facilities upgrade within three months. Upon request, the original conventional munitions storage base Barksdale Air Force Base would be upgraded

to nuclear weapons storage base. Currently, B – 52 bombers deployed at this base had to load a nuclear warhead in other places. In addition, in order to enhance nuclear development ability under test – ban condition, the U. S. DoE actively developed a computer simulation technique to promote Stockpile Management Plan task. In July, the NNSA cooperated with Cray Company to develop the next generation supercomputers called Trinity. This project was a part of the NNSA Advanced Simulation and Calculation (ASC) program, mainly for the largest scale and the most powerful needs stockpile management simulation without underground nuclear test, to ensure safety, security and effectiveness of the U. S. nuclear deterrence. The new computer was expected to be delivered in mid – 2015, whose performance was at least eight times than the performance of existing Los Alamos Cello supercomputer. In December, the U. S. DoD granted 2 supercomputing systems procurement contracts of High Performance Computing Modernization Program (HPCMP) to equip two U. S. DoD Supercomputing Resource centers and continue to promote supercomputing capacity. The new technology would enhance U. S. nuclear weapons maintenance and development capability.

2. Develop new nuclear safety equipment, and improve nuclear security and detection capabilities. During 2014, the United States continued to strengthen development and manufacture of nuclear safety equipment, and continuously improved nuclear security and detection capabilities to meet requirements of dealing with nuclear counter – terrorism and nuclear arms control test. In December, Lawrence Livermore National Laboratory invented a new password generation method, which was a way to provide quantifiable security and user

control concepts for nuclear weapons.

This method distributed each nuclear weapons component with a unique number, and then used constantly fluctuated radiation field emitted by nuclear weapons to generate secure random numbers. If the nuclear weapon components were removed or replaced, the system would not recognize the components, and other protective components would fail. In June, the U. S. DoE announced the development of a technology for testing nuclear warhead status, which would become a useful tool for nuclear disarmament inspectors. This method used a neutron scanner to determine nuclear warheads status without leaking nuclear warheads secret. This technology had received $3. 5 million funding from the NNSA. Furthermore, to enhance nuclear response ability, the NNSA participated in the first nationwide Radiation Response exercise in August. More than 200 people from 38 countries participated in the exercise, and more than 21, 000 copies of environmental radiation data were successfully collected and processed within one day. Radiation response network is a dynamic, cloud – based radiation data analysis system that provides federal, state and local users with standardized service in order to manage, archive, analyze and map with radiation data. The establishment of this system was due to Fukushima nuclear accident. The United States recognized all levels of governments and relevant aspects need to cooperate closely to better cope with crisis in case of emergency. The purpose of this exercise was to let experts at all levels to be involved and gather information as soon as possible after nuclear accident and terrorist attack.

2014年俄罗斯核力量综述

刘丽军　孙同辉

〔内容摘要〕2014年，面对内外矛盾，俄罗斯继续强调核力量在国家安全战略中的地位和作用，提供充足的核力量建设经费，加强新型武器平台的研发，一批新系统加入现役。年内，俄罗斯还多次组织了实战演练，既显示自身的核打击能力，又验证武器装备的可靠性和安全性。在履行与美国达成的新战略武器条约上，俄罗斯仍按期削减和销毁核武器系统，同时还在加强核安全保障上做出新的努力。

主题词：俄罗斯　核力量　建设　评估

作者单位：中国国际问题研究院军控与安全研究中心

一、继续加大国防投入，加快核力量发展

（一）增加国防预算，突出核力量发展

2014年，俄在经济紧缩的情况下，仍坚持增加国防预算，并调整军事采购政策。2014年3月，俄财政部公布数据表明，俄罗斯2013年国防开支增长15.6%，2014年增长18.4%，达766亿美元。10月，俄国家杜马透露，2015年俄计划增加32.8%的国防预算，达到804亿美元，占GDP的4.2%，这是

2001 年以来国防预算增长最快的一次。增长的资金多半将用于武器和装备现代化、演习及改善军队服务条件。在增加国防预算的同时，俄开始调整军事采购政策。俄国防部副部长鲍里索夫表示，2016—2025 年国家武器发展计划中将减少武器和军事装备的种类。基于目前工业和科技基础，将在半年内确定新版武器装备发展计划的主要指标。武器和军事装备种类的缩减可以减少维护和维修费用，以及降低军人的训练支出。2014 年，负责军事工业集团的俄副总理罗戈津宣称，俄罗斯正在加速复兴核威慑力，其军事投入将重点用于 2020 年之前的核力量升级。

（二）修订军事学说，继续保持核力量结构

针对新的安全环境，俄罗斯在本年度内修订了现有军事学说。2014 年 12 月，俄安全委员会会议通过了新版军事学说。俄军事学说首次于 1993 年通过，并在 2000 年和 2010 年进行过修订。此次修订的新军事学说，把西方国家建立和部署战略导弹防御系统、实施“全球快速打击”计划、部署太空战略武器等视为当前主要外部威胁；而北约东扩及加强在俄边境地区和邻近水域的进攻性潜力为俄新安全威胁。虽然新军事学说还首次提出“非核遏制”的概念，但俄前国防部副部长与陆军前总参谋长巴卢耶夫斯基称，此次是对现有军事方针进行修改，而非制定新的军事方针。在俄罗斯的军事方针中没有涉及预防性核打击的条款，俄仍坚持在核反击中使用核武器。根据现有方针，俄使用核武器的条件：一是俄及盟友遭受核武器或其他大规模杀伤性武器的袭击；二是俄面临可使其遭受灭顶之灾的常规武器袭击的威胁。

在坚持核武器使用原则的同时，俄在2014年还多次声明了保持现有核力量结构的意向。2014年1月，俄总统普京在莫斯科工程物理学院透露，俄罗斯国防政策的主要方向是发展核综合体，包括扶持核三位一体。由战略轰炸机、洲际弹道导弹和潜射弹道导弹组成的传统意义上的核“三位一体”，仍是俄罗斯军事防御的基石。

二、强调核威慑现实作用，确保装备采购独立性

（一）面对潜在威胁，强调核威慑的作用

2014年，俄在与周边关系严峻的情况下，多次突出了核武器的威慑作用，以此遏制因克里米亚问题而遭到的外部威胁。普京多次强调了以核武器应对外部威胁的决心。5月，普京在视察核部队参演的军事演习中强调，此次军演旨在模拟实施大规模报复性核打击，以应对敌军攻击。这被认为是俄因乌克兰问题而对西方的威胁。10月，美国众议院议员在给奥巴马总统的信中指出，俄正在加紧向克里米亚部署战术核武器，而且普京在近几个月中“已提升了其使用核武器的威胁，这自冷战以来是罕见的”。

（二）规范武器装备采购，提高核系统自主性

为了减少对外部技术的依赖，特别是减少与其交恶的乌克兰工业技术的依赖，俄修订了新的军事装备指导政策，以增强武器装备的自主性。2014年9月，俄安全理事会负责人表示，俄在新的军事指导政策中将增加有关替换武器进口国必要性方面的内容。俄罗斯安全理事会副秘书长波波夫表示，由于恶劣

的政治环境，一部分西方合作伙伴的可靠性只是暂时的。为此，俄安全理事会成立了一个特别工作小组，以修订军事指导政策。2014年5月，俄军事电子产品公司负责人表示，俄将不会在其核威慑力量和导弹防御设施中使用国外电子元器件。他称：“在核弹领域，已经完全决定不再使用国外电子元器件。其所需的电子元器件将100%在俄罗斯境内研发和生产。”2014年8月，俄北方机械制造生产联合体宣称，不再需要依赖乌克兰的设备供应，已经完全具备独立建造“亚森”级核攻击型潜艇和“北风之神”级改进型的首艇“弗拉基米尔大公”号战略导弹核潜艇。俄媒体对此称，消除对进口的依赖是企业的首要任务，俄在战略武器、军事和特殊装备上的生产技术独立性，是确保国家安全的最重要因素之一。

三、灵活运用军控手段，遏制现实战略威胁

（一）挑战现行军控体制，确保国家安全利益

近年来，俄罗斯坚持履行国际条约框架内的通告和透明义务，与美国开展核军控合作，但是在新型武器发展上时常采用“打擦边球”的模糊方式，对现行军控体制构成挑战。2014年4月，美国《外交政策》指责俄自2011年以来发展的RS-26“前沿”导弹和“伊斯坎德尔”（R-500）巡航导弹系统，违反了1987年签署的《中导条约》，虽然俄罗斯宣称这两种武器射程分别处于条约限制的上限，但是美方认为由于这两种导弹飞行路线可调，其实际已经违反了条约规定。2014年7月，美就此事向俄提出正式指控，而此前波兰和北约也对俄提出了抗议。而俄政府不仅否认了所有指责，而且指控美国的反导系统和无

人机等军备项目严重侵犯了国际条约。

（二）灵活运用军控政策，遏制现实战略威胁

俄罗斯近年来在军控政策上表现出了较大的灵活性，将其作为遏制现实威胁的有效手段。2014 年 7 月，针对因乌克兰问题西方对俄的新制裁，俄议员提出单方面退出新的《削减战略进攻性武器条约》。俄罗斯下院部分议员认为，莫斯科方面应退出双边战略核军备削减条约，以惩罚美国对俄罗斯参与乌克兰问题的制裁。同时，美国众议院在 2014 年 5 月已经批准立法，寻求否决国防部提供资金执行条约要求的武器削减。俄方态度无疑有向美国表明俄军控态度的意义。

四、发展新型作战系统，保证核威慑的持续性

（一）加快新型导弹测试，扩大战略导弹库存

2014 年，俄罗斯为配合装备更新计划，加快了对新型导弹的发射试验。2014 年 6 月，俄军事工业委员会透露，俄海军计划在 2014 年下半年和 2015 年完成海基洲际弹道导弹“布拉瓦”的 5 次发射，但该计划在此后被多次调整。2014 年 9 月、10 月和 12 月，俄海军三次从“北风之神”级潜艇试射“布拉瓦”导弹，击中位于库拉试验场的目标。特别是，第三次发射是在俄第二艘“北风之神”级潜艇“亚历山大·涅夫斯基”号搭载了所有 16 枚导弹情况下进行的，而此前发射的潜艇只搭载 1 枚或 2 枚导弹。俄新型的 RS－24“亚尔斯”导弹（北约代号 SS－29）也进行了测试。2014 年 3 月和 12 月，俄战略导弹部队两次从俄西北部普列谢茨克发射场的机动发射装置上发射“亚尔斯”

导弹，均准确命中位于俄堪察加半岛的预定目标。“白杨” - M 和 RS - 24 弹道导弹将是俄罗斯“三位一体”战略核力量陆基部分的主体，到 2016 年，其在战略导弹部队武器库中的比例将不低于 80%。2014 年 12 月，成功试射了 RS - 24“亚尔斯”洲际弹道导弹。两次试射的主要目的是确认在 2013 年和 2014 年生产的“亚尔斯”导弹系统的作战可靠性，并确认该导弹系统的作战和性能特点。此外，俄罗斯新型巡航导弹发展也被加快。2014 年 1 月，俄空军官员透露，俄正准备进行一系列新型巡航导弹试验。俄国防部长谢尔盖·绍伊古曾表示，俄计划 2020 前将巡航导弹武库增加 30 倍，包括新型的 Kh - 101 巡航导弹。

（二）发展新型导弹，确保武器技术优势

为了保证俄罗斯在战略导弹武器技术上的优势地位，俄近年在高超声速导弹技术等方面加大了投入。2014 年 5 月，俄军工部门宣称，其计划在 2020 年前研制一型高超声速导弹的首个样机。俄国防部和工业与贸易部已批准该项目。而此前俄罗斯已经立项启动了相关项目来研发高超声速导弹技术。2014 年 11 月，俄罗斯战术导弹集团总经理奥布诺索夫公开宣称，俄罗斯计划在未来 6 年内研制首批空射型高超声速导弹，该导弹最大速度可达到 8 马赫，并将配装俄首批 PAK DA 下一代远程轰炸机。

五、升级现有作战系统，发展新型打击平台

（一）实施信息化改造，升级系统作战能力

俄对现有武器系统的改进主要是通过现代的信息化技术提

高其作战性能，延长服役年限。目前，俄正在对其图－160与图－95战略轰炸机进行升级。2014年12月，俄空军接收第一批次经过现代化改造的战略轰炸机，包括1架图－160和多架图－95。图－160的改进主要针对航电系统和武器系统进行了部分替换。现代化的第二阶段将于2016年启动，主要是增加大功率发动机。俄计划将全部重型战略轰炸机更换新的控制指挥、导航以及瞄准系统，使其既可以用于核威慑，又可以执行常规的导弹发射及投放炸弹的任务。

（二）发展新型导弹系统，提高打击与生存能力

为应对美国导弹防御系统的威胁，俄近期重启了铁路机动型导弹的研制计划。2014年12月，俄军方透露，莫斯科热工技术研究所正在设计一种导弹发射列车“巴尔古津”（Barguzin）导弹系统。按照设计，一个“巴尔古津”系统师包括5个团，团可携带6枚“亚尔斯”或“亚尔斯－M”导弹。根据发展计划，该导弹列车可在2019年左右实现部署。目前，俄罗斯正在就研制导弹列车的问题进行技术研究与成本估算。2013年，俄罗斯战略导弹部队指挥官卡拉卡耶夫中将曾称，俄罗斯总统普京已下令开始设计新的导弹列车。此外，为应对美国的“全球快速打击”计划，俄还发展了新型“萨尔玛特”重型弹道导弹。据称，该导弹可飞越南极和北极，并搭载机动弹头，能突破几乎任何反导系统。该导弹将在2017年年底进行试验，并部署在俄克拉斯诺亚尔斯克地区和奥伦堡州。

（三）筹划发展新型战略轰炸机，提高空中打击能力

俄罗斯新型战略轰炸机的研制工作在2014年全面启动。

2013 年俄国防部与图波列夫设计局签订了未来远程航空系统（PAK DA）研制合同，PAK DA 的全面建造工作于 2014 年开始，2019 年将完成首飞，2023 年将完成国家试验并交付俄空军。2014 年 4 月，俄联合飞机制造公司总裁波戈相透露，俄将很快启动首架 PAK DA 远程机的部件制造，该机制造厂商是喀山航空制造联合体，其与图波列夫设计局都属于联合飞机制造公司。该机将拥有极强的战斗力，能突破现代化防空系统，并且将配备最复杂的无线电电子战系统和高精度武器。2014 年 5 月，俄罗斯空军总司令透露，该型机将设计为亚声速飞行，但可携带高超声速武器，以及正在试验的 Kh－101 和 Kh－102 巡航导弹。

六、加大新型装备采购，确保作战力量部署

（一）加紧新型装备建造，全面更新导弹系统

俄为完成阶段性更新核作战系统的任务，在 2014 年继续保持了新型装备的采购势头。2014 年 12 月，俄国防部长绍伊古在国防部委员会扩大会议上表示，俄战略核力量年度内新增 38 枚洲际导弹，其中 22 枚潜射导弹，战略导弹部队的升级装备比例达到了 56%；战略导弹部队现在有 3 个团装备了“亚尔斯”洲际导弹。2014 年底，俄海军将拥有 3 艘“北风之神”级战略导弹核潜艇。首艇“尤里多尔戈鲁基”号已经开始全面战斗值班。另外两艘核潜艇，“奥列格公爵”号和“弗拉基米尔公爵”号已列装。在远程航空战斗力上增加了 7 架现代化战略轰炸机图－160和图－95MS。2016 年新型导弹系统将达到 60% 的比例；2021 年增至 98% 。俄战略导弹部队发言人叶戈罗夫称，升级工

作主要包括针对导弹防御系统的突防系统，以及部队与武器的指挥系统和保障装备的升级。

此外，俄海军“北风之神”级潜艇的建造进一步加快。2014 年 2 月，俄北德文斯克造船厂总经理布德尼琴科表示，2014—2015 年俄罗斯将开建 4 艘“北风之神”级战略核潜艇。其中 2 艘“奥列格大公”号和“苏沃洛夫公爵”号在 2014 年内完成了龙骨铺设。目前，“北风之神”级潜艇首舰“尤里·多尔戈卢基”号于 2013 年 1 月服役于北方舰队，第二艘“亚历山大·涅夫斯基”号于 2013 年 12 月服役于太平洋舰队，第三艘“弗拉基米尔·莫诺马赫”号目前正在进行测试，第四艘“弗拉基米尔大公”号目前正在建造之中。预计在 2020 年前，俄海军将共接收 8 艘该级潜艇。

（二）推进导弹武器部署，稳步增强作战能力

为保持战略核威慑能力的持续性，俄本年度内稳步推进了新型武器系统的部署。俄陆基战略导弹的新近部署工作主要分两个阶段。第一阶段为 1997—2013 年，主要部署装配单弹头发射井和公路机动型的“白杨 M”导弹。首先是部署井基型导弹以取代位于塔吉谢沃第 60 导弹师的 SS－19（RS－18“匕首”）导弹。该计划于 2013 年完成。首枚公路机动的 SS－27MOD1 导弹于 2006 年在莫斯科东北部的捷伊科沃第 54 近卫导弹师完成部署，到 2010 年已完成 18 枚导弹（2 个导弹团）的部署。在完成 78 枚“白杨－M”导弹部署后，将开始第二阶段换装工作，即部署多弹头的 RS－24“亚尔斯”导弹（“白杨－M”改进型）。首枚公路机动型 RS－24 导弹于 2010 年在捷伊科沃完成部署。2012 年，俄罗斯开始准备增加部署 3 个 RS－24 导弹师。首

个 RS－24 导弹团（配备 10 枚导弹）于 2014 开始部署，以替换位于莫斯科西南部科泽利斯克的第 28 近卫导弹师的 SS－19 导弹。之后开始换装位于杜巴罗夫斯基的第 13 导弹师，以替换其部署的 SS－18 导弹。此外，俄罗斯也正准备采用 RS－24 导弹替换部署于伊尔库茨克第 51 近卫导弹师、新西伯利亚第 39 近卫导弹师和下塔吉尔第 42 导弹师的 SS－25（“白杨”导弹）导弹。第 39 近卫导弹师于 2012 年开始换装，目前已经完成。第 51 近卫导弹师也于 2012 年开始换装，3 个导弹阵地中的一个正在改造。而第 42 导弹师，3 个导弹阵地中的 2 个正在改造。剩下的第 4、14、35 导弹师目前还未提及换装工作，未来可能将全部退役。

在稳定推进陆基力量部署的同时，俄还加快了新型海基战略导弹部署。2014 年 4 月，俄海军署于 667BDRM 型（“德尔塔”Ⅳ级）战略核潜艇上的“莱涅尔”（Liner）潜射弹道导弹开始服役。2014 年 6 月，在“布拉瓦”导弹尚未批准作战部署的情况下，“北风之神”级“尤里·多尔戈鲁基”号已经开始装备该导弹在巴伦支海执行作战任务。2014 年 10 月，俄北德文斯克船厂透露，“弗拉基米尔·莫诺马赫”号“北风之神”级潜艇已全面完成国家的试验计划，准备交付俄罗斯海军。

七、改进核基础设施，提高作战保障能力

（一）升级改造指控系统，提高核指挥可靠性

为提高指挥效率和核冲突情况下的指挥可靠性，俄近年持续对核作战指挥系统进行了改造升级。2014 年 1 月，俄国防部表示，俄战略导弹部队在部署陆基“亚尔斯”导弹后，正在采

用第四代作战控制系统来增强通信和传送命令的可靠性和有效性。新型自主作战控制系统的使用将使战略导弹部队完成对固定指挥所的现代化改造。从 2016 年开始，战略导弹部队将与工业部门合作，计划引进第五代基于作战命令数字传输的一体化自主作战控制系统。该系统将能够快捷地重新调整导弹目标，提供信息支持并管理俄罗斯战略导弹部队的日常活动。新型自主作战控制系统将直接传送命令给发射系统，绕过中间所有的组件，包括在核攻击或电子压制的情况下。俄罗斯国防部表示，第四代和第五代先进的自动化系统外形紧凑、功耗低，并能够隐秘传输数据，不受外界因素影响。

（二）扩大装备生产储存设施，增强作战保障能力

2014 年，俄为配合新型作战平台的扩大生产和导弹系统的服役，扩大了相应的武器装备生产和储存设施。2014 年 1 月，挪威媒体披露，俄再次在距挪威边境不到 120 千米的北莫尔斯克的欧克尔纳亚（Okolnaya）湾建造一个新型核导弹库，用于存放有核弹头的“布拉瓦”弹道导弹。目前在这里已建好两个新导弹库，可存放 100 余枚“布拉瓦”导弹。新型核导弹库及其配套设施预算为 1600 万美元。2013 年 11 月，俄开始在这里建造导弹仓库，而其配套设施于 2014 年 10 月开工。俄退役海军少将弗拉基米尔·扎哈罗夫透露，在欧克尔纳亚湾保存“布拉瓦”导弹比在加吉耶沃重建新设施要便宜很多，并且更为方便。此外，为了加快现代核潜艇的建造速度，配合第五艘“北风之神”级核潜艇“奥列格大公”号的建造，俄北方机械制造厂对生产设施进行了现代化改造，在 2014 年 7 月完成了 50 和 55 车间、船台、船台线的更新。

八、开展战备训练与巡逻，保证战略威慑强度

（一）开展战备执勤巡逻，实施战略威慑试探

2014 年，俄针对军事训练实际和战略威慑需要，开展了大范围的战备巡逻和训练。2014 年 1 月，两架俄罗斯空军的战略轰炸机，协同预警机和战斗机沿着日本列岛外围巡航 9 小时；4 月中旬，俄 6 架图 –95 轰炸机由 3 条路线沿着日本列岛周边飞行一周；4 月底，2 架图 –95 抵近荷兰飞行；5 月，在乌克兰局势紧张时，俄在太平洋地区加强了军事活动，其中包括向美国加州海岸和关岛附近海域派出远程轰炸机战备执勤；10 月，俄 4 架图 –95 轰炸机和 4 架伊尔 –78 空中加油机飞越大西洋和北海，美国空军官员认为，图 –95 可能飞向了几个预定的核导弹发射点，此举是俄空军主动对北约称为“欧洲领空”的区域进行试探，以估计西方盟国的防御反应时间。

（二）组织部队发射训练，对装备和部队进行检验

除了按计划发射试验新型导弹武器外，俄在年度内通常还会组织例行性的部队发射训练，以提高核力量战备水平。2014 年 5 月，俄从南部导弹综合试验场发射 1 枚 SS –25“白杨”公路机动导弹；11 月，俄从西北部发射场试射了 1 枚“白杨” –M 型导弹，展示了导弹的高精度和完善的训练水平；同样在 11 月，俄北方舰队“图拉”号核潜艇从巴伦支海向堪察加半岛的库拉试验场发射 1 枚与“轻舟”（Skiff）同型的“西涅瓦”（Sineva）导弹。这些发射活动有效地检验了现役装备的可靠性，提高了部队的战备训练水平。

（三）举行综合性战略核军演，提高核力量战备水平

年度内，俄组织了多次战略性核军演，在提高战略核力量综合性作战能力的同时，有针对性地向外界宣示了核威慑。2014 年 3 月，俄启动了历时三天的包括核战争的大规模军事演习，演习内容包括了大范围的核进攻。俄国防部表示，在战略导弹方面，演习人员已被部署在导弹发射单位做好了发射准备，并将演练各种行政和支持部门的运行。演习部队还将执行对生化和放射性威胁的检测，以及确认并防止能够破坏进攻的各种常规威胁。2014 年 5 月，在与西方持续紧张局势的背景下，俄进行了一场包括陆基与海基导弹发射的核应对演习。此次演习模拟了俄罗斯在受到攻击后如何进行大规模核打击报复。海陆空基战略核力量均组织了实弹发射。2014 年 6 月，俄国防部表示，俄战略导弹部队将在未来 6 个月内进行 120 次演练。这旨在提高夏季作战训练期的强度，战略导弹部队将进行超过 40 次的人员培训、约 20 次指挥所演练、10 次指挥所与作战人员演习、50 次战术与特殊战术训练演习。这些演习有效提高了俄战略核力量的战备水平，遏制了西方对俄的一再威胁。

九、开展核安全演练，加强核设施安保措施

（一）开展核安全演练，提高防事故能力

为了预防核事故发生和处置，俄年度内组织了例行性核事故处置演练。2014 年 7 月，俄海军在太平洋演习期间进行核灾难应急响应训练。俄罗斯国防部宣称，俄远东的东部军区按计划进行了核事故处置的指挥和人员演习，以模拟核灾难的后续

反应。本次演习包括俄罗斯太平洋舰队的核装备，是一次对现代危机响应预案的评估，以将核事故的影响降至最低。俄罗斯之前举行过核应急响应演习，但这次正值俄罗斯与乌克兰和北约面临剑拔弩张的紧张局势之时，因此引起了广泛关注。

（二）加强核设施安保，预防核恐怖事件

由于近年来俄国内外矛盾区域严峻，因此俄提高了核设施的安全保卫能力，以预防核恐怖和失控事件。2014 年 3 月，俄宣布，年度内开始部署机器人保护战略核导弹基地。按照计划，这种无人操作的、移动安保系统将部署在全国 5 个导弹发射基地。机器人可以为安保部队提供后援，发现入侵者，“摧毁”移动目标和执行监测任务。自冷战结束以来，由于乌克兰问题，俄与西方关系空前紧张，在这种情况下，俄加快了机器人部署，来提高核武器场址安全，以防止核武器失控。

A Review on Russia Nuclear Forces:2014

*Liu lijun and Sun Tonghui*①

In 2014, Russia met serious domestic and external challenges, which made Russia more dependent on nuclear capability, and the development of nuclear weapons has sped up.

I. Continue to Increase Defense Expenditure

In recent years, to tackle with the deterioration of security environment, Russia has continuously increased its defense budget, and increased its input into nuclear capability development.

1. **Increase defense budget**

In 2014, though facing tough economic austerity, Russia still kept on increasing defense budget and adjusted military purchase policy. In March. 2014, the Ministry of Finance of Russia announced that in 2013 Russia defense budget had been increased 15.6%; in 2014 it had been increased 18.4%, reaching 76.6 billion dollars. In

① Liu Lijun and Sun Tonghui are researchers of the Centre of Arms Control and International Security Research at China Institute of International Studies.

October. 2014, Russian Duma said in 2015 Russia had planned to increase 32. 8% of defense budget, which would reach 80. 4 billion dollars and take up 4. 2% of GDP. This was the largest defense budget growth since 2001. The increase was mainly for the modernization of weapons and equipments, military manoeuvre and the improvement of military service conditions. While increasing defense budget, Russia has started to adjust military purchase policy. In September 2014, Borisov, Vice Defense Minister of Russia said that during 2016—2025 types of weapon and military equipment would be decreased in national weapon development plan. Based on the current industry and technology, Russia would fix a new weapon equipment development plan within six months. The reduction of weapon and military equipment types would decrease maintenance and service expenditure, and lower the training expense of the troops. In October 2014, Rogozin, Russia Vice - Premier who is in charge of military industrial group, said that Russia was increasing the revival of nuclear deterrence, its military input would focus on nuclear capability upgrading before 2020.

2. **Maintain nuclear forces structure**

Facing new security environment, Russia has revised its military doctrine. In December 2014, Russia National Security Council adopted the new military Doctrine. The first Russia military doctrine was adopted in 1993, and was revised in 2000 and 2010. The revision of the new military doctrine this time regards the missile defense system that the western countries built and deployed, Prompt Global Strike Plan and deployment of space strategic weapons as major external threat; meanwhile, NATO's eastern expansion and the strengthening of the offensive posture along Russian border area and its neighboring water area are new security threats to Russia. Although the new military doctrine proposed Non-Nuclear Deterrence Concept for the first time, Baluyevsky, Russian former Vice-Minister of Defense and the former Chief of Russian Army said that this was a revision of the current military doctrine, not making a new military doctrine. In Russian military doctrine, there's no clause relating to preventive nuclear strike, Russia still insists on using nuclear weapon in nuclear counterattack. According to current policy, the conditions under which Russia would use nuclear weapon are: (1) when Russia and its allies suffer from nuclear or other mass – destruction weapon attack; (2) when Russia is facing potential and crucial conventional attack.

While insisted on the principle of using nuclear weapons, Russia stated several times in 2014 its willingness to maintain current nuclear power structure. In January 2014, Russian President Putin said at Moscow Engineering Physics Institute that the main direction of Russian defense policy was to develop nuclear complex, including supporting nuclear triad. The traditional nuclear triad, which included strategic bomber, ICBM and SLBM, is still the foundation of Russian national defense.

Ⅱ. Emphasize the Realistic Function of Nuclear Deterrence

In 2014, as the external security environment was worsened by Ukraine issue, Russia emphasized several times the significance of nuclear capability. At the same time, in order to enhance nuclear deterrence, Russia has updated the nuclear weapon systems.

1. **Emphasize the Meaning of Nuclear Deterrence**

In 2014, Russia emphasized several times on the deterrent function of nuclear weapon. In 2014, Putin emphasized that the determination to resisting external threat with nuclear weapons was necessary. In May 2014, during a military exercise with nuclear forces, Putin stressed the purpose of this military exercise was to perform retaliatory nuclear strike against hostile troops. This is considered to be Russia's threat to the west because of Ukraine issue. In October 2014, a member of the U. S. House of Representatives wrote a letter to President Obama and pointed out that Russia was speeding up the deployment of strategic nuclear weapons in Crimea, and in recent months Putin "has already increased threat of using nuclear weapons, which was unusual since the Cold War."

2. **Regulate Equipment Purchase**

To reduce the dependence on foreign technologies, especially the dependence on Ukraine technologies, Russia has revised the new military equipment guiding policy, in order to enhance the capability of weapon systems. In September 2014, the Russia Security Council expressed that Russia would increase the indigenous weapons to replace imported ones in the new military equipment policy. Popov, the Deputy Scretary - General of Russia Security Council, said that due to the threatening political conditions, the reliability of some western partners is just temporary. Therefore, Russia Security Council founded a special task team in order to revise the military policy.

In May 2014, Russian military electronic product company said that Russia would not use foreign electronic components in Russian nuclear deterrent forces and missile defense facilities. He said that in nuclear bomb field, it has been decided that foreign electronic components would never be used any more. Required electronic components will be 100% researched and produced in Russia. In August 2014, Russia North Machinery Manufacturing Production Association declared that Russia would never need the equipment supply from Ukraine, and had been able to independently build Arsene level nuclear attack submarine and the first boat is "Archduke Vladimir" strategic missile nuclear submarine of 'Boreas' class advanced version. Russia media reported that the primary task for enterprisewas to eliminate the dependence to import. The independence of production technologies of strategic weapons, military affairs, and special equipments is the most significant factor of ensuring the national security.

Ⅲ. Flexibly in Arms Control

In 2014, while complimenting its traditional arms control obligations, Russia also flexibly used blurring methods to challenge current arms control system, in order to deal with realistic strategy threat.

1. **Challenge Current Arms Control System**

In recent years, Russia has insisted performing the notice and transparency obligations in the international treaty framework, and developed well arms control cooperation with the U. S., but Russia has adopted a blurring method of working around the edges in new weapon development, and posed challenge to current arms control system. In Apr; l. 2014, U. S. *Foreign Policy* accused that, since 2011, the RS – 26 "Frontier" Missile and "Islamic Kandel" (R – 500) Cruise Missile System violated the INF Treaty signed in 1987. The U. S. has insisted that as the flight routes of these two missiles are adjustable, actually they violated the regulations of the Treaty. In July 2014, the U. S. formally accused Russia of this issue, and before this Poland and NATO also both protested Russia. However, Russia not only denied all accusations, but also accused that the armament project such as the U. S anti – missile system and unmanned aerial vehicle etc has seriously violated international treaty.

2. Flexibly in Using Arms Control Methods

In recent years, Russia has expressed its flexibility on arms control policy, and considered it as an effective method of deal with realistic strategic threat. In July 2014, due to the new sanction on Russia, Russian legislators proposed unilateral withdrawal of the new *Strategic Offensive Arms Reduction Treaty* (NEW START) . Some members in Russian Low House believed Moscow should withdraw bilateral strategic nuclear reduction treaty, in order to punish the U. S. sanction on Russia's involving in Ukraine issue. Meanwhile, the U. S. House of Representatives adopted resolutions to seek a way of denying weapon reduction. Russian attitude undoubtedly expressed its arms control attitude towardsthe U. S.

Ⅳ. Develop New Operation System

To ensure the update of nuclear capability and guarantee the effective strategic nuclear deterrence, Russia continuously developed new weapons in recent years and constantly tested in 2014.

1. **Accelerate New Missile Tests**

In 2014, according toits update plan, Russia accelerated the launching test of new missiles. In June 2014, Russian Military Industrial Commission said, Russian Navy had planned to complete the five launchings of sea – based intercontinental ballistic missile Bulava in the second half of 2014 and first half of 2015, but this plan has been adjusted several times since then. In September, October, and December of 2014, Russian Navy test hit the targets in Kura testing site by Boreasclass submarine launching test Bulava missile. The third launching test was done with Russian second Boreasclass submarine Alexander Navski, carrying 16 missiles, while the former launching submarine only carried one or two missiles.

Russian new RS – 24 Yars Missile (NATO name: SS – 29) was alsotested. In March and December 2014, Russian Strategic Missile Troops twice launched Yars missiles on the mobile launcher in Plesetsk launch site in northwest Russia, and both accurately hit the intended targets, which located in Russian Kamchatka Peninsula. "Topol" – M and RS – 24 ballistic missiles would be the major part of the land base of Russian "triad" strategic nuclear power. In December 2014, Russia successfully launched RS – 24 Yars intercontinental ballistic missile. The main purpose of the tests was to confirm the operational reliability of the Yars missile systems, which were produced in 2013 and 2014, and confirm the characteristics of this missile systematic operation and performance. Besides, the development of Russian new cruise missile was also being accelerated. In January 2014, Russian Air Force Officer said that Russia was preparing for a series of new cruise missile tests. Sergei Shoigu, Minister of Defense expressed that the cruise missile arsenal would expand 30 times in number by 2020, including the new Kh – 101 cruise missiles.

2. **Develop New Missile Technology**

To ensure Russia's advantageous position in strategic missile weapon technology, in recent years Russia has increased its input into hypersonic missile technology and some other fields. In May 2014, Russian Ministry of Defense declared that they would research and produce the first hypersonic missile by 2020. Russia Ministry of Defense and Ministry of Industry and Trade both approved this program. Before this Russia has launched relevant programs to research and develop hypersonic missile technology. In November 2014, Obnosov, the General Manager of Russian Tactical Missile Group declared that Russia had planned to research and develop the first air – launched hypersonic missiles in the coming six years, the maximum speed of which could be Mach 8, and would be used by Russian first next generation of long – range bombers.

V. Upgrade Current Operation System and Platform

While developing new weapon system, in recent years Russia has sped up the upgrading and updating development of operation platform, which will comprehensively enhance Russia's strategic operation level in the future.

1. **Upgrade System Capability with Information Technology**

Russian current weapon system improvement enhanced its performance and extended service lifeby modern information technology. At present, Russia has been upgrading its Tu – 160 and Tu – 95 strategic bombers. In December 2014, Russian Air Force received the first batch of modernized strategic bombers, including one Tu – 160 and several Tu – 95. Improvement of Tu – 160 mainly was to replace parts of avionic system and weapon system. The second stage of modernization would be launched in 2016, mainly to enhance high – power engines. Russia planned to change new command and control, navigation and targeting system for all heavy strategic bombers, to use them not only in nuclear deterrence, but also in completing conventional missile launching and bomb releasing tasks.

1. **Develop New Missile Systems**

To handle with the threat of U. S. missile defense system, Russia restarted the research and development of railway – based mobile missiles. In December 2014, Russian military said that Moscow Thermal Technology Research Institute was designing a missile launching train Barguzin missile system. One Barguzin system includes five regiments in the design, and every regiment could carry six Yars or Yars – M missiles. According to the development plan, this train would start its service around 2019. At present, Russia is doing technology research and cost evaluation of the problems met in missile train research. In 2013, Russian Strategic Missile Forces Commander, General Karakayev said Russian President Putin had ordered to design new missile train. Besides, to handle with the U. S. Prompt Global Strike Plan, Russia also developed new Sarmat heavy ballistic missile. It was reported that this missile was able to fly across South Pole and North Pole, and carry maneuver warheads, which could break almost all anti-missile systems. This missile would be tested at the end of 2017, and would entre into service in Krasnoyarsk Region and Orenburg Region.

2. **Plan and Develop New Strategic Bomber**

The research and development of Russian New Strategic Bomber was fully launched in 2014. In 2013 Russian Ministry of Defense and Tupolev Design Bureau signed a contract of PAK DA research and development program. The overall manufacturing work of PAK DA started in 2014, and the first flight will be completed in 2019, then in 2023 the trials would be completed and PAK DA delivered to Russian Air Force. In April 2014, Pogosyan, President of Russia United Aircraft Corporation, said that Russia would soon launch the manufacture of the first PAK DA airplane, the manufacturing factory of this aircraft is Kazan Aviation Manufacturing Complex, which belongs to United Aircraft Corporation, whick ais affiliated to Tupolev Design Bureau. This aircraft has extremely strong fighting capability, could breakthrough modern air defense system, and would be equipped with the most complex radio electronic warfare system and high precision weapons. In May 2014, Russian Air Force Chief Commander said that this type of aircraft would be designed for subsonic flight, but could carry hypersonic weapons, and test Kh-101 and Kh-102 cruise missiles.

Ⅵ. Enlarge New Equipment Purchase

With its defense budget increase, Russia has continuously enhanced its weapon purchasing in recent years, which ensured the capability of new missile weapon systems.

1. **Speed up New Equipment Construction**

To complete the task of nuclear operation system, in 2014 Russia kept the purchase momentum of new equipment. In December 2014, Russian Minister of Defense Shoigu, said at the enlarged meeting of the Defense Committee that Russian strategic nuclear power would have 38 intercontinental missiles within 2014, among which there were 22 underwater missiles; the Strategic Missile Troops had three regiments equipped with Yars intercontinental missiles. By the end of 2014, Russian Navy would own three Borea sclass strategic missile nuclear submarines. The first Yuri Dolgoruki has started comprehensive operation duty. The other two nuclear submarines, Prince Oleg and Prince Vladimir were uder construction. In the air operation field, Russia increased seven modernized strategic bomber Tu – 160 and Tu – 95MS. In 2016, new missile system will cover a ratio of 60% ; and in 2021 it will be increased to 98%. Egoroff, the Russian Strategic Missile Troops spokesman declared that the upgrading work mainly includes the penetration system of missile defense system, the command system of troops and weapons, and the security equipment.

Besides, the construction of Russian Navy's Boreas class submarine was accelerated. In February 2014, Bud Chernichenko, the

General Manager of Russian Severodvinsk Shipyard said during 2014 to 2015 Russia would start to construct four Boreas class strategic nuclear submarine, among which the Prince Oleg and Duke Suvorovwere completed the keel – laying in 2014. Currently, the first Yuri Dolgoruki of Boreas class submarine started its service in Northern Fleet since January 2013, the second Alexander Navski started service in Parcific Fleet in December 2013, the third Vladimir Monomakh is currently under trial, and the fourth Prince Vladimir is under construction at present. It is estimated that before 2020, Russian Navy would receive eight submarines of this class.

2. **Promote Missile Deployment Speed**

To keep the constancy of strategic nuclear deterrence capabilities, Russia carried forward the new weapon system deploymentin 2014. The newly deployment of Russian land – base strategic missiles are mainly divided into two stages. The first stage is 1997 – 2013; Russian mainly deployed and equipped single warhead launch and road mobile Topol – M missiles. First is to deploy well – based missiles to replace the SS – 19 (RS – 18 Dagger) missile which were located in Tatishchevo the 60th Missile Division and this deployment was completed in 2013. The first road mobile SS – 27MOD1 missile completed deployment at Teykovo 54th Guard Missile Division whichwas located at northeast Moscow in 2006, and by the year of 2010, Russia deployed 18 missiles (2 missile groups) of this kind. After the deployment of 78 Topol – M missiles, Russia started the second stage of the replacement program, that was to deploy multi – headed RS – 24 Yars Missile (Topol – M improved version). The deployment of the first road mobile RS – 24 missile was completed in Teykovo in 2010. In 2012, Russian started to prepare the deployment of three more RS – 24 missile divisions. The first RS – 24 missile division (equipped with 10 missiles) started the deployment in 2014 to replace the SS – 19 missile in the 28th Guard Missile Division which located in Kozelsk, southwest of Moscow. After that Russia would replace the SS – 18 missile by the 13th missile division located at Du Barofsky. Russia is also going to use RS – 24 missile to replace the SS – 25 (Topol missile) by the 51st guard missile division in Irkusk, 39th guard missile division in Novosibirsk, and 42nd missile division in Nizhniy Tagil. The 39th guard missile division started the replacement in 2012. The 51st guard missile division also started the replacement in 2012, and one of the three missile positions has been under reconstruction now. And for 42nd missile division, two of the three missile positions are under reconstruction now. The rest 4th, 14th, and 35th missile division have not been assigned replacement work and would possibly be out of commission in the future.

While steadily promoting land – base power deployment, Russia also has accelerated new sea – based strategic missile deployment. In April 2014, Russian Navy's SLBM 667BDRM (Delta classⅣ) strategic nuclear submarine started its service. In June 2014, as the Bulava missile have not been approved to have operation deployment, the Boreas class Yuri Dolgoruki started to equip this missile and perform operation tasks in Barents Sea. In October 2014, the Russian Severodvinsk Shipyard declared Vladimir MonomakhBoreas class submarine has fully completed national trial plan, and would be submitted to Russian Navy.

Ⅶ. Improve Nuclear Infrastructure

To match the nuclear operation system modernization, Russia started to improve the modernizaton capability of the nuclear operation system, and has gradually expanded nuclear operation supporting infrastructures.

1. **Upgrade Command System**

To enhance commanding efficiency and reliability under nuclear conflict, Russia has gradually improved and upgraded the nuclear operation commanding system. In January 2014, Russian Defense Ministry declared that after land – base Yars missile deployed, Russia Strategic Missile Troops would use the fourth – generation operation control system to enhance the reliability and validity of tele – communication. The using of the new automatic operation control system would assist Strategic Missile Troops to complete the modernization of fixed command post. Since 2016, Strategic Missile Troop would cooperate with industrial sectors and plan to import the fifth – generation integrated automatic operation control system which would be based on digital transmission of operation command. This sytem would fast and conveniently re – adjust missile targets, provide information support and manage the daily activities of Russian strategic missile troop. The new autonomous operation control system would directly send commands to launching system, and bypass all middle components, including when under nuclear attack or electronic jamming. Russian Defense Ministry declared that the advanced fourth and fifth generation automatic system have compact appearance, low power consumption, and could secretly transmit data without external influence.

2. Expand Production and Storage Facilities

In 2014, to match the expanding production of new operation platforms and the service of missile systems, Russia enlarged its corresponding weapon production and storage facilities. In January 2014, Norway media published that Russia had built another new nuclear missile arsenals, for storing Bulava ballistic missile with nuclear warheads at the Okolnaya of Severomorsk which was no more than 120km to Norway border. So far there are two new missile arsenals, which could store more than 100 Bulava missiles. The budget of the new nuclear missile arsenal and its supporting facilities is 16 million dollars. In November 2013, Russia started to build missile arsenal here and its supporting facilities construction started in October 2014. Vladimir Zakharov, Russian retired Rear Admiral said that storing Bulava missile in Okolnaya was much cheaper and more convenient than building new facilities in Gadjievo. To accelerate the construction speed of modern submarines, and match the construction of the fifth Boreas class nuclear submarine Prince Oleg, Russian Northern Machinery Factory modernized its production facilities and completed the upgrade of 50 and 55 workshop, slipway and slipway line in July 2014.

Ⅷ. Enhance Operation Training and Patrol

In order to ensure readiness level of Russian nuclear forces and presented the strategic deterrent strength, Russian nuclear troop carried out comprehensive operation readiness training and performed guard duties.

1. **Carry Out Operation Patrol and Deterrent Test**

In 2014, according to the military training plan and strategy deterrent need, Russia carried out large – scale operation readiness patrol and training. In January 2014, two strategic bombers of Russian Air Force with airborne warning plane patrolled 9 hours around Japanese archipelago outline; In the middle of April, six Russian Tu – 95 bombers flew around Japanese archipelago outline along three routes; At the end of April, two Tu – 95 flew close to Netherland; In May, when there was tension in Ukraine, Russia strengthened the military activities in Parcific region, which included sending bomber to perform patrolling duty at the neighboring waters close to California Coast and Guam; In October, four Russian Tu – 95 bombers and four IL – 78 air refueling tankers flew across the Atlantic and the North Sea. The U. S. Air Force officer estimated that Tu – 95 might fly to several missile launching sites. And this move is considered as Russia Air Force attempt to totest the defense reaction time of NATO and its western allies.

2. **Organize Launching Training**

Besides launching trial of new missile weapon as planned, Russia also organized routine launching training in the year to enhance nuclear operation readiness level. In May 2014, Russia launched a trial of SS – 25 Topol road mobile missile from southern missile test field; in November, Russia launched a Topol – M missile from northwest launching site, which presented high accuracy and perfect training level of the missile troops. Same in November, Russia Northern Fleet Tula Submarine launched a Sineva missile that was the same type as Skiff to the Kura testing field in Kanchatka Peninsula from Barents Sea. These launching activities effectively checked the reliability of the current equipment, and enhanced the operation readiness level of the troops.

3. **Carry out Strategic Nuclear Exercise**

In 2014, Russia organized several strategic exercise, which not only improved strategic nuclear power comprehensive operation capabilities, but also presented the nuclear deterrence to external world. In March 2014, Russia launched a three – day large – scale military exercise including nuclear war, and the exercise included large – scale nuclear strike. Russian Defense Ministry declared that in the strategic missile field, the soldiers had launched missiles and had been well prepared for the launching. The exercise troop had also checked biochemical and radioactive threat, and also ensured and prevented different conventional threats. In May 2014, under the continuous tense situation with the Western countries, Russia had a nuclear training, which included land – based and sea – based missile launching. This exercise marked how Russia performing large – scale retaliation strike after being attacked. Sea, land and air – based strategic nuclear troops all organized live launching. In June 2014, Russian Defense Ministry declared that Russian strategic missile troop would have 120 exercises in six months. The purpose was to increase the intensity of summer comfbat training. Strategic missile troops would conduct more than 40 times of training, and about 20 command post exercises, 10 command post and war fighting exercise, and 50 tactical and special tactical exercises. These exercises effectively had enhanced Russia's operation readiness of strategic nuclear power.

Ⅸ. Enhance Nuclear Security Measures

In recent year, Russia has focused on the nuclear security in the in – use nuclear power, speacially focused on improving nuclear facilities security, in order to increase nuclear security level.

1. **Carry out Nuclear Security Exercise**

To prevent and deal with nuclear accidents, Russia organized routine nuclear accident exercise in the year. In July 2014, Russian Navy performed nuclear disaster emergency response training during Pacific Exercise. Russian Defense Ministry declared that, the eastern military region performed nuclear accident exercise according to the plan in order to test the subsequent reaction of nuclear disaster. This exercise included the nuclear facilities of Russian Pacific Fleet and was an evaluation to the modern crisis response plan, in order to minimize nuclear accident effect. Russia had performed nuclear emergency response exercise before, but this time Russia and Ukraine were under tense conditions at sword points with NATO, therefore it brought wide concern.

2. **Prevent Nuclear Terrorist Attack**

As Russian domestic and external challenges getting severe, Russia increased the security protection capability of its nuclear facilities to prevent nuclear terrorism. In Mar. 2014, Russia declared that it had started to use robots to protect strategic nuclear missile base within the year. According to the paln, this unmanned, mobile security protection system would be used in five missile launching bases all over Russia. Robots could be security troop's equipment. Once any intruder detected, they would destroy the moving objectives and perform supervision tasks. Since the end of Cold War, due to Ukraine issue, Russan relations with the West has become unprecedented tense. Under this situation, Russia sped up its robot deployment to enhance nuclear weapon site security.

2014 年英法核力量发展综述

戴艳丽　刘　敏　孙爱平

〔**内容提要**〕作为中等核力量国家，英国和法国在核力量的发展上都有着各自的方式，但在面临外部威胁和核力量发展所采取的措施方面，又都有着诸多共同点。2014 年，两国在军事预算持续普遍削减的背景下，坚持核力量的升级与发展。

主题词：英国　法国　核力量　发展　综述

作者单位：中国国际问题研究院军控与国际安全研究中心

一、坚持战略威慑，确保核力量投入

虽然英法两国国内对保持核威慑战略和核力量发展存在诸多争议，但两国都坚持战略核威慑思想，并在军事预算普遍削减的大背景下，保证了核力量的稳定发展。

（一）制定新国防战略，巩固核威慑思想

2014 年，英法两国都在考虑针对现实威胁环境，修订各自的国防战略，并采取多种手段公布战略核威慑思想。1 月，英国会委员会表示，《2010 国防战略与安全评估》（SDSR）没有对

英国的国防地位做出战略性的论述，应当在《2015 国防战略与安全评估》中得到修订，与此相关的文件还包括 2015 年可能计划发布的《国家安全战略》及《综合开支审查》等。2015 年，英国在阿富汗的作战行动将结束，英国军队需要进行新平衡发展。而外界评论认为，新战略将在对英国军力进行评估的基础上，突出核战略威慑力量的地位与作用。2014 年，英国还因苏格兰独立公投而产生了对核力量部署与去留的广泛争论。英国携带“三叉戟”导弹的潜艇驻军在苏格兰西北部城市格拉斯哥的威廉王子海军基地，如果苏格兰独立，英国可能要花费数百亿美元来迁移海军基地。作为美国最重要和最亲密的盟友，英国的核威慑力量将遭受危险，这无疑威胁到英美对俄的战略威慑基础。而在 2014 年俄罗斯由于乌克兰问题而导致的与北约关系恶化，对英国战略核威慑提出了更高要求。英国国防部长哈蒙德表示，英国反对苏格兰独立，也没有将其核力量移出苏格兰的应急计划，这无疑增强了外界对英国政府的信心，稳定并巩固了其战略核威慑思想。

（二）削减军事预算，但确保核力量投入

在全球经济紧缩的大背景下，英国和法国都持续削减了国防预算，但在具体实施过程中，都仍努力保持对核力量的较大投入。2013 年 12 月，法国通过了未来五年军事支出计划法案，虽然该法案努力保持军事预算不受政府紧缩计划影响，但是 2014 年 6 月现任政府向国会提交的财政修正法案确定了削减 10—20 亿欧元年度国防预算。2014 年，英国也面临了军事预算削减的问题。2013 年 12 月，英国国防参谋长霍顿将军就预算削减使武装部队能力下降提出批评。2014 年 2 月，英国海军参谋

长赞贝拉斯上将也就此警告称，如果政府不对军队进行额外投资，英国将有可能退出世界军事强国之列，海军潜艇、战机等的规模水平可能因此下降。虽然预算被削减，但是英法两国都努力保证在核力量发展方面的投入。其中，法国战略核力量建设经费已经超出其国防开支的 10%，占其国民生产总值的 0.17%。2014 年6 月，法国军备总局（DGA）国防采办局宣称，其将继续投资发展核武器，包括目前正在研制的 M51 潜射弹道导弹及 ASMP－A 空面导弹，预计将于21 世纪30 年代中期具备作战能力。法国军备总局局长科莱·比永也表示，目前，欧洲导弹集团正研究在“阵风”战斗机上搭载 ASMP－A 导弹。

二、对核威慑能力评估，讨论核力量作用

为应对外界威胁形势的变化和预算削减的现实，英国和法国近年来都开始讨论削减核力量规模，但仍坚持了现有的核力量组成结构和形式。

（一）对核威慑能力评估，建议缩小核规模

针对新的威胁形势，英国组成专门的评估委员会，对其由“三叉戟”导弹构成的核威慑能力进行评估。2014 年 7 月，英国“三叉戟”委员会对英国核威慑能力进行为期三年的评估后认为，英国应减少核弹头的数量，但应保留目前基于“三叉戟”导弹的武器平台。该委员会反对英国将核武器作为应对不确定未来的保险，但建议英国与美国或法国合作维持持续的海基核威慑能力，以在英国及其盟国的国防中发挥关键作用。此外，该委员会还反对英国研发新的替换平台、投送系统和核弹头，

以节约成本。该委员会认为，英国维持其核威慑能力的全部费用占其国防预算的9%—10%，但到21世纪20年代，由于国防预算的增加，该比例将有所下降。此外，该委员会还认为，如果英国进一步削减“三叉戟”核弹头的数量，将不会影响其核威慑能力的可信度。

（二）保持核力量结构，讨论核力量作用

英国和法国在各自的国防文件中都确认了各自单一的及“两位一体”的核威慑力量构成，即保持适当规模的海基（弹道导弹核潜艇）和海、空基（改进型中程空对地导弹）复合的核力量形式，但两国内部关于保持现有核力量规模和现代化的争议不断出现。2014年7月，由英国前国防和外交事务领导成员组成的独立小组发布报告认为，虽然英国应当保持其由“三叉戟”核潜艇组成的核武库，但对其进行现代化更新应该推迟到2016年以后。英国的一个专门委员会透露，目前，英国部署了40枚海基“三叉戟”导弹，总量少于120枚核弹，而这些武器的作用主要表现在以下三个方面：一是当一个进攻性有核国家的重新崛起，同时该国家又拥有压倒性优势的常规力量，如俄罗斯；二是当一个现有或新兴的核国家具备全球打击能力，并对英国造成直接的战略竞争；三是如果未来出现大规模、压倒性力量，涉及使用大规模杀伤性武器，并对英国构成威胁。

三、重视对作战平台维护，改进作战系统能力

英国和法国较为重视对战略武器平台的改进与维护，以此确保核力量保持在较高的战备状态。

（一）保持系统平台维护，确保武器采购计划

为了保证战略核力量的良好战备状态，英法两国都坚持对战略导弹潜艇等系统平台例行维护，以确保其正常运行。2014年3月，英国国防部表示，对“前卫”级核潜艇反应堆进行测试时，发现在冷却水中出现低放射性元素，这一问题在2012年维护时也曾发现，为此英国将花费1.2亿英镑为“前卫”级核潜艇更换新堆芯，这一工作将于2015年完成。此外，英国还采取措施，减少由于美国导弹燃料生产减少造成的对“三叉戟”导弹采购的影响。2014年6月，美海军战略系统项目负责人本尼迪克特透露，由于航天飞机项目不再需要燃料，出现“行业疲软”的问题，这可能造成“三叉戟”导弹燃料价格上升80%，因此美国可能限制英国每年的武器采购计划，以最低限度地保持燃料市场的活跃。但英国对此表示，这一问题不会改变英美的导弹合作，也不会影响英国的核力量更新计划。英国国防部表示：“美国已经为英国提供导弹推进固体燃料超过40年，具有极佳的安全性和可靠性。英国也拥有足够的‘三叉戟’导弹燃料可满足未来数十年的需求。”

（二）改进武器系统能力，为系统提供运行保障

2014年，英法两国还积极改进导弹潜艇等战略武器平台，并为系统正常运行提供保障。2014年6月，英国国防部与巴布科克公司签订五年合同，为海军潜艇开发新型武器运输和发射系统（WHLS）和水下信号发射器（SSE）。该公司宣称，其将帮助国防部降低资本运营成本、维持最小的库存量，并保障部队的需求。此外，此次签订的合同还涉及英国及海外港口的工

程技术支持、设备安全管理、设备维护文档与手册、报废管理和库存管理等方面。该公司还将为设备维修人员、使用人员提供技术支持，为国防部未来提高该平台能力提供支持。这些措施将确保战略武器系统保持在良好的运行状态。

四、开发新型武器系统，保持核威慑系统先进性

由于英法两国战略核力量发展政策只允许保留较少的战略武器规模，因此两国对战略武器系统质量非常重视，希望通过开发新型战略武器系统，确保核作战系统的高度先进性，以此确保核威慑的长期有效性。

（一）升级基础生产设施，为新型战略系统作准备

按照英国国防部的计划，取代现有“前卫”级核潜艇的新一代弹道导弹核潜艇“继承者”级潜艇的首艘将在 2028 年交付，并将持续服役到 2060 年。英国在 2014 年开始升级相关生产设施，为新型战略系统生产奠定基础。2014 年 3 月，英国国防部宣布，将为本国潜艇工业投资超过 3 亿英镑，对 BAE 系统公司巴罗弗内斯船厂进行现代化升级，为期 8 年，以确保其能够为皇家海军建造下一代核动力潜艇。英国计划在 2020 年代新建 4 艘下一代弹道导弹核潜艇，以取代可携带“三叉戟”导弹的“前卫”级核潜艇。英国政府将提前对新潜艇的建造、组装和相关物流设施进行升级或翻新。政府提供的基础设施费用是“继承者”潜艇项目的一部分，该项目旨在维持英国的战略核威慑能力。“继承者”项目有待于在 2016 年获得最终批准，但现在就要开始准备，以便首艘新一代潜艇能够在 2028 之前正式服

役。此外，2014 年 1 月，美国海军与通用动力电船公司即将完成下一代弹道导弹核潜艇的规范设计工作，英国是该项目的主要参与者，其与美国合伙从电船公司采购导弹发射部件。其中，美国计划建造 12 艘新一代弹道导弹核潜艇，每艘有 16 个导弹发射管；而英国计划建造 4 艘新一代潜艇，每艘有 12 个导弹发射管。

（二）开发新型导弹技术，确保战略威慑优势

为掌握新型导弹技术，确保占领战略威慑优势地位，英法对新型的高超声速导弹武器技术发展都表现积极。2014 年 11 月，法国国防部长让伊夫·勒·德里安称，法国已经开启新型空射核导弹项目的研究，新一代空射核导弹将关注隐身与高超声速技术。其透露，法国已启动代号为 ASN4G 的第四代“阿斯普姆”（ASMP）巡航导弹项目，包括新型的 ASN4G 导弹和搭载这种导弹的武器平台。法国将大胆地探索最前沿的隐身技术和高超声速技术，该项目与法国空军的未来发展形态紧密相关。新型的 ASN4G 导弹于 2014 年夏季正式开始研制，旨在突破 2035 年前各国的防空系统。法国空军参谋长德尼·梅西耶宣称，根据法国当前的技术水平，ASN4G 导弹将只能从隐身性能和高超声速这两大特性中选择其一，他个人更倾向于高超声速技术，因为该技术较为成熟。法国新型的高超声速导弹速度预计能达到 7 – 8 马赫。此外，英国也积极与美国展开新型导弹技术的合作，以提高其战略威慑潜力。2014 年 1 月，英国反映发动机公司与美国签署协议，评估该公司的“佩刀”吸气式火箭发动机的性能、应用和发展途径，以及其在高超声速飞行器中应用的潜力。该协议为英国公司提供了更进一步的发展空间。该公司

目前已成功演示验证了“佩刀”发动机的超轻型高性能热交换机技术。英国政府为该项目的下一阶段研发提供了1亿美元的经费支持。

五、加大核基础设施投入，增强核武器开发合作

在积极改进和发展核系统平台的同时，英法两国大力开发核武器研制基础设施，并通过对外技术合作提高核武器技术发展能力。

（一）研制核基础设备，提高核武器开发能力

在核禁试条件下，世界核武器国家几乎都通过开发核基础设施来模拟核试验和设计新型核武器，并以此为基础提高核武器储存技术，而这些基础设施中最重要的就是超级计算机。2014年6月，英国核武器制造商原子武器研究院（AWE）完成部署三个分布式内存的超级计算机，高性能计算公司SGI的ICEX系统进入全面运行状态。AWE是英国制造和维护核弹头的主要单位，其工作涉及核弹头的全寿期，从最初概念、评估和设计到部件制造和组装，再到服役支持、退役和处置。由于《全面禁止核试验条约》禁止核试验，因此AWE必须通过科学计划，不断开发验证核弹头安全和可靠的方法。AWE高性能计算项目主管称，SGI的超级计算机系统能够运行各种应用程序并改进科学建模，从而使科研人员能够快速推进研究和开发项目，使英国能继续在全面禁试时代保证“三叉戟”弹头的安全和有效性。

（二）加强核技术合作，共享武器开发数据

通过核技术合作，降低发展成本，提高开发能力已经成为英国和法国核武器的有效途径。2014年1月，英法两国在诺顿空军基地举行合作会议，英国首相卡梅伦和法国总统奥朗德签署公报宣布将加强国防合作。英法两国2010年在英国兰卡斯特宫签署了合作协议，此次协议进一步承诺将联合投资于国防装备采购、部队联合训练和继续建设英法联合远征部队。其中包括了启动为期2年的未来空战系统开发项目，投资1.2亿英镑进行可行性联合研究，以及法国投资于英国伯克郡奥尔德马斯顿的核武器设施，使两国能继续合作和安全测试核武器，更好地共享技术和科学数据，以进一步开展联合研发。此外，英国在本年度还多次与美国就新一代战略导弹核潜艇计划和“三叉戟”导弹维护进行沟通与合作。这些措施有效维护了英法两国战略核力量威慑的有效性。

六、加强核安全立法，提高国家核安全水平

在全球范围内核安全问题日益突出的形势下，英法两国都试图通过规范核安全制度，来提高国家整体核安全水平。2014年2月，法国政府发布一项应对核事故或辐射应急响应的国家计划。该计划由法国国防与国家安全部制定，还包括核安全局（ASN）与国防核安全局（ASND）、辐射防护与核安全研究所、政府专家以及三家核运营机构。根据发布的报告，核安全局负责监管运营商，法国政府负责保障事故中的人员安全。已经在工厂、场址以及区域（达到10千米）部署了应急计划。这项国

家计划的实施旨在加强对类似于日本福岛核事故的防御；加强法国以外核应急事件中对法国居民的安全防护；加强对严重燃料运输事故的响应能力。文件详细规定了各方的责任，并对一系列的案例进行研究，以帮助管理者在核事故中做出决策。其中包括了核武器安全事故的处置方法和流程，并对军队在核安全中的作用和责任作出了规定。

A Review on UK and French Nuclear Forces: 2014

Dai Yanli, Liu Min and Sun Aiping[1]

As the countries of middle range nuclear power, UK and France have their own way of nuclear power development, however, when in the face of external threat and the ways in the nuclear power development, they have quite a lot in common. In 2014, with the background of continuous reduction of military budget, they both confirmed the nuclear deterrence strategy, insisted on upgrading and developing their nuclear capabilities.

Ⅰ. Ensure Investment in Nuclear Capability

Although there are quite a lot disputes on remaining nuclear deterrent strategy in UK and France, both countries insisted on the strategy of nuclear deterrence and ensure the stable development of the nuclear power with the background of reduction of military budget.

① Dai Yanli, Liu Min and Sun Aiping are researchers of the Centre of Arms Control and International Research at China Institute of International Studies.

1. Make New National Defense Strategy

In 2014, both UK and France were considering the revision of their national defense strategy in view of the real environment of threat, and announced their thoughts of strategic nuclear deterrent. In January 2014, the British Parliament said that the *2010 Strategic Defense and Security Review* (SDSR) failed to make a strategic discussion on British national defense position, it should be revised in the *2015 Strategic Defense and Security Review*, the relevant documents also includes *National Security Strategy* and *Comprehensive Spending Review* that was released in 2015. In 2015, the British operation in Afghanistan would be ended; the British army would need a new balanced development. The outside criticisms thought that, based on the assessment of British military power, the new strategy will highlight the position and function of strategic nuclear deterrent. In 2014, because of the Scottish Independence Referendum, the British had wide disputes on whether remaining or discarding the nuclear deployment. The British submarines are carrying Trident stationed in Prince William Naval Base of the northwest Scottish city Glasgow. If Scotland is independent, UK may need to pay billions of U. S. dollars to relocate the naval base. As the most important and closest ally to The United States, the nuclear deterrence would be in danger, and this will undoubtedly threaten the strategic deterrent base of UK and The United States to Russia. However, the deterioration of relationship between NATO and Russia brought higher request to British strategic nuclear deterrence. Therefore, the British Defense Minister Hammond said that UK was opposed to Scottish independence, and have no plan to move out the nuclear power from Scottish, this will undoubtedly enhance the outside confidence to British government, also stabilized and strengthened their strategic nuclear deterrent thought.

2. **Ensure Nuclear Forces Investment**

Under the background of global economic pressure, UK and France both reduced their defense budget. However, in the detailed implementation process, they both tried to invest quitea lot in nuclear forces. In December 2013, France adopted its military spending budget for the next 5 years, although they tried to keep the military spending without the affecting of the government austerity, in June2014, the amended financial budget that the current government submitted to the congress determined to reduce 1 – 2 billion Euros defense budget every year. In 2014, UK also had to face the problem of defense budget cut. In December 2013, the British Chief of Staff General Horton gave criticism on the situation that the budget cut caused the declining of armed forces ability dropping. In February 2014, the British Navy Chief of Staff Admiral Zam Bellas also warned that if the government would not give an extra investment in the armed forces, UK would withdraw from the world class military power, the scale of submarine, fighter and etc. would be sharply reduced.

Although the budget was reducing, both UK and France have been trying to ensure the investment on nuclear forces development. For France, the budget for strategic nuclear forces were inreased 10% of the total national defense expense, took 0. 17% of its GDP. In June 2014, the French DGA defense procurement bureau announced that wiould continue to invest in nuclear forces development, including the M51submarine – launched ballistic missile and

ASMP – A air – to – surface missile under developing, which was expected to be with operation capability in the middle of 2030. The Director of French DGA Billon also said currently the European missile group was developing ASMP – A missiles.

Ⅱ. Evaluate Nuclear Forces Deterrence

In order to deal with the variety of external threats and the budget reduction, UK and France have begun to discuss the reduction of nuclear forces scale in recent years; however they both have insisted on the existing nuclear forces structure and form.

1. Evaluate the Nuclear Forces Deterrent Capability

In view of the new situation of threat, UK formed a special committee to evaluate the nuclear forces deterrent capability of the Trident missile. In July 2014, after three years' evaluation, the committee of Trident thought that UK should reduce the number of nuclear warheads, remain the weapon platform for the Trident missile. This committee opposited UK to use the nuclear forces to deal with the uncertain future, the committee suggest UK to keep the co – operation with The United States or France to remain the continuous naval nuclear power deterrence, so that to play a key role in British and the allies' national defense. Moreover, this committee also opposited UK to develop a new replace platform, delivery system and nuclear warheads, so that to save the cost. This committee also thought that the total spend for remaining the nuclear power deterrent capability is the 9 ~ 10% in British defense budget. Moreover, this committee also thought that if

UK reduced its warheads number of the Trident missile, it would not affect the confidence of its nuclear power deterrence.

2. **Remain the Nuclear Forces Structure**

UK and France have both confirmed their nuclear deterrent force structure in their own national defense documents, that is, to keep the proper nuclear forces of sea based, air based missile, however there have been more and more deputes on the existing nuclear forces structure and modernization in the two countries. In July 2014, an independent group which was formed by the former British defense leaders and foreign affairs leaders released a report, they thought although UK should keep the nuclear weapon formed by the Trident nuclear submarine, but the modernization for it should be delayed till 2016. A special British committee revealed in 2014 that, till now, British armed forces had deployed 40 the sea based Trident missiles, less than 120, and these weapons have the following 3 functions: firstly, if any offensive country with nuclear forces re – emergency, and this country has overwhelming superiority conventional force, such as Russia; Secondly, if any existing or emerging nuclear country has the global strike capability, and bring directly strategy competition with UK; Thirdly, if there occurs large scale overwhelming power, which revolves mass destruction weapons, and caused threat to UK.

Ⅲ. Maintain Operation Platforms

UK and Francehave paid much attention to the improvement and maintenance of the strategic weapon platforms to ensure high readiness of the nuclear weapons.

1. **Keep Maintenance of Systematic Platform**

To ensure good readiness of the nuclear weapons, both UK and France have kept routine maintenance for their strategic missile submarines and other systematic platforms. In March 2014, the UK Ministry of Defence claimed that low radioactive materials detected in the cooling water of Vanguard – class nuclear submarine. This was the second time that low radiactive materials were detected after 2012, and the UK government planed to invest £ 0. 12 billion to replace new reactor core for the Vanguard – class nuclear submarines. The work was expected to be finished in 2015. In June 2014, Benedict, the director of the U. S. Navy strategic system project disclosed that the space shuttle no longer need fuel, the industry might cause an 80% price increase of the fuel for the Trident missile. Therefore the U. S. government might limit the annual weapon purchase plan of UK government to keep the minimum vitality of the fuel industry. Yet, the UK government claimed that the limitation would neither change the missile cooperation between UK and the U. S. nor effect UK's innovation plan for its nuclear forces. The UK Ministry of Defence declared that, "The U. S has been supplied UK solid fuel for missile propulsion for more than 40 years with excellent security and dependability, and UK now has enough fuel to meet the need of the Trident missile in the next ten years."

2. **Improve the Ability of Weapon System**

In 2014, UK and Frence also resorted to improve their sea – based missile and other strategic weapon platforms to ensure normal operation of the systems. In June 2014, the UK Ministry of Defence signed a 5 – year contract with Babcock to develop new WHLS and SSE systems. Babcock had promised to help the UK Ministry of Defence to low the operational cost with the minimum inventory and meet the need. The contract also involved engineering technical support, equipment safety management, document and manual of equipment maintenance, scrap management and inventory management in UK and its overseas ports. The company would also offer technical support to the maintenance and operation personnel and help the Ministry of Defence to improve the platform ability. These measures would ensure a good readiness of the strategic weapon systems.

Ⅳ. Develop New Weapon System

Since the development policy for strategic weapons of UK and France only allowed the two countries to keep limited strategic weapons, the two governments have given great attention to the quality of strategic weapon systems. The two governments hoped to maintain the advance of the nuclear weapon operation systems to ensure a standing deterrence of nuclear weapons.

1. Upgrade Manufacturing Infrastructure

As planned by the UK Ministry of Defence, the new ballistic – missile Successor – class nuclear submarine, which would replace the Vanguard Class nuclear submarine, would be put into service in 2028 and was expected to be retired in 2060. The UK government started to upgrade related manufacturing facilities to lay foundation for the new strategic system. In March 2014, the UK Ministry of Defence declared that it would invest 0. 3 billion Pounds for the country's submarine industry to the Barrow – In – Furness shipyard of the BAE system for an 8 – year modernization project to ensure that the shipyard was able to build the next generation of nuclear submarine. The UK government plans to build 4 next – generation missile submarines in 2020 as replacement of the Trident missile on Vanguard class nuclear submarine. The UK government would also upgrade and renovate the building, assemble and logistic facilities of the submarine. The infrastructure expense supplied by the government was a part of the Successor class submarine project, which was expected to increase UK's deterrence of strategic weapons. The Successor project was to be approved in 2016, but its preparation has already started to ensure that the new submarine could be put into service before 2028. Besides, the U. S. Navy and General Dynamics Electric Boat would soon finish the specification design work of the next – generation missile ballistic submarine in which the UK was a major player and would purchase the missile launching part from the company together with the U. S. government. As a part of the plan, the U. S plans to build 12 new submarines each of which was equipped with 16 missile launcher, while UK plans to build 4 new ballistic missile nuclear submarines each of which was equipped with 12 missile launcher.

2. **Develop New Missile Technology**

To follow up the new missile technology and ensure their advantageous position of strategic deterrence, UK and France have been active in the development of the new hypersonic missile technology. In November 2014, Jean – Yves Le Drian, the French Minister of Defence claimed that the country had launched the research on the new air – launched missile, which highlighted the invisibility and hypersonic technology. France has begun the fourth generation of ASMP cruise missile project including the new ASN4G missile and the missile platform with the code of ASN4G. France would boldly explore the most advanced invisibility and hypersonic technology , which would have a great bearing to the future development French air force. The new ASN4G missile whose development was started in the summer of 2014 was aimed to break all the air defence system of the world developed before 2035. Denis Messier, the French Air Force Chief of Staff declared that, the ASN4G could only be equipped with either invisibility or hypersonic technology, which he prefered the later for it was more a mature technology. France's new hypersonic missile can fly at an expected speed of 7 to 8 Mach. Besides, the UK government has also been active in cooperation with U. S in the development of new missile technology to improve its strategic deterrence. In January 2014, the British Reaction Engine Company signed an agreement with the U. S to assess the performance, utility and development of its Sabre air – breathing rocket engine and the engine's potential use in super – speed aircraft. The agreement has supported the country with further developing space. The company has already successfully manifested the ultra light high – performance thermal switch technology of the "Sabre" engine. The UK government has offered $ 0. 1 billion fund for the next phase of development.

V. Increase Investment in Nuclear Infrastructure

While being active in improving and developing the nuclear system platform, UK and France have also resorted to develop infrastructure for nuclear weapon and improve the development ability of nuclear weapon through foreign cooperation.

1. **Develop Nuclear Infrastructure**

In a world where nuclear test is banned, nearly all nuclear countries simulate nuclear test and design new nuclear weapons through developing nuclear infrastructure and by which improve the stocking technology of the nuclear weapons. Among these infrastructures, the most important is the super computer technology. In June 2014, the UK nuclear weapon manufacturer AWE finished the deployment of three super computers, signing the full operation of the ICE X system of the high performance calculation company SGI. As the main participant in the manufacture and maintenance of the UK's missile AWE's work involves the complete cycle of the missile head spanning from the initial conception, assessment and design to the manufacture, assemble of accessories and to the support of the service, retirement and dispose. Since the nuclear test is banned by CTBT, AWE has to develop safe and dependable way for warheads test by scientific plan. The director of AWE claims that the system of the SGI super computer could run all application and improve scientific modeling to ensure rapid advance of research and development which would in turn ensure the safety and efficiency of the Trident missile in a time when nuclear test is banned.

2. **Enhance Cooperation of Nuclear Technology**

It has become an efficient method for UK and France to develop nuclear weapons by technical cooperation, development cost reduction and development ability improvement. In January 2014, the two countries held a cooperation conference in Norton Air Force Base, during which UK Prime Minister David Cameron and French President Hollande signed a communiqué on the cooperation in national defence. While the two countries have already signed a similar agreement in UK Lancaster House in 2010, they would be further committed to jointly invest in the purchase of national defence equipment, united army training and the continuant construction of the UK – French joint expeditionary forces with the signing of this communiqué. Included in this communiqué is a future air war development project with a start – up period of 2 years, a united research of feasibility with a investment of 0. 12 billion pounds and an France invested nuclear facility in Aldermaston, Berkshire, UK which would ensure the two countries' cooperation in safe test of nuclear weapons and better sharing of technology and scientific data for the purpose of further united research. Besides, UK has also been communicating and cooperating with the U. S. for the plan of the new strategic missile nuclear submarine and the maintenance of Trident missile, all of which have effectively safeguarded the effective deference of the strategic nuclear force of UK and France.

VI. Enhance Legislation on Nuclear Security

In a time when the global nuclear security has become increasingly more prominent, both UK and French have been trying to improve the country's overall nuclear security by standardizing nuclear safe system. In February 2014, the French Government released a national plan of handling nuclear accident and emergency response. The plan was jointly made by the French Ministry of Defence and Safety as well as ASN and ASND, Institute for Radiation Protection and Nuclear Safety, government experts and other three nuclear operators. According to the released report, the ASN is responsible for the inspection of the operators and the French government is responsible for personnel safety in accidents. The emergency plan has been deployed in factories and relative sites and zones (with a covering era of 10 kilometers) . The national plan is meant to enhance the handling and prevention of nuclear accidents similar to the Fukushima Nuclear Power Plant. The document has specified the responsibilities of interested parties and studied series of cases to help managing personnel judge in nuclear accidents, including the handling methods and procedure of nuclear weapon accident in nuclear security.

核武裝
Nuclear Armed State

2014 年印度核力量发展综述

谭　奕　王　飞

〔**内容提要**〕印度是核武装国家中核力量水平发展最快的国家，特别是远程投送手段不仅覆盖范围越来越大，而且投送方式也越来越多样化。在 2014 年度中，印度继续大幅加大了核力量发展投入，积极开展多种导弹试验，扩大核基础设施，以争取获得更强的战略威慑能力。

主题词：印度　核力量　发展　综述

作者单位：中国国际问题研究院军控与国际安全研究中心

一、加大国防投入，巩固战略核威慑

本年度内，印度继续较大幅度增加国防预算，加大核力量发展的投入，并积极争取核国家地位，以此巩固战略核威慑。

（一）增加国防预算，加大核领域投入

在国家经济增长放缓的大背景下，印度近年坚持大幅度增加国防预算，并有针对性地加大了战略核力量的投入。印度在 2014 年 2 月发布的《2014—2015 年中期联邦预算》中，列支国防预算达 2. 24 万亿卢比（约合 371. 5 亿美元），比 2013—2014

年国防预算增加9.98%。但在7月，印度宣布新的国防预算从上财年的2.03万亿卢比（卢比在2013年走软）提高到了2.29万亿卢比（约合383亿美元），实际增加12%，主要用于印度武装部队的现代化。而与此同时，印度宣布将核研究与核能方面的预算较上财年提高约27%，核领域相关企业投资也大幅提升。从2014年4月起的2014—2015财年，印度拨给原子能部（DAE）1045亿印度卢比（17亿美元）预算，其中874亿（14.55亿美元）用于核研究，其余部分用于核能发电。核研究领域经费的289亿卢比（4.83亿美元）用于孟买的“巴巴原子研究中心”（BARC）；112亿卢比（1.87亿美元）用于卡尔帕卡姆的“英迪拉·甘地原子研究中心”，共计有5个研究机构在DAE支持下运行。新的预算方案加大了印度核基础性采购。

（二）重新审视核政策，争取国际核地位

随着印度核力量的发展和壮大，印度国内开始对其现有核政策提出质疑，要求对其重新审视。2014年4月，印度国防研究与分析所发表报告，在明确印度现有核政策的基础上，提出了质疑和建议。其认为，印度核政策的基石是“可信的最低核威慑力”，与“不首先使用”和“不使用”核武器概念的结合使用，清晰地表明印度把核武器仅仅作为一种威慑能力，而不是威胁他国的一种手段。但印度国内对其中的“不首先使用”提出质疑，因为这一政策要求印度处于防守态势，即在遭遇攻击前应具备较高的响应能力，而且其认为主要对手巴基斯坦越来越倾向于使用战术核武器，而印度核威慑能力及在遭遇战术打击后是否会实施大规模报复性攻击值得怀疑。为此，该报告提出，定期发布关于核武库和系统的升级和运行声明；扩大印

度核武库到三位数的中间水平；发展战略预警组织和技术；建设多个良好伪装和升级的核基地，以使印度在承受住对手第一击后仍有能力给对手造成令其不可接受的毁伤。可见新的提议使印度的核政策更具攻击性。

此外，2014 年印度还积极突破限制，争取国家核地位和更多话语权。6 月，印度在核供应国集团（NSG）年会中积极争取突破核不扩散条约限制，与其他核国家建立更紧密联系。目前，美、英等国认为，拥有核武器的印度应该加入“核供应集团”，而其他一些国家由于印度未加入 189 国签署的、防止国家获得大规模杀伤性武器的条约，而对此表示怀疑。印度为此已批准国际原子能机构保障监督协议的附加议定书，扩大了对其民用核计划监督。但这并不会影响印度核武器计划和敏感核燃料活动。

（三）扩大核武器库存，提高核打击能力

近年来，印度不断扩充核武器，提高核打击能力，扩大战略威慑范围。2014 年 6 月，斯德哥尔摩国际和平研究所（SIPRI）公布的数据显示，印度正在不断升级核武库，核武器数量从 2010 年的 60—80 枚已经提高到 110—120 枚，而且还在扩大军用裂变材料的生产能力。2014 年 2 月，印度国防研究发展组织（DRDO）公布了其在 2014 年的导弹测试计划，其中包括了“烈火 -5”远程弹道导弹、“无畏”巡航导弹和 K -15 潜射弹道的多次发射试验。2014 年 8 月，印度国防部长科学顾问、“国防研究与发展组织”（DRDO）主管阿维纳什·钱德尔在印度南部城市海得拉巴出席“先进航空电子学国际会议”时也透露，印度将大幅扩展本国的导弹研制项目，在未来 5 年内，印

度将研制包括多种战略导弹在内的多种不同型号导弹。可见，印度将扩大核库存和发展远程打击能力，作为其战略核威慑的主要方式。

二、组织部队发射训练，提高核力量战备水平

2014 年度内，印度组织了多次导弹武器的实弹发射训练，在检验了导弹武器战备状态的同时，有效提高了战略核力量的战备水平。

（一）组织示范性发射，加快武器服役进程

近年来，印度大量列装新型导弹武器，为了加快这些导弹武器的服役进程，印度在本年度内组织了多次由科研部门和军方参加的示范性发射。2014 年 12 月，印度国防研究与发展组织（DRDO）在印度东部奥里萨邦沿海的惠勒岛发射了“烈火 4”导弹，部署在沿岸的雷达与光电系统成功追踪并监控了导弹飞行全过程的参数，导弹射程超过了 3500 千米。此次试射是印度陆军对该型导弹的首次用户试验，也是该导弹的第四次成功试射，此次试射由印度陆军战略部队司令部负责。此前的 2014 年 11 月，印度陆军组织了对“烈火 2”导弹的试射，此次发射由机动发射装置完成。此次试射也是印度陆军进行的用户试验，由印度陆军战略部队司令部负责，印度国防研究与发展组织提供后勤保障。

（二）进行导弹发射演练，提高部队战术水平

除了新型武器的示范性发射外，2014 年印度还对多年的多

种型号导弹进行了发射，并对多种发射战术进行了检验。2014 年 1 月、3 月和 11 月，印度陆军在东部奥里萨省昌迪普（Chandipur）外海的综合导弹试射场，多次发射“大地 2”型（Prithvi－Ⅱ）导弹。试射导弹是从产品库存中随机抽检，整个试射活动由专门成立的战略部队司令部执行，由国防研究与发展组织监督执行。DRDO 的雷达、光电系统和位于奥迪萨邦海岸的遥测站跟踪导弹弹道。特别是在 11 月的发射中，使用机动发射装置发射多枚导弹，试验了导弹齐射战术。此外，2014 年 9 月，印度陆军作为常规训练再次发射“烈火 1”导弹。这些发射活动有效提高了部队战备训练水平和战术运用能力。

三、加快新型核系统发展，发展全面核威慑能力

2014 年，印度加快了远程导弹武器和新型作战平台的发展，以完善“三位一体”核力量，争取形成全面的核打击能力。

（一）提高核打击射程，扩大核威慑范围

近年来，印度把提高核打击射程，扩大核威慑范围，作为核力量发展的主要方向。为此，2014 年，印度组织了多次远程导弹武器试验。1 月，印度战略部队司令部和国防研究与发展组织（DRDO）联合进行具备核能力的“烈火 4”弹道导弹的飞行试验，成功验证了该导弹的能力。此次试验是“烈火 4”导弹连续第三次成功飞行试验，同时也是该导弹最后一次研发飞行试验，之后将进入批量生产阶段。试验中，“烈火 4”导弹从惠勒岛奥里萨邦海岸发射，飞行高度达 850 千米，经过约 20 分钟飞行后命中目标，命中精度 100 米以内。沿岸的远程雷达和光

电跟踪系统对整个飞行试验过程进行跟踪和监控。“烈火 4”导弹填补了“烈火 3”导弹与“烈火 5”导弹之间的空白，提高了导弹杀伤力和作战半径。此次试验达到了所有任务目标。

印度国防研究与发展组织主席钱德尔表示，此次试验意义重大，意味着印度的威慑、有效性水平达到新的高度。此前，印度在 2012 年 4 月和 2013 年 9 月均成功试射了“烈火 5”远程弹道导弹，该导弹采用 3 级固体推进技术，最远射程超过 5000 千米。在 2014 年国防博览会的一个新闻发布会上，詹德表示“烈火 5”洲际弹道导弹预计将于 2015 年服役，要有 2—3 次试验才能完成研制试验。预计这些试验将在一年内完成。试验完成后，“烈火 5”导弹将服役。印度媒体声称该导弹射程覆盖中国腹地，可携带核弹头打到周边任何地区。此外射程更远、可携带多枚核弹头的“烈火 6”洲际导弹也在研制中。届时，印度将具备对所有核国家的战略威慑能力。

（二）测试新型潜射导弹，发展海基打击能力

2014 年，印度为加快海基核力量发展，开始对其新型潜射导弹项目进行测试。3 月，印度从孟加拉湾的水下平台成功试射 1 枚具备核能力的 2 级 K4 潜射弹道导弹，射程超过 2000 千米。该导弹由印度国防研究与发展组织（DRDO）研发，未来将部署在印度战略部队的多个平台上，包括自主研发的“歼敌者”（INS Arihant）号核潜艇。此前，印度成功研发 K15 潜射弹道导弹，射程只有 700 千米。装备核武器的 K－4 导弹计划部署在印度第一艘弹道导弹“歼敌者”号核潜艇，以及其两艘后续艇上。在“歼敌者”号核潜艇完成海试后，将会由该艇进行一系列 K4 导弹试射。

（三）筹备海基平台服役，完善全面核威慑能力

在发展海基打击武器的同时，印度还正积极发展海基战略武器平台的海试和服役，以建立全面的三位一体战略核威慑力量。2014 年 1 月，印度海军副参谋长巴布（Babu）少将透露："'歼敌者'号的港口试验即将结束，即将进行包括 K15 导弹发射等科目的海试。"12 月，印度媒体报道，"歼敌者"号已为首次试航做好全部准备。该潜艇排水量 6000 吨，动力系统采用功率为 83MW 的压水堆。首次试航将于数日内在维萨卡帕特南启程。"歼敌者"号潜艇的小型化反应堆于 2013 年 8 月临界，目前已达到满功率运行。在进行长距离潜航之前，"歼敌者"号将先进行数次水面试航。海上验收试验（SAT）包含对 K15 弹道导弹（射程 750 千米）的试射。此外，印度国防研究与发展组织（DRDO）在 2014 年 2 月确认了印度第二艘核动力潜艇的存在，该潜艇已在维沙卡帕特南军事造船厂进行了数年的建造。"歼敌者"号的服役以及 K15 和 K4 导弹的发展，无疑将使印度具备从地面、空中和水下发射具备核能力的远程弹道导弹的能力，大大提升了核打击能力，将使其成为继美国、法国、俄罗斯和中国之后实现"三位一体"战略核力量的国家。

四、发展多元打击手段，争取占领技术优势

为了提高战略威慑的灵活性和有效性，近年来印度还积极发展多元化的战略打击手段，并积极开发新一代导弹技术，争取获取对潜在对手的技术优势。

（一）发展多元打击手段，形成灵活威慑能力

除了各种弹道导弹外，印度还在开发多种远程核打击手段，以巩固其战略核威慑。2014 年 1 月，日本媒体报道，印度战略部队司令部已要求 40 架具备核打击能力的苏 30MKI 战斗机，与陆基和潜射弹道导弹协同使用。此外，为了扩大战略威慑手段的可选择性，印度还在发展具备核投送能力的巡航导弹武器。10 月，印度在昌迪普尔附近的试验场试射了 1 枚国产可携带核弹头的“无畏”型亚音速巡航导弹，该型导弹可打击 700 多千米范围内的目标。这是该型导弹第二次试射，此前在 2013 年 3 月进行的首次试射没有取得希望的所有设计参数，由于飞行偏离了预期的路线，试验不得不中途停止。此次试验是该型导弹的首次成功试验，这标志着印度已经掌握远程巡航导弹武器技术。

（二）发展新型导弹技术，获取对外战略优势

印度与大多数导弹武器国家一样，也在积极发展高超声速导弹等新一代导弹技术，以谋求对外战略优势。2014 年 8 月，俄罗斯战术导弹武器集团总经理奥布诺索夫透露，印度专家将参与俄罗斯高超声速导弹的研发工作。此前，在 5 月，俄印专家声称他们已经检验了研发高超声速版“布拉莫斯”巡航导弹的可能性，并预计研发工作将需要 10 年时间。12 月，俄印合资企业布拉莫斯航宇公司负责人称，印度 DRDO 正在与俄罗斯合作开发高超声速版“布拉莫斯”导弹，其认为当前应该集中研究推进技术，如超燃冲压发动机技术。外界普遍认为，该技术具备发展核导弹的潜力，一旦掌握该技术，将占据新的战略威

慑优势。

五、扩大基础设施建设，改善国家核安全

为了扩大核武器生产能力，以提高库存量，印度近年来加大了核基础设施的建设力度，并开始逐步改善国家核安全。

（一）扩建核基础设施，提高核生产能力

2014 年，印度扩大了核武器生产配套的基础设施规模，以满足核武器材料需求的增加。2014 年 6 月，法国媒体报道，印度正在发展隐蔽的铀浓缩工厂，以支持印度发展热核武器。分析称，这可能引发周边国家的忧虑，伊朗发展核项目遭到国际社会的检查和制裁，印度却凭借与美国签署的民用核能合作协议，不受国际原子能机构的监督。英国专家根据卫星数据发现，印度在南部迈索尔附近以稀有金属厂为名，正在扩建铀浓缩设施——新的六氟化铀工厂。完成后，每年将增产 160 千克纯度为 90% 的浓缩铀。斯德哥尔摩国际和平研究所强调："迈索尔附近的稀有金属厂似乎正在建造新的气体离心设施。建造新的海军推进用反应堆计划刺激了印度扩大其离心浓缩能力，但可能过剩的产能也意味着它有意将现有的钚与铀混合，制造出热核武器。"国际战略研究所核不扩散项目官员马克·菲茨帕特里克认为，不管印度所为是否为海军船只提供燃料，都将增强印度核武器的制造能力，拉大印巴间的距离，缩小与中国的竞争差距。

（二）改善管理制度，提高核设施安全

长期以来，国际核武器倡议组织对印度的核安全一直持批评态度，但近年来印度在这方面不断努力改进，并取得了一些成绩。自从 2005 年印度与美国开展民用核能合作以及 2008 年核供应国集团对印度取消核禁运以来，印度的核安全评价一直都不高。印度长期的能源战略基于广泛采用核能的方案，而对该国确保核安全能力的怀疑令核技术出口国感到不安。目前，印度核安全存在的问题包括："规章制度不严，多数属于指导意见而非硬性要求；可应用于武器的核材料数量增加；监管体系不完善，比如缺乏独立的监管机构等。"核武器倡议报告指出，尽管印度已承诺建立独立的监管机构，但印度的官僚作风让这一问题的解决进展非常缓慢。为此，印度政府开始推动印度民用核能领域标准化，并调整印度的核安全规定。这使其在核武器倡议的核安全指数评价上比 2012 年略有提高，该指数的评估指标包括核材料数量与存放地、安全与管控措施、符合国际规范程度、国内承诺与处理能力、风险环境等。

A Review on India's Nuclear Capability: 2014

*Tan Yi and Wang Fei*①

India is the fastest growing country in the level ofnuclear forces among the nuclear armed states, especially the remote delivery system is not only covering more and more large areas, but also the delivery system is increasingly developed. In order to get a stronger strategic deterrent capability, India has continued to increase investment in nuclear forces development dramatically, carry out various missile tests actively, and expand nuclear infrastructure in 2014.

I. Increase Defense Spending

In order to consolidate its strategic nuclear deterrence, India has continued to increase the defense budget and the spending of nuclear forces development substantially.

1. Increase the Defense Budget in Nuclear Field

In the background of the slowing economic growth of the coun-

---

① Tan Yi and Wang Fei are researchers of the Centre of Arms Control and International Research at China Institute of International Studies.

try, Indiahas insisted on increasing defense budget substantially in recent years and increasing strategic nuclear forces spending contrapuntally. India disbursed 2. 24 trillion Rupees (about $ 37. 15 billion) for *the defense budget in the Interim federal budget in 2014 - 2015*, which was issued in February 2014, which was increased 9. 98% over the defense budget of 2013 - 2014. But in July 2014, India announced that the new defense budget would be increased to 2. 29 trillion Rupees (about $ 38. 3 billion) from 2. 03 trillion Rupees (Rupee weakness in 2013) of the previous fiscal year, which was increased 12% actually. Meanwhile, India announced that the budget for nuclear research and nuclear energy development would be increased 27% over the previous fiscal year, and the investment of relevant enterprises in nuclear field would be increased dramatically. In the fiscal years of 2014 - 2015 started from April 2014, India allocated 104. 5 billion Indian Rupees ($ 1. 7 billion) to the Department of Atomic Energy (DAE) for budget, of which 87. 4 billion ($ 1. 455 billion) was used for nuclear research, and the rest for nuclear energy electricity. 28. 9 billion Rupees ($ 483 million) was used for Bhabha Atomic Research Centre in Mumbai (BARC) and 11. 2 billion Rupees ($ 187 million) for Kalpakkam Indira Gandhi Centre for Atomic Research, and 5 research institutes in total were running under DAE's support. The new budget plan would increase India's nuclear infrastructure purchase.

2. **Re - Examine Nuclear Policy**

With the development and growth of India's nuclear capability, India began to question its existing nuclear policy and ask for review. In April 2014, India's Defense Research and Analysis Institute published a report, brought questions and suggestions on the basis of India's existing nuclear policy. It believed that the cornerstone of India's nuclear policy was the combined use of nuclear weapon concept for credible minimum nuclear deterrence, no first use and do not use, which showed clearly that India regarded the nuclear weapons as a deterrent capability only, but not a threat method to other countries. But India domestic brought questions to the concept of no first use, because this policy required India to be the defensive status, which meant that India should have a higher response capability before an attack. And they thought that Pakistan – – India's main rival, has increasingly inclined to use the tactical nuclear weapons, while whether India would implement retaliatory attacks in the event of a large – scale tactical operation. Therefore, the report proposed that in order to enable India to withstand the opponent's first strike and even give the opponent an unacceptable damage, India would publish regularly the upgrade and running statement on the nuclear arsenal and system, expand India's nuclear arsenal to the intermediate level of three – digit, develop strategic early warning organization and technology, build more well camouflage and upgrade nuclear bases. The new proposal showed that India's nuclear policy was much more aggressive.

Moreover, India broke out the restriction actively and strove for the national nuclear status and more discourse power 2014. India strove for breaking out the non – proliferation nuclear treaty restriction and establishing more close connection with other countries at the Nuclear Suppliers Group (NSG) in June 2014. Currently, the United States, Britain and other countries believed that the nuclear – armed

India should join in the Nuclear Suppliers Group. Some other countries doubted it because it did not join in the treaty. For this, India has approved the additional protocol to the safeguard agreement of International Atomic Energy Agency so that it could expand the supervision of its civilian nuclear program. But this would not affect India's nuclear weapons program and sensitive nuclear fuel activities.

3. **Expand Nuclear Arsenals**

In recent years, India has unceasingly expanded its nuclear arsenals, improved nuclear strike capability and enlarged the scope of tactical deterrence. In June 2014, the released data from the Stockholm International Peace Research Institute (SIPRI) showed that India has been unceasingly promoting its nuclear arsenals, and the number of nuclear weapons had been increased to 110 – 120 from 60 – 80 as of 2010, and it has been expanding the weapon – grade fissile material production capacity. In February 2014, the Defense Research and Development Organization (DRDO) of India announced its missile test programs in the coming years, including the launch tests of "Agni – 5" ballistic missile, Fearless cruise missile and K – 15 submarine launched ballistic. In August 2014, Avinash Chander, Scientific Advisor to Indian Defense Minister, Director of Defense Research and Development Organization (DRDO), also said that India would substantially expand the country's missile development project when he spoke at the "International Conference of Advanced Avionics". In the next five years, India would develop a variety of missiles including strategic missiles. India would expand nuclear arsenals and develop remote strike capability as its major nuclear strategic deterrence methods.

Ⅱ. Organize Launch Training

In 2014, India organized live – fire training of missile for several times, examined the operation status of the missiles while improved the operation level of strategic nuclear capability.

1. **Organize Demonstration Launching**

In recent years, Indiahas mounted a large number of new missile weapons. In order to accelerate the process of these missile in service, India organized demonstration launch for many times participated by the research departments and the military. In December 2014, the Defense Research and Development Organization (DRDO) of India launched Agni 4 missile on the Wheeler Island of Orissa coast in eastern India. The radar and optoelectronic system deployed in the coast successfully tracked and monitored the whole flight process of the missile. And the test range of the missile exceeded 3500 kilometers. This test was the first user test of the missile of this type for the India Army, and was also its fourth successful test. It was tested by the Indian Strategic Command. In the previous November 2014, the Indian Army organized the test of Agni 2missile, the launch was completed by motorized launchers. This test was also the user test conducted by the Indian Armed Forces, undertaken by the Indian Army Strategic Command, and provided logistical support by the Defense Research and Development Organization of India.

2. **Implement Missile Launch Training**

In addition to the demonstration launch of the new weapons, India has launched a number of models of missiles in recent years, and examined their launching tactics. In January, March, and November of 2014, India Armed Forces launched Prithvi -2 missile for severaltimes in the testing field of the sea of eastern Chandipur of Orissa. The test missile was random sampled from the product inventory; the testing activity was executed by the special Strategic Command and the Defense Research and Development Organization. The ballistic missile was tracked by radar and optoelectronic system in Audi Orissa coast. Especially in November, a number of missiles were launched by mobile launchers and the missile tactics was tested. Moreover, India launched Agni 1 missile once more as the regular training. The launch activities improved the level of training of army and tactical capability effectively.

Ⅲ. Accelerate the Development of New System

In the current year, Indiahas accelerated the development of remote missile weapons and new operation platforms in order to perfect the triad nuclear forces and strive to form the comprehensive nuclear strike capability.

1. Improve Nuclear Strike Range

In recent years, Indiahas regarded the improvement of nuclear strike range and scope expansion of nuclear deterrence as the main direction of nuclear forces development. Therefore, in the current year, India organized remote missile weapon tests for several times. In Janurary 2014, the Strategic Forces Command and the Defense Research and Development Organization (DRDO) of India jointly conducted the flight test of Agni 4ballistic missile and its capability was confirmed successfully. This was the third consecutive successful flight test of Agni 4 ballistic missile, at the same time it was its last development flight test, after that it would enter the phase of mass production. In the test, Agni 4 ballistic missile was launched at Wheeler of Orissa coast, the altitude reached 850 km, and then hit the target after about 20 minutes' flight, the accuracy was within 100 meters. The remote radar and optical tracking system in the coast tracked and monitored the whole flight test. Agni 4 ballistic missile filled the gaps of Agni 3 missile and Agni 5 missile, and improved the missile lethality and operation radius. This test achieved all the mission objectives. Avinash Chander, Minister and Science Advisor of Indian Defense, Director of Defense Research and Development Organization (DRDO) believed that, the test was significant, which meant that the deterrence and the level of effectiveness of India had reached a new height.

Earlier, India successfully launched Agni 5 ballistic missile in April 2012 and in September 2013, which adopted solid propulsion technology of grade – Ⅲ, whose longest range was over 5000 km. In a news conference of National Defense Exposition in 2014, Chander expressed that Agni 5 intercontinental ballistic missile was expected to be in service in 2015, the development test would be completed after two or three tests. These tests were to be completed in a year. After the test completed, Agni 5 missile would be put into service. Indian media claimed that the range of the missile could cover Chinese hinterlands and hit any surrounding areas with nuclear warheads. In addition, Agni 6 intercontinental missile with long range and nuclear warheads was under developed. By then, India would have a national deterrent capability to all nuclear weapon states.

2. **Test New Submarine – Launched Missiles**

In 2014, India tested the new submarine – launched missile program in order to accelerate the development of sea – based nuclear forces. In March 2014, India successfully launched a submarine – launched missile of K4 – Ⅱ of nuclear forces from the underwater platform of the Bay of Bengal, and the range exceeded 2000 kilometers. The missile was developed by he Defense Research and Development Organization (DRDO) of India and would be deployed on many platforms in India's Strategic Forces, including the self – developed INS Arihant nuclear submarine. Earlier, India successfully developed K15 submarine – launched missile with the range of 700 kilometers. The K – 4 missile for equipping nuclear weapons was to be deployed on the INS Arihant nuclear submarine, which was the first ballistic missile of India and its two subsequent boats. After the sea tests of the INS Arihant nuclear submarine were completed, it would implement a series of K4 missile tests.

3. **Prepare Sea – Based Platform Service**

Indiahas developed the sea – based strike weapons and prepared the sea test sactively in order to establish the comprehensive triad strategic nuclear deterrent capability. In January 2014, Babu Major, Deputy Chief of Staff of the Indian Navy, said that the harbor tests of the INS Arihant were coming to an end, the sea tests including K15 missile launch and other subjects would come soon. In December 2014, India's media reported that the INS Arihant had done all the preparations for the first test. The displacement of the submarine was 6000 tons; its power system adopted the pressurized – water reactors of 83MW. And it would leave Visakhapatnam in a few days. Miniaturized reactors of the INS Arihant submarine were critical in August 2013, had reached full power operation currently. Before the long distance lurk, the INS Arihant submarine would be tested over the sea for a few times. Sea Acceptance Test (SAT) contained the tests of K15 ballistic missile (range of 750 km). In addition, the Defense Research and Development Organization (DRDO) of India confirmed the existence of the second nuclear forces submarine in February 2014, which had been built in a military shipyard for several years in Visakhapatnam. The service of INS Arihant and the development of K15 and K4 missiles would undoubtedly make India possess the launch capability of remote ballistic missile of nuclear forces from ground, air and underwater. This improved its nuclear strike capability increasingly and would make India become the triad strategic nuclear country after the United States, Russia.

IV. Develop Diversified Means of Striking Capability

In order to promote the flexibility and effectiveness of strategic deterrence, India has actively developed diversified strategic striking methods and positively developed a new generation of missile technology in recent years for getting technical advantages to its potential opponents.

1. Develop Diversified Means of Striking and Deterrent Capability

In addition to a variety of ballistic missiles, India has been developing a number of nuclear striking means in order to consolidate its strategic nuclear deterrence. In Janurary 2014, a Japanese media reported that the Strategic Forces Command of India had got 40 Su 30MKI fighters with nuclear strike capability to be conjunctionally used with the land – based and the sea – based ballistic missiles. Furthermore, India has been developing the cruise missile weapons with nuclear projection capability in order to expand the strategic deterrence means. In October 2014, India tested a Fearless type subsonic cruise missile, which could carry nuclear warhead in the test field near Chandipur, the missile could hit its targets within the range of over 700 kilometers. This was the second test of the missile, earlier in March 2013 the first test did not achieve all the desired requirement. The test had to be stopped halfway due to deviation from the expected flight path. The scond test was the first successful test of the missile, which marked Indiahad mastered remote cruise weapon technology.

2. **Develop New Missile Technologies**

India has been developing actively hypersonic missile and other missile technology of a new generation to seek its strategic advantages over other countries. In August 2014, Obnossov, General Manager of Russian Tactical Missile Group, revealed that Indian experts would participate in the research and development work of Russia hypersonic missiles. Earlier in May 2014, the experts of Russia and India said that they had examined the possibility of developing cruise missile of hypersonic version Brahmos, and predicted the research work would take 10 years. In December 2014, the head of BrahMos Aerospace Company of Russian – Indian joint venture said that Defense Research and Development Organization (DRDO) of India was working with Russia to develop the hypersonic version of Brahmos missile. He believed that they should be focused on the propulsion technology such as the ultra scramjet technology. It was generally believed that the technology had the potential to develop nuclear missile, once the technology was mastered they would occupy new strategic deterrence advantages.

V. Expand the Infrastructure Construction

In order to expand the production capacity and improve the capability of its nuclear weapons, India had increased the construction strength of nuclear infrastructure and began to improve national nuclear security gradually.

1. **Expand Nuclear Infrastructure to Improve Nuclear Production Capacity**

In 2014, India expanded the infrastructure scale of production of nuclear weapons to meet the increasing demand for nuclear weapons materials. In June 2014, French media reported that India was building up a new uranium enrichment plant, which was enough to support India's development of thermonuclear weapons. The analysis showed that it could lead to worries from its neighboring countries. Iran was inspected and sanctioned by the international society because of the nuclear projects, while India could do this without the supervision of International Atomic Energy Agency. British experts found that India was expanding uranium enrichment facilities—the new uranium hexafluoride plant in the name of rare metal plant near Mysore in southern India in accordance with the satellite data. It would increase the production of 160kg enriched uranium with 90% purity. Stockholm International Peace Research Institute stressed it seemed that the rare metal plant near Mysore was building new gas centrifuge facility, the construction of new naval propulsion reactor plan stimulated India's capability of expanding centrifuge enrichment, but the excess capacity could also mean that it intended to mix the existing plutonium and uranium to produce thermonuclear weapons. Mark Fitzpatrick, Project officer of Nuclear Nonproliferation Project in International Institute for Strategic Studies, believed that regardless of whether India only provided fuel for naval vessels or not, it would enhance India's manufacturing capability of nuclear weapons, widen the distance between India and Pakistan and narrow the competitive gap with China.

2. **Improve the Management Institution to Enhance Security and Safety**

Ever since a long time ago, the International Initiative Organization for Nuclear Weapons had been critical of India's nuclear safety and security, but in recent years India has constantly strived to improve and achieved some success. The assessment of nuclear safety and security of India had not been high since India developed civil nuclear cooperation with the United States in 2005 and the Nuclear Suppliers Group cancelled the nuclear embargo on India in 2008. The long – term energy strategies for India were widely used nuclear scheme, while the doubts about the capability to ensure nuclear safety and the security made the nuclear exporters uneasy. Currently,

India's nuclear safety and security problems contained that the majority of strict rules and regulations were guidance rather than mandatory requirements; the number of nuclear material of weapons had been increased; the regulatory system was imperfect such as lack of independent regulatory agencies and so on. The initiative report of nuclear weapons noted that India's bureaucracy made the progress in solving this problem very slow even though India had promised to establish an independent regulatory agency. Therefore, the Indian government began to promote the standardization of India's civilian nuclear energy, and adjusted India's nuclear safety requirements. This made its assessment of nuclear safety and security index on nuclear weapon initiative a bit higher than 2012. The assessment norms of this index included the amount of nuclear material storage sites, security and control measures, degree of compliance with international norms and domestic commitments and processing capabilities and risk environment and so on.

地区核问题
Regional Nuclear Issues

2014 年朝鲜核形势评估

刘俊波

〔内容提要〕2014 年朝核问题总体上继续保持对抗与对话交织、紧张与缓和并存的态势，基本保持稳定。朝鲜采取前所未有的全方位外交攻势，但与美日韩等有关各方的互动未能突破原有的框架和范式。与此同时，围绕朝核问题这个核心，价值观外交、网络安全等一些外在因素或新议题凸显，并呈现由外围向中心扩散的趋势，催生朝核形势呈现出新的局面。

主题词：朝鲜　核问题　年度　形势

作者单位：中国国际问题研究院

一、美朝互动未能突破接触水平，朝核问题对话和谈判未能开启

围绕朝核问题六方会谈的重启，2014 年年初以来，中国进行了新的外交努力，重点是积极劝和促谈，敦促美朝双方降低对话门槛，为重开对话创造必要条件。在美朝官方正式对话无法恢复的情况下，美朝迂回接触的力度加大。朝鲜利用一轨半或二轨对话的方式与美方进行接触，美也在对话与接触分离的原则下寻求对话的条件。朝鲜外务省副相李勇浩与美国前国务

院官员和学者分别在乌兰巴托和新加坡进行非正式会谈，就如何寻求重启对话进行商讨，朝方暗示愿意冻结核试验以换取对话。双方还以激活“2·29协议”为起点，就如何履行“行动对行动”原则、为重启对话注入动力进行具体沟通。为进一步推进美朝对话，朝鲜在11月初以释放美国人质为契机，成功邀请美国国家情报总监克拉珀访问平壤，实现了美朝最高情报官员的会晤。朝鲜更是在情报交流之际，向美方抛出希望探讨一揽子解决朝核问题的设想。朝方高官特别表示，希望双方在日后继续进行对话。

美朝双方的非正式接触一度活络，但始终未能上升到对话和谈判的层次。朝鲜为了开启对话，在核问题上表现出一定灵活态度，数次公开表示愿意无条件重返六方会谈。2014年10月，朝鲜常驻联合国日内瓦办事处代表徐世平在接受媒体访问时表示，朝方已经准备重启朝鲜半岛核问题六方会谈。11月，朝鲜最高领导人金正恩特使崔龙海在访俄期间向俄罗斯外长拉夫罗夫表态说，朝鲜准备根据2005年9月通过的六方会谈共同声明，在不设先决条件的情况下恢复六方会谈。但在拥核问题上根本立场并未改变，朝鲜继续推进核武力建设，致力于推动国际社会承认其核拥有国地位。朝鲜不仅频繁试射中程弹道导弹，还威胁进行新形式的核试验。在与美方的私下接触中以及朝鲜劳动党中央书记姜锡柱访欧期间，再次要求美国应在接受朝鲜核武器国家地位的基础上进行有关谈判。这种论调加大了美国对朝鲜接触意图的疑虑和警惕。

基于这一认识，美国不愿轻易降低对话门槛，奥巴马政府有条件重启会谈的立场没有发生根本改变。美国继续坚持战略忍耐的基调，重申不为对话而对话，坚持要求朝鲜首先采取三个预先步骤证明弃核意愿。美国国务院高官明确表示，美国政府的立场不是仅让朝鲜站到对话桌边，而是促使朝鲜放弃核计划，显示美国坚持的“朝鲜必须首先做出无核化承诺”的立场没有松动。在日内瓦《框架协议》签订 20 周年纪念研讨会上，新任美国国务院六方会谈特使悉尼·塞勒再次强调，如果朝鲜宣布重返六方会谈，推迟核试验和导弹试射计划，并中断核项目，朝鲜的态度会被认为发生了根本性变化。塞勒称，如果朝鲜展现认真态度，将可重返六方会谈桌前。

一年来，美朝双方通过非正式接触进行了摸底式交流，朝鲜在一定程度上也提出一些新的设想，但彼此之间的分歧仍较为明显，立场差异难以在短时间内根本弥合，重启六方会谈及有关对话的动力虽然在接触过程中悄然聚集，但横亘在对话之间的坚冰仍未消除，双方的接触始终未能为对话找到入口，六方会谈的僵局远远没有突破。

二、价值观外交、网络安全等外围因素呈现中心化趋势

2014 年朝核问题的一个特点是，原来在朝核问题中处于边缘或外围的人权、黑客等问题呈现趋中心化态势，价值观外交、网络安全问题、南北体制竞争问题凸现出来，并与核问题相互交叉，进一步造成朝核形势复杂化。

首先是价值观外交成为朝核形势的另一条主线。2 月 17 日，联合国人权理事会朝鲜人权状况国际调查委员会发表朝鲜人权报告，宣称朝鲜当局正犯下反人类罪，提出联合国安理会应把朝鲜人权问题提交给国际刑事法院，对有关责任人进行“目标制裁”。3 月下旬，联合国人权理事会通过该决议，认为应按照国际司法程序对朝鲜侵害人权的责任人进行起诉。欧盟和日本

在此基础上起草朝鲜人权决议草案，并提交联合国大会。11 月 18 日，联合国大会第三委员会通过了欧盟和日本提交的人权决议案，谴责朝鲜境内长期持续存在有系统、普遍和严重侵犯人权行为，决定将联合国朝鲜人权问题调查委员会的报告提交安理会，并鼓励将朝鲜局势移交国际刑事法院。12 月 18 日，联合国大会全体会议通过朝鲜人权决议案，要求联合国安理会进行讨论。12 月 22 日，联合国安理会就朝鲜人权问题举行会议。这是安理会第一次就核问题以外的朝鲜局势举行会议，朝鲜局势被列入安理会议程。

面对前所未有的人权压力，朝鲜展开积极外交攻势。9 月上旬，朝鲜劳动党中央委员会书记姜锡柱访欧，提出愿恢复与欧盟中断 11 年之久的双边人权对话。9 月下旬，朝鲜在时隔 15 年后派出外相出席联大一般性辩论，就相关问题进行阐述，并为本国人权问题辩护。10 月 7 日，朝鲜在纽约联合国总部举行首次人权说明会，罕见地承认有劳动教改所，承认在改善人权方面有所不足，强调愿意与国际社会保持对话与合作。与此同时，朝鲜也对国际压力做出强硬姿态。在人权报告出台伊始，朝鲜外务省发言人称该报告为“极其危险的政治挑衅”。11 月 20 日，在报告通过后，朝鲜声明将采取一切必要措施，来维护国家的主权和安全，全面强化包括核武装力量在内的自卫国防力量，朝鲜将以坚决地反击予以回应，美国和韩国将成为首当其冲的打击对象。朝鲜外务省官员甚至威胁称，“美国及其追随势力推行的非理性人权攻势，将迫使我们采取核试验等后续措施”，威胁将人权问题与核反制相联系。随着人权问题的持续发酵，朝核形势也变得越来越难以确定。

其二是网络安全与美国内政治问题重叠，对朝核问题带来潜在负面影响。早在 2014 年 6 月 11 日，索尼影视娱乐有限公司首发电影《采访》的第一条预告片，由于该电影以刺杀朝鲜最高领导人金正恩为假想内容，引发朝鲜的强烈反应。在预告片公布之时，朝鲜便称这部影片“肮脏且受到诅咒”。6 月 25 日朝鲜发出警告，称好莱坞上映有关刺杀朝鲜领导人金正恩的喜剧电影属于“战争行为”。朝鲜外务省发言人声明称，“如果美国政府默认或支持电影上映，我们将采取果断而无情的对策”。11 月 22 日，在影片上映前夕，索尼公司遭黑客攻击和恐怖袭击威胁。美国政府称之是“威胁国家安全的严重事件”，并迅速将矛头指向朝鲜。联邦调查局（FBI）声称有足够证据证明朝鲜政府应对索尼公司遭受的网络攻击负责，美国国内大肆炒作朝鲜“在线恐怖主义”，国会则借机渲染对朝鲜进行高强度的金融制裁。12 月 19 日，奥巴马谴责朝鲜的网络攻击行为，表示将对索尼影像娱乐公司遭到黑客攻击事件作出“适当回应”，威胁对朝鲜进行新的制裁，奥巴马甚至表示，考虑是否将朝鲜重新列入恐怖主义名单。

索尼遭黑客攻击事件虽然只是一个局部性、阶段性的事件，由此引发的美朝争吵也很快消散，没有上升为朝核问题的重要议题。但由于网络安全问题的敏感性及美国国内的政治环境，在实际上却对本已脆弱的美朝关系造成新的冲击，不仅导致美国内政治气氛更加保守，也对朝核形势造成间接的负面影响。

其三是统一问题在南北关系中急剧凸显，一定程度上冲淡了朝核问题这个主题，也弱化了解决朝核问题的动力。自从张成泽事件后，韩国国内“朝鲜崩溃论”升温，进而滋生出“统一可能很快到来”的论调。韩国总统朴槿惠在 2014 年新年致辞中大谈统一问题，提出“统一大发论”。韩国外交部长官尹炳世也表示，讨论朝鲜半岛统一的气氛正在形成。在访问德国期间，朴槿惠发表“德累斯顿宣言”，被外界视为是韩国向国际社会发出的统一宣言。7 月，韩国政府宣布成立“统一准备委员会”，具体探索统一方向。12 月 2 日，朴槿惠在主持召开韩国统一准备委员会会议时强调，2015 年是韩朝解放 70 周年，是推动韩朝关系向前发展、促成朝鲜“实质性变化”的重要时机。

面对韩国的统一攻势，朝鲜做出强烈反应。4 月，朝鲜媒体发表“十问”，批评朴槿惠搞体制对抗，警告吞并式统一会带来战争。9 月 28 日在出席联大一般性辩论时，朝鲜外相李洙墉要求韩国放弃有关半岛统一的不现实方案的言论和想法，重申南北朝鲜统一的唯一方式是按照联邦制原则两大体制共存，并表示，半岛核问题只有在朝鲜的主权和生存威胁解除后才能解决，强调核武器不是为了威胁谁，也不是用来交换的筹码。11 月 6 日，针对韩国政府表示要在 2015 年 8 月制定“统一宪章”的声明，朝鲜告诫韩国应立即停止这样的敌对行动。

韩国高调推行“统一论”重新点燃了南北体制竞争的战火。在朝核问题陷入僵持的情况下，统一议题过分突出，并在一定程度上主导南北争论，不仅直接影响到半岛总体形势的缓和，也间接影响到朝核形势的演变。

三、朝鲜推行多元化、全方位外交攻势，各方互动呈现新局面

朝鲜在过去一年加快对外关系的调整步伐，大力推行多元化外交，一方面试图突破由于第三次核试验带来的国际封锁状态，一方面也在努力为国内政策重心的转移争取良好的国际条件。朝鲜最新一轮外交攻势具有明显的全方位性质，既带有巩固传统外交地盘的色彩，如东南亚、非洲、中东等地，更重要

的是明确重点，将韩、日、俄等作为主攻方向。

朝鲜主动出击，三度发起对韩外交攻势。在 2014 年伊始，朝鲜国防委员会向韩方发出“重大提案”，提议双方从 1 月 30 日开始采取实际措施，全面停止相互刺激和诽谤中伤，停止针对对方的一切军事敌对行为，采取相互措施防止发生核灾难。朝鲜常驻联合国代表申善昊随后敦促韩国积极响应“重大提案”，表示朝鲜一直在尽一切努力落实其提出的各种提案，以结束不稳定的停战机制，建立朝鲜半岛和平机制。2 月 12—14 日，朝韩举行高层会谈，推动实现了南北离散家属团聚。6 月 30 日，朝鲜国防委员会向韩国政府提出“特别提议”，提议在朝韩“7·4 共同声明”发表 42 周年之际，全面停止军事敌对行为。不仅如此，朝方还呼吁在仁川亚运会期间暂停韩美联合军演。10 月 4 日，在仁川亚运会闭幕之际，朝鲜派出以黄炳誓为首的“三人高级代表团”突访韩国，与韩国高级官员会谈，并与韩国总理见面。这是金正恩执政以来朝鲜访问韩国的最高级别代表团。朝鲜劳动党中央书记兼统一战线部部长金养健在与韩国官员的会谈中表示，朝方代表团本次访问韩国，希望此行成为巩固韩朝关系的良机。朝方同意韩方提出的进行第二轮南北高层接触，并建议在 10 月底至 11 月初举行会谈。

在对日关系上，朝鲜以重启绑架问题谈判为切入，以邦交正常化为目的，积极推进朝日协商。3 月底，日朝在沈阳恢复绑架问题谈判，解除了第三次核试验后封存的日朝接触进程。5 月 29 日，日朝达成“斯德哥尔摩协议”，这成为日朝关系的一个重大突破。按照协议，朝鲜承诺重启对所有绑架日本人的全面调查，并于 9 月向日方提交特别调查报告；日方则承诺部分放松对朝单边制裁。7 月 4 日，朝鲜成立特别调查委员会，日本也决定放松对朝单方制裁。但日朝双方在谁先采取行动等问题上纠缠不休，朝鲜许诺的调查报告也一拖再拖，迟迟没有出笼，引起日本的严重不满。特别是日本国内被绑架人质的家属向政府施压，要求不要再被欺骗。9 月 29 日，朝鲜日朝邦交正常化谈判大使宋日昊表示，调查仍处于早期阶段，希望日本派工作组到朝听取说明。10 月底，日本派出政府工作组访朝，这成为时隔 10 年后，日本政府首次就绑架问题派团赴朝。

对俄关系成为朝鲜 2014 年外交的一个突破口和亮点。从 2 月 7 日，朝鲜最高人民会议常任委员会委员长金永南出席索契冬奥会开幕式起，朝鲜与俄罗斯高层往来开始增多，朝俄在跨西伯利亚铁路与朝鲜铁路联通、过境输送天然气等问题上进行密切合作。朝鲜还与俄举行“高级别接触”。5 月，俄罗斯总统普京签署总统令，免除朝鲜欠苏联时期的 100 亿美元债务，解决了拖延 20 多年的朝鲜债务谈判，这成为俄朝关系取得实质性进展的标志性事件。此后，俄朝经济合作加速。6 月，俄朝举行的政府间贸易和经济合作会议，正式确立到 2020 年双边贸易额增加 10 倍，达到 10 亿美元的目标，并讨论了俄海军停靠罗津港的问题。在李洙墉访俄之后，10 月下旬，朝俄启动银行间卢布结算，双方达成总额为 250 亿美元的改造铁路网和矿产开发项目等。11 月下旬，金正恩的特使崔龙海开启为期一周的“俄罗斯之旅”，就提升两国政治、军事、经贸合作等多项议题进行讨论，据报道，崔龙海甚至提出与俄建立联盟关系的倡议。双方一系列高层互访与多领域合作推动两国关系进入了新高潮。

四、未来一年朝核形势面临的机遇与风险

2015 年的朝鲜半岛局势，特别是朝核形势总体且基本上不

会脱离 2014 年的基调。特别是由于朝鲜和韩国的客观需求，半岛的良性互动有望逐步建立，并直接影响到朝核总体形势。朝与有关各方的互动在一段时间内尚有余力，这可在一定程度上成为维持局势总体趋稳的基本动力。但风险在于朝核问题的本质并未发生根本改变，这将潜在制约朝鲜与各方的互动。特别是鉴于美国国内政治因素，美朝对话的动力极度脆弱，而朝韩之间因统一问题引发的体制竞争若重新显性化，将直接影响到局势缓和或有关各方关系改善的“可持续性”，朝核形势的风险届时将大大增加。

朝鲜的魅力外交仍有一定“续航能力”，半岛总体缓和的态势有望继续维持。朝鲜的“并进路线”正在深入推进，国内新经济政策正在逐步落实，在经济发展成为金正恩执政的一个重要标签的背景下，改善外部环境成为客观必需。而与此同时，朝鲜 2014 年的外交攻势尚未取得令人满意的成果，朝韩改善进程卡壳，朝日缓和推进不顺，朝俄协议尚待具体落实，在朝美关系上更没有实质性突破。相反，朝鲜在人权、网络等领域受到的外交压力显著增大，进一步压缩了朝在国际上的活动空间。这客观上要求朝鲜必须加紧对外关系的缓和，推进外交突破。特别是，2015 年正值二战结束 70 周年，也是半岛光复 70 周年，韩国总统朴槿惠执政 3 年，亟需在南北关系上有所建树，韩国在推动南北良性互动问题上的紧迫性和必要性同时增大，这有助于朝核形势的缓和。而与朝鲜互动的其他几方，如俄罗斯、日本，因各有需求，仍会在一段时间内继续与朝鲜的接触甚至合作，这有助于推动朝鲜半岛局势及朝核形势趋于平缓。

朝鲜与各方互动不足成为重大制约，缓和的“可持续性”成为一个问题。虽然朝鲜大力推动全方位外交，但目前看来更多是经济意涵，具有策略性取向，在核问题这样的战略问题上，朝鲜的立场并未发生根本松动，这将成为制约朝鲜外交攻势成效的根本性因素。朝鲜虽然试图通过策略性调整促成与美的正式对话，但美国在核问题上的坚定立场使得双方的根本分歧难以弥合。尤其是考虑到美国当前的国内政治环境，战略忍耐政策虽然饱受批评，但美朝对话的动力严重缺乏。美国与古巴、伊朗关系的改善在外交上或许对美朝关系前景具有利好意义，但奥巴马在古巴、伊朗核问题上的巨大投入耗费了其灵活处理朝核问题的资源；特别是在政治上的利差意义，反而限制了奥巴马在对朝政策上的灵活性。受国内因素制约，美国对朝政策的调整变得更加困难。同时，南北关系中因为统一问题的突出，也使朝韩之间的结构性矛盾凸显出来，体制竞争是否会由隐形向显性转变，或将成为影响南北关系演变的一个关键因素。而朝鲜与日、俄关系的调整难以根本帮助朝鲜脱困，更难以撬动朝核问题的根本变化，且日、俄本身发展与朝关系能否顺利也会成为一个问题。届时，朝鲜是否重新向挑衅的道路上回摆就难以排除。

在朝鲜的核战略取向不变的情况下，朝鲜的核能力会越来越成为一个关注的焦点。一年多来，关于朝鲜核能力的评估五花八门。虽然朝鲜尚未对核弹头小型化进行过试验，但美国军方有声音认为朝鲜已经掌握核武器小型化技术，并表示美国需要重新判断本国及盟友受到攻击的可能性。而 2014 年上半年朝鲜在核试验场地的活动表明，朝鲜正在进行“新形式”的核试验准备。从场地结构看，有评估认为朝鲜不久将进行“齐射试验”。与此同时，朝鲜 2014 年正在改造卫星发射场地及设备，以便为发射比 2012 年 12 月发射的“银河三号”长出四分之一的更大型火箭做物质准备。2013 年底、2014 年初，朝鲜进行了两次火箭引擎试验。这些迹象都显示朝鲜继续致力于核弹头小型化及远程投射能力。另外，朝鲜在发展潜射弹道导弹等方面的问题，也引发外界高度关注。这些技术上的变化会对各方的应对政策产生何种影响，将会成为未来影响朝核形势的重要因素。

An Analysis of DPRK Nuclear Situation: 2014

*Liu Junbo*①

The DPRK Nuclear issue in 2014 continued an interweaving of confrontation and dialogue, and a coexistence of tension and relaxation. Although the overall situation tends to ease up, no big progress was made. The striking feature was that the DPRK took an unprecedented all – round diplomatic offensive to explore a new breakout, but its interactions with the United States, ROK and the others were still limited to the preexisting frame and model. Meanwhile, some new factors like human rights issue and Cyber security loomes larger in the overall interactions, what's more, those marginal issues began to creep from the marginal to the light spot of the DPRK nuclear issue, which indirectly creating a new evolution of the nuclear situation.

---

① Liu Junbo is Deputy Director of the Department for Asia – Pacific Security and Cooperation Studies , CIIS.

I. The U. S. – DPRK Interactions Failed to Surpass the Level of Engagement

To resume the Six Party Talks, China, since early 2014, made new diplomatic efforts to persuade DPRK and the U. S. to lower the bar for the talks so as to create necessary conditions for the re – opening of the dialogue. When official talks between the U. S. and DPRK remains infeasible, circuitous engagement occupies a bigger stage. By use of 1. 5 track and track 2 approach, DPRK tries to reach out to and secure the stable contact with the U. S. , while the U. S. also looks for the window opportunities of the negotiation with the DPRK through exploratory dialogue based on the principle of separating informal dialogue and official talks. Ri Yong Ho, Vice Foreign Minister of DPRK, held an informal talk with former U. S. officials and scholars in Ulan Bator, to discuss measures to resume the Six Party Talks. Ri inferred that DPRK could stop the nuclear test in exchange for the resumption of the Talks, and the two countries would walk back to the 2. 29 Agreement to have a concrete discussion of how to implement the "action for action" principle and to add new momentum to the Talks. By taking advantage of the release of the detained American citizens, the DPRK successfully invited Director of National Intelligence Clapper to visit Pyongyang, and achieved the meet between the intelligence officials. During the visit, DPRK even proposed to Clapper a package solution for the final settlement of the nuclear issue. The DPRK officials emphasized once again their wish to continue the talks with the U. S. when the U. S. official departure from

Pyongyang.

For some time, DPRK and the U. S. were active in having unofficial talks, but this is still far away from negotiation. DPRK shows some flexibility in the nuclear issues and expresses its willingness to resume the Six Party Talks. So Se Pyong, permanent representative of the DPRK to UN office in Geneva, announced DPRK's readiness to resume the Six Party Talks at a Press in October 2014. When meeting with Mr. Sergey Lavrov, Russian Minister of Foreign Affairs, Choe Ryong Hae, special envoy of Kim Jong Un, top leader of the DPRK, stated that DPRK will resume the Six Party Talks without setting any presuppositions following the Declaration of Six Party Talks in September of 2005. However, DPRK's stands in nuclear issues does not change, it will continue with the buildup of nuclear program and strike to earn the recognition of the international society on its status of being a nuclear weapon state. The DPRK frequently launches intermediate – range ballistic missile in the spring of 2014 and threatened to conduct new from of nuclear test. Kang Sok Ju, secretary of the Central Committee of the Workers' Party of Korea, beated over the old tune by reiterating the requirement of reopening negotiations based on DPRK's status of a nuclear power state when meeting with EU officials during his trip to Europe. Those arguments deepens the U. S. doubt and alert on DPRK's real intentions for talks.

Therefore, the U. S. was reluctant to relax its requirement to dialogue, and the position of the Obama Administration on the conditional resumption of the Six – Party Talks remained unchanged. The continued its strategic patience and reiterated its position of not engaging in talks for the sake of talks, and kept requiring DPRK to take three pre – steps to show its willingness in abandoning nuclear forces. Senior officials from the U. S. Department of State. indicated clearly that the purpose of the U. S. is not to have DPRK back to the negotiating table but to demand it to abandon its nuclear program, which shows that the positions of the U. S. in having DPRK making commitment in abandoning nuclear weapons does not change. At the seminar on 20th anniversary of Geneva Agreed Framework, the new special envoy from the Department of State of the U. S. , Sydney Seiler, re – emphasizes that the attitude of DPRK will be accepted as fundamentally changed only when it came back to the Six – Party Talks, freeze the nuclear test and missile launching, and terminate the nuclear project. Seiler said that if DPRK take it seriously, the U. S. could go back to the negotiating table.

The two sides had a diagnostic engagement and communication during the past whole year and DPRK had raised some new thoughts, however, differences seemed more obvious and the discrepancy were difficult to change in a short time. Even though dynamics of resuming the Six – Party Talks accumulated during the communication, the solid ice is still to be melted. The two sides are still searching for the door of dialogue to open, and the stalemate of the Six Party Talks was far from being broke out.

Ⅱ. The DPRK Nuclear Situation under the Cross Effect

One feature of the DPRK nuclear situation in 2014 is that those marginal and outside factors like the human rights and cyber security issues are centralized, and questions such as the value oriented diplomacy and system competition between DPRK and ROK looms larger, The situation was further complicated when those issues interact with the nuclear issue.

Firstly, value diplomacy becomes one main thread of the nuclear situation. On Februrary 17, Commission of Inquiry on Human Rights in the Democratic People's Republic of Korea (DPRK) of the United Nations Human Rights Council issued a report, stating that DPRK committed a wide array of crimes against humanity, and called for urgent action by the security council to address the human rights situation in the country, referral to the International Criminal Court, and to issue targeted sanctions on those responsible. Late in March, the United Nations Human Rights Council launches a resolution to sue those responsible in the DPRK human rights issue. EU and Japan decided to draft a resolution on DPRK human rights on this base and handed it over to General Assemble of the United Nations. On November 18, the 3rd committee of the United Nations General Assemble passed the draft human rights resolution by EU and Japan, condemning the continuous systematic, all – pervading and serious anti – humanity in DPRK, decided to handed over report of the COI to the Security Council and encouraged addressing it to the International Criminal Court. On December 18, the resolution on DPRK human rights issues passed in the General Assembly and was required to be discussed by the Security Council. On December 22, Security Council held a meeting on DPRK's human rights problem, which is the first meeting on DPRK except for its nuclear issues.

Facing the unprecedented stress from human rights issues,

DPRK takes active diplomatic actions. During his visit to EU, Kang Sok Ju (L), secretary of the Central Committee of the Workers' Party of Korea, expressed the willingness to resume the bilateral dialogue with EU on human rights which suspended for 11 years. Late in September, DPRK sent its foreign minister to General Assembly Debate after 15years, to explain and defend it human rights issues. On October 7, DPRK held a press in United Nations New York, surprisingly to admit its labor reform system and the shortage in improving human rights, and expressed its willingness in having dialogues and cooperation with the international community. Meanwhile, DPRK kept tough facing the international stress. When the report was issued, spokesman from DPRK's Foreign Ministry defined it as a very dangerous political provocation. And on November 20, right after the issue of the resolution, DPRK announced to take all necessary measures to protect its sovereignty and security through strengthening its defense capabilities including nuclear weapons and responding with strong counter attack, targeting firstly at the U. S. and ROK. Official of the DPRK Foreign Ministry even threatened to link the human rights issues with nuclear reaction, saying that the unreasonable attack in human rights by the U. S. and its followers will force DPRK to take further actions like nuclear test. With the development of the human rights issues, DPRK's nuclear situation became much more uncertain.

Secondly, the overlapping of cyber security andthe U. S. domestic politics brings negative influence on DPRK's nuclear issues. On June 11, 2014, Sony Pictures Entertainment released a trailer for its new movie "*The Interview*", arising strong reactions from DPRK for its assumption of an assassination of Kim Jong Un, top leader of the DPRK. DPRK defines the movie "dirty and cursed". On June 25, DPRK threatened that the release of movie was a kind of war, and its spokesman from Foreign Ministry announced to take resolute and merciless counter measures if the U. S. government admit or support the movie. On November 22, before the movie debut, Sony Pictures Entertainment was ha – jacked and threatened by terrorist attack. The U. S. government considered it as a "serious event threatening its national security" and targeted quickly at DPRK. FBI said it had enough evidence to accuse DPRK for the hacker of Sony. The U. S. violently propagated DPRK's online terrorism, and the House of Representatives exaggerated to raise financial sanctions against DPRK. On December 19, President Obama condemned DPRK for its cyber attack activities on Sony and said that it will take appropriate response to the event, and threatened to take new sanctions on DPRK. Obama even said he may consider to put DPRK back on the list of State Sponsor of Terrorism.

Although hacker of Sony is a partial and periodical event, the quarrel triggered by that was diluted soon, without rising to be a main topic of DPRK's nuclear issue, however, the interlude on Sony cyber attack in fact posed negative impact on the fragile U. S. – DPRK relationship due to the sensitivity of cyber issue in nature and the political environment of the U. S. It forced the U. S. to be more conservative, and lays indirect negative influence on the DPRK nuclear situation.

Thirdly, the reunification issue occupies more role in the DPRK – ROK relationship, which took precedence over the nuclear topic and to some extent weakened the momentum and efforts in dealing with nuclear problem. Since the purging of Chang Sung – taek, the voice of collapse of DPRK was heated up again in ROK, giving birth to views that the Korean Peninsula may soon be united. Park Geun – hye mentioned unification bonanza when delivering the 2014 New Year Speech. Yun Byung – se, ROK's minister of foreign affairs also announced that the environment for discussing the reunification is right at the track. Park Geun – hye's Dresden Declaration is considered to be a declaration of reunification by ROK to the international society. In July, ROK declared to establish the Unification Preparation Committee to conduct researches on reunification direction. On December 2, when hosting the committee meeting of the Unification Preparation Committee, Park Geun – hye emphasized that 2015 is the 70th anniversary of liberation of Korean Peninsula, and is also a vital occasion to push the ROK – DPRK relationship forward and facilitate the fundamental change of DPRK.

DPRK reacts strongly against ROK's reunification offensive. DPRK's media raised 10 questions in April criticizing Park Geun – hye's system antagonism and threatened that the absorption reunification will trigger war. When attending the General Assembly Debate on September 28, Ri Su Yong, foreign minister of DPRK, demanded ROK to abandon all those unrealistic remarks and opinions on peninsula reunification, and reiterated that the only way to unification is federation, which means the two systems co – exist in one country. He also indicated that only when the threats to DPRK's sovereignty and security were removed, could the nuclear problem be solved. He stated that nuclear forces are neither for threat nor for exchange. On November 6, DPRK warned ROK to stop their intention to issue a reunification charter by August of 2015.

ROK's high profile on reunification of Korean Peninsula once again sparked the flames of war on system competition between DPRK and ROK. At the time when the nuclear issue falls into dilemma, the over – salience of reunification issue not only influenced the mitigation of the peninsula situation but also may affect the evolution of the nuclear situation.

Ⅲ. The DPRK Practiced a Diversified and All – round Diplomacy

In 2014, DPRK sped up its adjustment of foreign relationship and conducted a pluralistic diplomacy. On one hand, it tried to break through the international blockade after the third nuclear test; on the other hand, attempted to create better circumstances for the shift in emphasis of its domestic policies. The new round of diplomacy becomes more all – around, consolidating the traditional relationships like in the Southeast Asia, Africa, and Middle East, and also targeting at the key countries like ROK, Japan and Russia in particular.

DPRK takes the initiative and carried out diplomatic offensive on ROK for three times. Early last year, National Defense Commission of DPRK submitted a crucial proposal to ROK, suggesting both sides take practical measure since January 30, including stopping mutual slander; stopping military counter measures, and take measures to prevent nuclear disasters. Sin Son Ho, permanent representative of

DPRK to UN, urged ROK to actively respond to the proposal, and stated that DPRK was making all efforts to implement the proposal so as to set up a peace mechanism for the peninsula. From February 12 to 14, DPRK and ROK held senior level meeting to advance the reunion of separated families. On June 30, National Defense Commission proposed a special proposal to ROK, in which the DPRK put forward to stop all military countermeasures at the 42th anniversary of the "7. 4 Joint Statement" . What's more, DPRK also called on the suspending of the ROK – U. S. joint military drill during the Incheon Asian Games. Right at the closing of Incheon Asian Games 2014, on October 4, DPRK paid a sudden visit to ROK by sending a 3 – member delegation headed by Hwang Pyong – so to meet with ROK high level officials and the Prime minister. This is the highest delegation since Kim Jung Un's taking into office. Kim Yang Gŏn, Secretary of the Worker's Party, expressed his willingness to take the visit as a good chance to consolidate their relationship with ROK. DPRK agreed with ROK's proposal of having the 2nd round of high level meeting and suggested to be held in late October or early November.

On relationship with Japan, DPRK takes the negotiation on kidnapping issue as a breakthrough point to normalize the relation and advance the bilateral dialogue. Late in March, Japan and DPRK resumed negotiation on kidnapping issue, which is the first contact after the 3rd nuclear test. On May 29, the two sides reached Stockholm Agreement, which was one of the breakthroughs of the bilateral relations. According to the Agreement, DPRK promised to restart the investigation on all kidnapped Japanese and submit investigation report by September, while Japan agreed to relax its unilateral sanctions against DPRK. On July 4, DPRK set up a special investigation group and Japan decided to release its sanctions. However, the two contradicted over who should take the first step, and DPRK postponed for several times the release of the investigation report, arousing complaints from the Japanese side. On September 29, DPRK's Ambassador for the Negations of Normalization of DPRK – Japanese ties Song Il Ho stated that the investigation was still at the early stage and asked Japan to send working team for further explanation. Late in October, Japan sent a government working team to DPRK, being the first delegation after 10 years of the kidnapping issue.

Russia was one breakthrough for DPRK's diplomacy last year. Since Kim Yong Nam, Chairman of the Presidium of the Supreme People's Assembly of DPRK, attended the opening ceremony of the 2014 Winter Olympics in Sochi, DPRK and Russia maintained frequent contact at high level. The two sides conducted some project cooperation on the connection of trans – Sybria railway and the DPRK railway, and trans – border gas transportation. High – level dialogues between the two were also held. In May, Russian President Putin signed a president proclamation to exempt DPRK from the 10 billion U. S. D debts to former Soviet Union, ending the 20 years' negotiation on debt issue, which became a threshold in DPRK – Russian relationship. Since then, economic cooperation between the two speeds up. Later In June, the two countries held a governmental meeting on trade and economy cooperation, confirming that the bilateral trade will be increased by 10 times to 1 billion U. S. dollar till 2020, and also had a discussion of berthing the Russian navy at Rajin Port. The high point in the Russia – DPRK relations happened when Choe Ryong Hae, special envoy of Kim Jong Un started his Russian trip late November. Cho had several discussions with Russian senior officials to promote cooperation in political, military, and trade etc. He even proposed to establish alliance with Russia. All those visit and cooperation pushed the bilateral cooperation to a new high level.

IV. The Opportunities and Risks of DPRK Nuclear Issue in 2015

The 2015 DPRK nuclear situation will still follow that of the last year. Basing on the objective needs of both DPRK and ROK, a healthy interaction could be realized and that may affect the overall nuclear situation. There is still room for DPRK's interaction with the others, which is the basic stabilizer to keep the situation steady to some extent. But the risks still exist as the situation does not change fundamentally in nature, and the nuclear paradox will restrict the positive interactions. Especially under the dynamics of the domestic politics in the U. S. , momentum to dialogue is quite fragile between the U. S. and DPRK, and the risks may be escalated when the system competition between DPRK and ROK activated, and the sustainability of the relaxation on Korean Peninsula and the positive interaction among the parties may also be affected by then.

Firstly, the charm diplomacy by DPRK still has life of endurance, and the overall relaxation of the peninsula is expected therefore. The Byungjin Policy is advanced and the new economic improvement measures are carried out. When the economic development changes to be one crucial logo for Kim Jong Un, to cultivate a favorable external environment will become a necessity for DPRK. In the meantime, DPRK did not gain satisfied result from its diplomatic measures last year, DPRK – ROK relation hits a bottleneck, its relations with Japan goes unsmoothly, DPRK – Russia agreement waits to be implemented, and esp there is no breakthrough in the DPRK – U. S. relation.

What's worse, pressures increases on topics like human rights and cyber security, limiting the space of DPRK, which means objectively the DPRK has to restore relationships with the outside. Perticulally, as the 70th anniversary of the end of war and liberation, year of 2015 is a special token for the peninsula. Park Geun – hye has taken the position as ROK president for 3 years and is eager to make achievements in the relationship with DPRK, so ROK also has urgency and necessity in promoting healthy interaction on the peninsula, which will benefit the nuclear situation. The other parties, e. g. Russia and Japan will continue to maintain contact or cooperate with DPRK based on their own respective needs, which will also be a good parameter for the situation.

Secondly, the lack of momentum for interaction between the DPRK and the other parties makes the sustainability of mitigation of situation under question. Though DPRK takes a multifaceted diplomacy, it is more focused on economy and is regarded as a tactics change. DPRK's position on nuclear program etc strategy issue has never changed, which still is the fundamental obstacle for the effectiveness of its diplomacy. DPRK tries to obtain official dialogue withthe U. S. through tactics changes, but the U. S. ' firm position on denuclearization makes the dialogue unfeasible at present time. Especially when considering the domestic political environment of the U. S. , although the strategic patience is under criticism, it is a pity that there is no motivation in the U. S. government for talks with DPRK.

The improvement of U. S. – Cuba, U. S. – Iran relationship sounds good to DPRK diplomatically, but the great investment of Obama on Cuba and Iran has consumed political resources, which politically may restrains the Oabam's flexibility of policies towards DPRK. Constrained by the domestic parameters, adjustment or changes of policies to DPRK by the U. S. is hard to be realized. At the same time, system contradiction between DPRK and ROK increases with the unification issue. Whether the system competition become implicit and trigger the structural contradictions between the North and the South will be a key point for peninsula situation. Japan and Russia are not core parties of the DPRK nuclear issue. DPRK's relation with them will not help it out of the dilemma, not to mention the change of nuclear situation. Their relationships are also restricted by several parameters, so it is still uncertain whether the relation could be smooth. Meanwhile, the cool of China – DPRK relations also compressed DPRK's space. All those failure in diplomacy may make it possible for DPRK to go back to provocation.

Thirdly, when DPRK refuses to change its strategy in nuclear program, its nuclear capability will be more and more focused by the international society. For the past year, assessment of DPRK's nuclear capacity varies a lot. Though DPRK had never tested a miniaturized nuclear warhead, some from the U. S. military believe that DPRK has successfully miniaturized nuclear warhead and the U. S. needs to reassess its danger of attack on the U. S. and its alliance in the region. Activities of DPRK in its nuclear test site also showed they may be preparing to conduct some new – form of nuclear test.

Judging from the tunnel structure, some believe that DPRK will conduct salvo test in the future. It remodeled the test site and appliance for satellites last year, preparing for launching 1/4 longer satellite than the Unha – 3 satellite launched in December 2012. In late 2013 and early 2014, DPRK conducted 2 tests of rocket engines, which shows that DPRK will devote to miniature nuclear warhead and long range launching. What's more, DPRK's ability in developing submarine – launched ballistic missile is also one of the attentions. In the coming few years, influence of technological changes in DPRK nuclear program on other parties' policy may become another key factor for the nuclear situation.

2014 年伊朗核问题评估

宫旭平　高　原

〔**内容提要**〕作为当前全球安全治理的一个焦点，2014 年伊核问题进入密集谈判解决的新阶段。尽管两次延迟签署协议，但是伊核问题还是取得了实质性新成果：一是伊朗如期执行日内瓦第一阶段协议；二是伊朗首次允许 IAEA 核查其军事层面问题。鉴于此，美欧等西方国家开始减少对伊制裁，伊朗与西方国家关系有所改善，但是双方在限制伊朗铀浓缩规模、能力和解除对伊制裁时间表上的分歧，最终导致协议延迟到 2015 年 6 月 30 日讨论。中国积极参与谈判，贡献中国智慧。2015 年，从国际关系格局发展趋势和伊朗新战略来看，伊核问题签署协议也许只有“一步之遥”，但也不排除其他因素可能影响伊核问题如期解决的进程。

主题词：伊朗　核问题　防扩散　综述

作者单位：北京空军指挥学院　长春空军航空大学

经过 10 年的艰辛谈判，2013 年 11 月，伊朗和中、美、俄、法、德六国签署了日内瓦第一阶段协议，这份历史性协议，确定了今后伊核问题的总基调，也把伊核问题推进了一个走向全面和持久解决的正常轨道。2014 年伊朗核谈判可以概括为三阶段和九轮谈判，已经形成密集外交谈判来解决伊核问题的新模式。

一、伊朗积极与六国谈判协商，伊核问题发生积极变化

鲁哈尼政府自2013年担任伊朗总统以来，致力于改变国内经济状况和改变伊朗国家形象，并制定了在未来30年内成为世界十大经济体之一的战略目标。这也是伊核问题在2013年取得突破的主要原因之一。在2014年1月份的瑞士达沃斯论坛上，鲁哈尼表达了与美国积极沟通和参与国际事务的意愿。因此，鲁哈尼政府一面遵循协议，配合国际原子能机构进行核查，一面在谈判中争取自身和平利用核能的权利。伊核问题发生积极变化的具体表现：

其一，伊朗如期执行日内瓦第一阶段协议。2014年1月20日，伊朗鲁哈尼政府停止20%浓度的铀浓缩活动，切断了纳坦兹铀浓缩工厂的原料供应。据国际原子能机构报告，伊朗在燃料浓缩中试厂和福尔多燃料浓缩厂没有再进行铀－235丰度超过5%的六氟化铀浓缩。仍保持铀－235丰度达到20%的六氟化铀形式的核材料的数量为160.6千克。这种材料中的一部分正在被稀释，其余部分正在被转化为氧化铀。在燃料浓缩厂、福尔多燃料浓缩厂或燃料浓缩中试厂（生产区）没有安装另外的IR－2m型离心机或IR－1型离心机。仍保持铀－235丰度达到5%的六氟化铀形式的核材料的数量为7609千克等。没有安装新离心机。[①] 2月9日，一项来自IAEA的声明表示，伊朗已履行协约的第一项要求，同时，双方达成《七项具体合作措施》

① 《在伊朗伊斯兰共和国执行与〈不扩散核武器条约〉有关的保障协定和安全理事会决议的相关规定》S/2014/116。

的协定，伊朗于 5 月 15 日前执行该协定的所有措施。报道称，IAEA 的调查主要涉及三个方面：第一，针对核武器部件研制问题的调查；第二，关于核武器实验的调查；第三，有关伊朗自 2003 年以来仍然在地下开展核试验的调查。调查人员将对相关人士展开询问，查看资料文件并进行实地考察。伊朗方面，报道援引伊朗伊斯兰共和国通讯社的消息称，伊朗将提供矿山、核以及激光反应的设施与资料来源。最后，报道补充道，2 月 18 日，美国将同其他五大国与伊朗代表在维也纳展开会谈，希望可以向达成限制伊朗铀浓缩的永久协约迈出第一步，以换取对伊朗制裁的全面解除。

其二，伊朗首次采取措施防止核项目用于军事用途。为了表明伊朗核项目不会用于军事用途，伊朗原子能机构主席阿里·阿克巴·萨利希在国家媒体上首次宣布，愿意采取相关措施防止阿拉克城附近的核反应堆投入军事用途。[①] 具体举措是在设计上做出一些改变，从而生产更少的钚，减轻外界的焦虑与担心。因为从轻水反应堆中提取的钚与从重水反应堆中提取出来的相比，不易用于武器生产。这次改变的政治意义十分重大。

重水反应堆核废料钚元素可用于制造核武器，因此，阿拉克重水反应堆一直是伊核问题各方争议的焦点之一。第三轮谈判之后，4 月 19 日，伊朗原子能组织主席萨利希表示，围绕伊朗阿拉克重水反应堆的争议已基本解决，伊朗将改造该反应堆，大幅减少钚元素生产量。改造后，阿拉克重水反应堆钚元素的生产量将下降近 80%。5 月 6 日，伊朗日前已向国际原子能机构提交阿拉克重水反应堆有关设计信息。

5 月 23 日，联合国原子能监管机构表示，伊朗已降级处理

① 伊朗核机构：愿采取措施防止核设施投入军事用途，环球网 2014 年 02 月 08 日。

了可以快速转化为核武器内核的高纯度浓缩铀库存的大部分，从而使得该国剩余的浓缩铀仅为制造一枚核武器所需量的约五分之一。国际原子能机构在一份机密报告中称，伊朗目前拥有不足40千克这种高纯度浓缩铀。这份报告显示，伊朗6年来首次回应了外界对该国核计划“可能的军事层面”的关切。这是2008年以来，伊朗首次与IAEA就有关伊核计划“可能的军事层面”的突出议题进行技术交流。自2014年1月以来，伊朗已经削减了将近80%的高纯度浓缩铀。5月23日的新进展无疑为六国与伊朗最终达成一项核武解决方案奠定了基础。[①]

尽管伊朗积极推进伊核问题解决，但是伊朗没有放弃和平利用核能的权利。

首先，伊朗确立了核谈判的红线。伊朗鲁哈尼政府为了改变长期被西方世界经济遏制的状况，积极营造与西方缓和的氛围，一改内贾德政府的强硬立场，采取温和渐进的路线，调整伊核谈判的总体思路，按照第一阶段协议，稳步推进，在今年第三轮谈判中，与会各方已经就协议中多达60%的内容达成共识。即使是在这种情况下，伊朗坚守在核问题上的立场和底线。在第50届慕尼黑安全会议上，伊朗外长扎里夫表示，伊朗不会放弃研发新型离心机的权利。

4月9日伊朗“核技术日”时，伊朗最高领袖哈梅内伊在接见一批核专家时发表讲话表示，伊朗之所以接受谈判，其目的是向世界展示伊朗无意将核研究用于军事目的。他向伊朗核谈判代表团表明了意图，不应该屈服于“强加于他们的条件”，他说谈判应该继续，但“谈判不会使伊朗停止或放慢核研究和

---

① 《外媒：国际原子能机构报告肯定伊朗核问题进展》，《参考消息》2014年5月25日。

核开发”。[1] 他强调一定要认识到伊朗和平利用核能的权利。维护伊朗国家利益和伊朗科学家在核能领域所取得的成就是不容协商的红线。

其次，伊朗继续与俄罗斯合作发展核能。2月11日，鲁哈尼总统在伊朗庆祝伊斯兰革命35周年的讲话中表示，伊朗将继续努力获得“和平的”核技术。[2] 3月19日，伊朗总统鲁哈尼表示，伊朗不会放弃自己的铀浓缩权利。5月12日，在第四轮伊核谈判前，鲁哈尼总统再次发表电视讲话表示，伊朗与西方讨论只能是伊核的透明度问题，核技术不能用来谈判，伊朗在核技术问题方面不会退让一步，伊朗不接受“核隔离”。[3]

11月11日，伊朗与俄罗斯在莫斯科达成协议，俄罗斯原子集团公司将在伊朗境内新建8座反应堆，其中4座位于现有俄罗斯建设的布什尔设施，另外4座将建于另一地点。俄罗斯是唯一与伊朗保持核合作的国家。2015年，俄美关系因为克罗米亚入俄和乌克兰问题日趋紧张，伊朗一方面加强与俄罗斯在和平利用核能方面的合作，一方面也有利用俄罗斯来牵制美国之意。

伊朗意识到要成为中东地区强国，根本在于重新整合因制裁而负重的经济。现任总统鲁哈尼改变了伊朗在国际社会上的“恶棍”形象。而伊朗最高领导人哈梅内伊仍态度强硬，他虽支持核谈判，却也警告称，伊朗绝不会停止或放缓核研发计划。同时伊朗新政府面临国内分歧和压力。国内强硬势力指责伊朗

---

① 《伊核第三轮谈判获60%共识　伊朗拒绝放弃核计划》，环球网，2014年04月10日。

② Iran marks 35th anniversary of Islamic revolution. News. xinhuanet. com, from ipad, 2014年02月11日.

③ 《外媒：伊朗总统鲁哈尼称伊不接受“核隔离”》，《参考消息》2014年05月12日。

首席谈判代表、外长扎里夫对西方的政策“太软”，尤其是没有阻止欧盟高级外交代表阿什顿在访问伊朗时，接见伊朗的持不同政见者。

二、各方进行高密度的外交博弈谈判，技术谈判与外交谈判互为关联

经过10年艰苦的谈判，2013年11月24日，六国与伊朗在日内瓦就解决伊核问题第一阶段措施达成协议，可以说这是一份历史性决议。在此协议基础上，2014年伊核问题的发展演变可大致分为三个阶段。第一阶段从1月20日到4月9日。在这一阶段有三轮谈判。

2月18—20日，国际六国代表团由欧盟外交政策高级代表阿什顿率领，伊朗代表团的负责人是外长扎里夫，双方在维也纳举行了2014年首轮谈判。由于乌克兰局势突然发生变化，本轮伊核会谈也因此加快了讨论进程，但该谈判还取得一些成果：第一，双方达成一项全面解决伊核问题的框架性协议，设定了最初四个月的议题和时间表，并约定下一轮会谈的日期和地点。第二，伊朗已经通知六国自己准备研发比“IR—2M”型离心机更先进的离心机，因此，伊朗是否能够继续研究和开发一种新型离心机是本轮谈判的重点之一。第三，展开了技术讨论，技术专家将在3月初举行会谈，商讨全面协议的相关细节。

3月18—19日，第二轮谈判在维也纳举行。该轮对话将就全面协议的要素进行深入讨论。主要包括4个方面的内容：伊朗铀浓缩活动、阿拉克重水反应堆、民用核合作和西方对伊朗实施的制裁。由于西方怀疑阿拉克重水反应堆生产用于制造核

弹的钚，因此要求伊朗冻结该反应堆的建设。同时西方要求伊朗的铀浓缩活动接受国际监督，确保伊朗只进行5%的铀浓缩活动，以防止伊朗获得丰度为90%的武器级浓缩铀。[①] 会后，各方专家继续在实质性领域工作，技术专家也继续就相关细节进行磋商。

4月8—9日，第三轮对话会在维也纳举行。伊朗外交部长扎里夫称，与会各方已经就协议中多达60%的内容达成共识。9日，扎里夫与欧盟高级代表阿什顿发表联合声明，称此次谈判对涉及问题进行了全面细致的讨论。阿什顿说，各方将寻求“就全面协议的具体内容开展工作”。4月19日，伊朗原子能组织主席萨利希说，围绕伊朗阿拉克重水反应堆的争议已基本解决，伊朗将改造该反应堆，大幅减少钚元素生产量。

可以说，前三轮谈判还是比较顺利的，谈判达成一定成果。

第二阶段，从5月13日到7月19日，谈判进入“深水区”。

5月13—16日，六国与伊朗展开第四轮谈判。各方开始全面协议的草拟工作。谈判开始进入“深水区”。由于各方在一些问题上的分歧过大，会谈未能实现起草全面协议的目标，没有达成实质性成果。这轮谈判没有前三轮那样六国和伊朗共同参加的闭幕会，也没有发表共同声明和确定下一轮谈判的确切日期。

6月16—20日，第五轮谈判在维也纳举行。此次谈判前，伊朗不仅与美国举行了双边会谈，还分别与俄、法、德三国进行了双边会谈，这是伊朗史无前例地在多边会谈前进行双边协商，六国与伊朗的谈判取得了一定的进展，双方在各自协议案

① “伊核谈判在维也纳缓步前行”，《光明日报》，2014年3月21日。

文的基础上提出了共同文本框架，并确定了下次谈判的日程表。这轮会谈艰巨但具有建设性，但分歧很大，主要在铀浓缩和解除制裁时间表等方面。

7 月 2—19 日，第六轮谈判在维也纳举行。按照协议，谈判到 7 月 20 日到期，但是经过近三周的谈判，各方没能在协议到期前达成全面协议。在此轮谈判期间，7 月 13 日，美伊双方也进行了多轮谈判，但是由于分歧过大，最终未能在核心问题上达成一致。7 月 18 日，欧盟外交和安全政策高级代表阿什顿与伊朗外长扎里夫发表共同声明，商定将谈判的最终期限延后 4 个月，延期至 11 月 24 日。这标志着伊核谈判进入了下一阶段。分歧主要集中在离心机数量和铀浓缩问题上。美国国务卿克里发表声明说，在谈判期限延长的 4 个月期间，美国将解除对伊朗 28 亿美元的资产冻结，而作为回报，伊朗承诺将其四分之一的 20% 浓缩铀稀释为燃料。

第三阶段，从第七轮谈判开始，伊朗谈判进入关键阶段。

9 月 4 日，伊朗和美国在日内瓦举行双边会谈，确定了第七轮谈判的时间。9 月 11 日，伊朗与六国中的英国、法国和德国参加了首轮会议。本次在维也纳召开的闭门会谈将延续美国与伊朗上周在日内瓦会谈的精神。美国国务院发言人此前曾表示，在瑞士日内瓦会议上，两国“深入交流了核心意见”，但并未给出更多细节。

9 月 18—26 日，第七轮谈判在美国纽约举行。各方都充分体现出早日达成全面协议的政治意愿，但是谈判未取得明显进展。此时，出席联合国大会的伊朗总统鲁哈尼在记者会上表示，谈判进程极为缓慢，希望谈判时应当展现适当的灵活性。他强调伊朗将继续发展用于和平目的的核计划。

10 月 14—16 日，第八轮谈判在维也纳举行。伊朗、美国外长和欧盟政策负责人举行了三方会谈。16日，伊朗和俄罗斯也举行了副外长级会谈，但是会谈没有取得阶段性成果。

11月18—24日，第九轮谈判在维也纳举行，这是2014年最后一轮马拉松式谈判。11月24日是伊朗核问题全面协议谈判的截止期限。六国和伊朗外长当天在维也纳虽未能达成协议，但决定将谈判再次延期至2015年6月30日。各方将争取在2015年3月达成政治协议，之后商谈技术细节。此次延期，各方不只是制订了简单的时间表，还规划出了具体的路线图：2015年3月，争取达成政治性框架；6月底，完成所有技术细节和草案。

这次谈判没有达成既定目标既有政治上的因素，也有技术上的因素。11月20日，国际原子能机构总干事天野之弥在机构理事会会议上提交报告时说，伊朗仍未向该机构作出任何解释和提供信息，以澄清其对伊朗可能秘密发展核武器的怀疑。11月，机构与伊朗近期分别在德黑兰举行两次技术会谈，讨论伊朗2014年5月同意但尚未落实的两项重要实际措施，即向机构提供有关伊朗可能开展高爆试验的信息，以及提供伊朗有关中子输运研究的信息。伊朗方面没有给出满意的答复。根据伊朗2014年5月与国际原子能机构达成的方案，伊朗应于8月25日前采取5项措施向机构提供其核计划中的相关信息，其中包括上述两项措施。伊朗此前已经执行了另外3项措施。①

伊核问题谈判现为两种形式并存。一种是国际原子能机构从技术上对伊朗核设施进行核查，确定伊朗是否有未申报的核

① 2013年11月，伊朗与国际原子能机构在德黑兰签署合作路线图，允许机构核查人员检查部分核设施。根据这份路线图，双方分阶段地采取了多项具体合作措施。

材料和核活动，从而确定伊朗核计划是否全部用于和平目的。另一种是伊朗与六国在联合国框架下举行对话。两者既相互独立，又相互关联。

三、反恐背景下美国主导伊核谈判，欧盟积极配合减少对伊制裁

（一）美继续改善与伊朗的关系，努力达成限制伊朗“核抱负”的全面协议

奥巴马政府在伊核问题上一直采取制裁和谈判双轨战略。美国在实施对伊朗史上最严厉的石油制裁后，也向伊朗鲁哈尼政府抛出橄榄枝。2013 年美伊关系可以说取得了突破性进展，两国元首自伊朗 1979 年发生伊斯兰革命以来首次直接通话。2 月 2 日美国国务卿克里也和伊朗新政府外长扎里夫在德国举行的第 50 届慕尼黑安全会议间隙会晤并开始接触，磋商伊核问题后续谈判事宜。

6 月 9—10 日，在高度保密状态下，美伊双方在日内瓦威尔逊总统酒店进行了为期两天的闭门会谈，这是伊朗就核问题与六国会谈外美伊两国首次会谈。美方代表团将由副国务卿伯恩斯与白宫顾问苏利文率领。伊朗代表团则由副外长、核谈判副代表阿拉格希率领。

6 月 16 日，在第五轮维也纳会谈后，美伊又进行了新一轮双边直接会谈。8 月 7 日，美国奥巴马政府的首席核谈判官员将于 7 日在日内瓦与伊朗官员举行会谈。美国国务院称，美国代表团将包括副国务卿谢尔曼与副国务卿伯恩斯。11 月 9 日，美国国务卿克里与伊朗外长扎里夫在阿曼首都马

斯科特会晤。

10 月，奥巴马给伊朗最高领导人哈梅内伊写信，敦促他克服长达 10 年的不信任，通过谈判达成一份限制德黑兰“核抱负”的协议。同时，表示美国可以同伊朗联手打击“伊斯兰国”。这或许是奥巴马为与伊朗达成和解，从而改变中东局势所做的最后尝试。

尽管美国积极推动伊朗核问题解决，但是它也不忘挥舞“大棒”。10 月 23 日，美国副国务卿谢尔曼表示，如果无法达成以限制伊朗核项目换取放松对伊制裁的协议，美国将加大对其经济制裁，甚至可能对其核设施进行军事打击。①

（二）鉴于伊朗开始执行协议，美欧逐步减少制裁

1 月 20 日，美国务院发表声明说，国务卿克里已经批准“必要的”缓和制裁举措，并将于当天通知国会。美国务院随后公布了放松制裁的具体指导文件，其中包括允许伊朗现有 6 名客户在现有数量上继续购买伊朗原油；与美国伙伴国和伊朗一道建立“财政渠道”，以便伊朗支付人道事务交易和医疗费用、伊朗海外学生大学学费和联合国会费。

此外，在伊核问题协议落实的 6 个月期限内，美国停止针对伊朗石化产品出口、黄金等贵金属进出口，以及汽车行业商品和服务的制裁措施。同时，美国政府将发放许可证，准许伊朗部分航空企业进口零部件和购买安全保障所需要的检修和相关服务。

伊朗政府约 5.5 亿美元的海外资产已经解冻。这是伊核问

① “美国警告：若伊朗核谈判不成功或进行军事打击”，新浪军事，2014 年 10 月 27 日。

题第一阶段协议 1 月 20 日生效以来解冻的第一笔伊朗海外资产。按协议，约 42 亿美元的伊朗海外资产将逐步解冻。

10 月 24 日，美国波音公司最新公布的三季度报告显示，该公司时隔 35 年首次向伊朗出售技术信息。这是美国减缓对伊制裁以来的首个实质性动作，也是美伊关系“解冻”的迹象。

欧盟：在石油贸易相关领域，欧盟将不再禁止向伊朗原油运输相关业务提供保险服务，不再禁止进口、购置及运输伊朗石化产品及相关服务，此外，还解除了向伊朗提供运输工具的禁令。在金融领域，欧盟解除了成员国及其金融机构与伊朗政府、央行和公共部门之间的贵金属交易禁令。

鉴于临时核协议开始生效，欧洲国家与伊朗的关系也开始正常化。

英伊关系：即 2013 年两国元首通话之后，9 月 24 日，英国首相卡梅伦与伊朗总统鲁哈尼在纽约联合国总部举行会面，这是两国领导人 30 多年来首次会面。卡梅伦认为，伊朗的领导人可以帮助打击“伊斯兰国”带来的威胁。他认为，伊朗能够帮助确保叙利亚和伊拉克变得更加稳定与包容，而如果伊朗愿意参与，那么西方国家就应该表示欢迎。

从以上分析可以看出，在反恐背景下，美欧等国希望通过伊朗打击“伊斯兰国”，保持中东稳定。

四、中国积极参与谈判，贡献中国智慧

在解决伊核问题上，作为国际核不扩散成员国，中国一直积极参与谈判，始终发挥建设性作用，中方在谈判中担任了有关议题的牵头人，具体负责协调有关问题的谈判，贡献

着中国智慧。2011 年，中国首次成为草案的共同提案国。2013 年，中国国家主席习近平和伊朗总统鲁哈尼通话，赞赏伊朗政府的新举措。中国外交部长王毅出席了日内瓦历史性协议的签署仪式。

2014 年，中国继续支持伊核问题的和平解决。2 月，中国副外长李保东参加第一轮伊核谈判，并提出 5 点主张，坚持对话谈判道路；寻求全面、公平、合理的长期解决方案；秉承分步对等原则；营造有利的对话谈判气氛；寻求标本兼治、综合治理。[①] 中国外交部军控司官员也参与了 2014 年六轮核谈判，中方在谈判中就各方的难题、僵局提出了许多建设性方案。

7 月 14 日，习主席在巴西福塔莱萨同美国总统奥巴马通电话，两国元首就伊朗核问题的形势交换意见。中国在伊朗拥有重要的经济利益，中国愿与美方加强沟通和协调，推动各方相向而行，争取尽早达成一项全面持久解决伊核问题的协议。

五、伊朗和六国的主要分歧和发展趋势

伊核谈判的意义早已超越核问题本身，不仅关乎伊朗与西方关系正常化，而且对于地缘政治、反恐与区域稳定乃至国际格局均有重大影响，可谓“牵一发而动全身”。

目前，阻碍全面协议达成的关键分歧有两点：一是如何限制伊朗铀浓缩的规模和能力：二是怎样制定解除对伊制裁的时间表。伊朗的诉求是快速彻底地解除制裁，同时保留相当数量的核设施和离心机。伊朗最高领袖哈梅内伊则认为，伊朗未来

① 《外交部副部长李保东提出中国关于全面解决伊核问题五点主张》，人民网，2014 年 2 月 19 日。

需要大量离心机。与此同时，美国等西方国家则认为，伊朗已经安装了1.9万台离心机，因此最多允许伊朗继续运行其中的数千台，而且现有制裁措施不会立即解除。

2015年，从国际关系格局发展趋势和伊朗新战略来看，伊核问题签署协议也许只有“一步之遥”，但也不排除其他因素，如乌克兰问题、叙利亚问题和打击“伊斯兰国”等问题可能影响伊核进程。因此，一种可能是达成全面协议，第二种可能是再次延期，第三种可能是谈判破裂，回到原点。

A Review on Iranian Nuclear Issue: 2014

*Gong Xuping and Gao Yuan*①

As one of focuses of governance global security, in 2014, the Iranian nuclear issue entered into a new stage of intensive talks. Although the agreement had been postponed twice, some new substantial achievements have also been obtained. First, Iran performed the first stage of Geneva agreement on schedule. Second, Iran permitted IAEA to inspect the facilities. In view of this, the U. S. and the other western countries began to lift the sanctions on Iran. At the same time, Iran began to improve relations with western countries. Because of the differences on the scale, ability of Iranian uranium enrichment and the schedule of lifted sanctions on Iran, the agreement was delayed to sign on June 30th, 2015. China has involved actively in the negotiations and provided Chinese wisdom. From the trend of the development pattern of international relations and Iranian new strategy, in 2015 the agreement may have only "one step" to sign, but other factors which would affect the Iranian nuclear issue.

After ten years of hard negotiations, in November of 2013, Iran

① Gong Xuping is an associate professor of Air Force Command College of the PLA, China, and Gao Yuan is a lecturer of Air Force Aviation University of the PLA and P5 +1 signed the first phase of the Geneva agreement on Iranian nuclear program. This historic agreement put the general tone of the I-ranian nuclear issue, pushed the Iranian nuclear issue into normal track of a comprehensive and lasting solution. In 2014, the Iranian nuclear negotiations can be summarized as three stages and nine rounds of negotiations. It has been formed the new pattern of intensive diplomatic negotiations to solve the Iranian nuclear issue.

I. Iran Negotiated Actively with P5 +1

Since he became IranianPresident in 2013, Rouhani has devot-ed to change the domestic economic situation and change Iranian na-tional image, and developed the strategic goal of one of the world's ten largest economies in the next 30 years.

This became the main reason that the Iranian nuclear issue had a breakthrough 2013. In January 2014 in Davos, Rouhani expressed the willingness to communicate with the United States and participate in international affairs. Therefore, Rouhani followed the agreement and cooperated with IAEA. On the other hand, fought for the right to peaceful use of nuclear energy.

First, Iran complimented the first stage of Geneva agree-ment. On January 20, Iranian government stopped 20% uranium en-richment activities, cut off the Natanz uranium enrichment plant raw material supply. According to the IAEA report, Iran in the fuel en-richment and more fuel enrichment plant did not have uranium -235 more than 5% of uranium hexafluoride. Part of the material was diluted, the rest are being converted into uranium oxide. More fuel enrichment plants or enrichment (production) were not installed in IR -2 -1 type centrifuge or IR type centrifuge. Remains of U -235 at abundance of 5% uranium hexafluoride forms was 7609 kg, etc. the new centrifuges were not installed. On February 9, according to a statement from the IAEA, Iran had performed the agreement of the first requirements. At the same time, the two sides reached "seven specific cooperation measures" of the agreement. On May 15, Iran would implemented the agreement by all of the measures.

According to the report, the IAEAinspection mainly involved three aspects sources as well as laser reaction. Inspectors would be on those related inquiries, check of the data file and site trips. Citing Iranian Islamic Republic News Agency said, Iran would provide mining, nuclear facilities and data source. Finally, the report added, the United States with other five countries would hold the talks with Iran in Vienna. The talks would move toward the comprehensive agreement on Iranian uranium enrichment and exchange for the lift of sanctions on Iran.

Second, Iran took measures to prevent the Iranian nuclear program from military purpose for the first time. In order to show that Iranian nuclear program would not be used for military purpose, Chairman of Iranian Atomic Energy Agency, Salehi announced in a state media that Iran was willing to take relevant measures to prevent the nuclear reactor near Arak city from military purpose. Specific measures were made to change on the design of the reactor. The plutonium extracted from light water reactor compared with heavy water reactor was extracted, which would not be easy for weapons production. The change was of great political significance. Used plutonium in heavy water reactor could be used to make nuclear weapons. Therefore, Arak heavy – water reactor has been the focus of the dispute.

After the third round of negotiations, On April 19, 2014, Chairman of Iranian Atomic Energy Agency Salehi said dispute over Iranian Arak heavy – water reactor hadbeen basically solved. Iran would restructure the reactor. Plutonium production would be reduced drastically.

After its restructure, the production of plutonium from Arak heavy – water reactor would drop nearly 80%. On May 6, Iran submitted the Arak heavy – water reactor design information to the International Atomic Energy Agency. On May 23, the nuclear watchdog said, Iran had been relegated to deal with most of the highly enriched uranium stocks.

The International Atomic Energy Agency said in a confidential report that Iran had less than 40 kg of this kind of highly enriched uranium. The report suggested that Iran had responded to the outside world for the first time in six years about its nuclear program "possible military dimension" concerns.

This was the first time since 2008 that Iran and the IAEA on Iranian nuclear program to have a technical communication. Since January 2014, Iran has cut its nearly 80% of highly enriched uranium. On May 23, the new progress for the six countries and Iran eventually reach a nuclear solution to lay the foundation. Although Iran has been active in thenuclear issue to be solved, Iran did not give up the right to peaceful use of nuclear energy.

At first, Iran established its red line on nuclear talks. In order to change the status of the economy, which has long been curbed by the western world. Rouhani government has actively tried its best to a good atmosphere with western countries. Iran has changed its tough stance by Ahmadinejad's government and taken a modest incremental route. It has adjusted plan of the nuclear negotiations. Agreement in accordance with the first stagemade its steady progress, as much as 60% of the content in the agreement was agreed in the third round of negotiation.

Atthe 50th Munich security conference, Iranian Foreign Minister Zariff said that Iran would not give up the right of research and development of new type centrifuge.

On April 9, Iranian Supreme Leader Khamenei said in ameeting address to nuclear experts, "Iran has accepted negotiations, its purpose is to show the world that Iran had no intention to do nuclear research for military purpose".

He showed that the Iranian nuclear negotiation delegation should not give in to "imposed on their conditions". He said the negotiation should be continued, but the negotiation would not make Iran to stop or slow down the nuclear research and nuclear development. He stressed that international community must recognize Iranian right to the peaceful use of nuclear energy. Iranian national interests and scientist's achievements in the field of nuclear energy can not be the red line of negotiation.

Secondly, Iranhas continued to cooperate with Russia to develop nuclear energy. On February 11, President Rouhani celebrated the 35th anniversary of the Islamic Revolution in Iran. In his speech, Rouhani said Iran would continue its efforts to get the peaceful nuclear technology.

On March 19, Iranian President Rouhani said that Iran would not give up their right to enrich uranium. On May 12, before the fourth round of the Iranian nuclear negotiations, in a televised speech, Rouhani said again that the issue, which Iran and the west could be touched upon, was the transparency of the Iranian nuclear issue. Nuclear technology could not be used for discussion. Iran would not step back down. Iran would not accept a "nuclear isolation".

On November 11, Iran struck a deal with Russia in Moscow. Russian Atomic Group Company would help Iran to build eight new reactors, four of them would be inside of Bushehr facilities, which were built by Russia, the other four would be built in another places. Russia is the only country that has nuclear cooperation with Iran. In 2014, the U. S. – Russian relations became deteriated because of the Crimean. One hand, Iran has enhanced its nuclear cooperation with Russia, on the other hand, Iran has intended to contain the U. S. by the cooperation with Russia.

To become a great power in the Middle East, the most important thing for Iran is to make economic integration because of sanctions. President Rouhani has changed Iran "villain" image in the international community. And Iranian Supreme Leader, Khamenei, is still tough. Though he supported the nuclear talks, he also warned that Iran would not stop or slow down the nuclear research and development plan. At the same time, Iranian new government faced domestic division and pressure. Iranian opposition forces criticised Foreign Minister and Iranian chief negotiator Zariff for his "too soft policy towards western countries". They could not stop senior EU diplomatic representative Ashton to meet with Iranian dissidents during a visit to Iran.

Ⅱ. Technical and Diplomatic Negotiations Interlinked

After ten years of tough negotiations, on November 24, 2013, the six countries held talks with Iran in Geneva to solve the Iranian nuclear issue by the first stage measures to reach an agreement. This was a historic resolution. On the basis of this agreement, the Iranian nuclear issue in 2014 could be roughly divided into three stages. The first phase is from January 20 to April 9. At this stage there were three rounds of negotiations.

On February 18 to 20, the six – nation delegation led by European Union high representative for foreign policy Ashton, Iranian Foreign Minister, head of the delegation Zariff held 2014 in the first round of talks in Vienna. Because Ukraine situation suddenly changed, the Iranian nuclear talks therefore accelerated the discussion process. The talks obtained some results: the two sides reached a comprehensive solution to have a framework agreement, set the first four months of issues and schedule, date and place of the next round of talks. Iran informed the research and development of more than "IR –2M" type advanced centrifuge, therefore, whether Iran could continue to research and develop a new type of centrifuge was one of the highlights of the talks. Negotiation launched a technical debate, technical experts would hold a meeting in early march, to discuss the details of a comprehensive agreement.

On March 18 to 19, the second round of talks was held in Vienna. This round of dialogue was a comprehensive agreement for further discussion, includeing four aspects: the content of the Iranian uranium enrichment activities, Arak heavy - water reactor, civilian nuclear cooperation with western sanctions against Iran. As western countries doubted on Arak heavy - water reactor plutonium production, they required to freeze the construction of the reactor. At the same time, the western countries also required Iran to accept international inspection on uranium enrichment activities to ensure that Iran could only have 5% of the uranium enrichment activity, to prevent Iran from acquiring a 90% weapons - grade enriched uranium. After the meeting, the experts continued to work in the field of materials, technical experts also continued their consultations on relevant details.

On April 8 - 9, the third round of dialogue was held in Vienna. Iranian Foreign Minister Zariff said the parties had agreed as much as 60% of the content in the agreement. European Union High Representative Ashton and Zariff issued a statement, saying that the talks made a comprehensive and detailed discussion. Ashton said that the parties would seek to "work out the specific content of a comprehensive agreement". On April 19, Salehi, Chairman of Iranian Atomic Energy Agency said the dispute over Iran Arak heavy - water reactor hadbeen basically solved. Iran would restructure the reactor, sharply reduced its plutonium production. The first three rounds of negotiations achieved certain results.

The second phase was from May 13 and the negotiation entered into a "deepwater zone".

On May 13 to 16, the fourth roundof negotiations was held between the six countries and Iran. The parties began to draft the comprehensive agreement. Negotiation entered into the " deepwater zone" . Due to the large differences among the parties on certain issues, the talks failed to achieve its goal of drafting comprehensive agreement, without any substantive results. As compared withthe first three rounds of talks, Iran and other six countries did not issue a joint statement and only determined the date of the next round of talks.

On June 16 – 20, the fifth round of talks was held in Vienna. Before the talks, Iran held bilateral talks with the United States, Russia, France, and Germany. Some progress was made in the talks, the respective agreement text on the basis of a common framework was proposed. They also setup the new schedule and determine the dates of next negotiations. This round of talks was very tough but constructive, and differed widely mainly in the uranium enrichment and sanction lift schedule, etc.

On July 2 to 19, the 6th round of talks was held in Vienna. After nearly three weeks of negotiations, the parties failed to a complete an agreement prior to the comprehensive agreement. During this round of talks, due to the large differences, they failed to overcome the core issue and to reach an agreement. On July 18, the EU's Foreign and Security Policy High Representative Ashton and Iranian Foreign Minister, Zariff issued a joint statement, agreed to negotiate a deadline to prolong the negotiation for another 4 months to November 24. Differences mainly were focused on quantity and uranium enrichment centrifuges. The U. S. Secretary of State John Kerry said in a statement that during the extention of negotiations for four months, the United States would lift $2.8 billion assets freezing on Iran, in return, Iran promised to dilute a quarter of its 20% enriched uranium.

On September 4, Iran and the United States held bilateral talks in Geneva, the seventh round time was determined. On September 11, Iran and the six countries including Britain, France and Germany held the first round of meetings. The closed – door talks held in Vienna continued the spirit of talks between the United States and Iran a week ago. The U. S. Department of State spokesman said during the meeting in Geneva the two countries had had "in – depth communication on core issues".

On September 18 to 26, the seventh round of talks was held in New York. All sides showed their political will to give full support to a complete agreement as soon as possible, but no obvious progress was made in talks. At this point, when attending the conference of the UN general assembly, Iranian President Rouhani said at the press conference, the negotiation process was very slow, and he hoped that the negotiations should be displayed properly with flexibility. He stressed that Iran would continue to develop its peaceful nuclear program.

On October 14 and 16, the eighth round of negotiations was held in Vienna. Officials from the U. S., EU, and Iran held their three parties talks. On October 16, Iran and Russia held vice foreign ministerial levels talk. But there were no results achieved at this stage.

On November 18 to 24, the ninth round of talks was held in Vienna, this was the last round of negotiations in 2014. November 24 was the deadline for negotiations of the Iran nuclear issue to have a comprehensive agreement. On that day, foreign ministers from the six countries and Iran met in Vienna. Though failed to reach the comprehensive agreement, they decided to postpone the negotiaion again to June 30, 2015. The parties would strive for political agreement in March 2015 after detailed technical issues. The purpose of the postpone was to not only make a simple schedule, but also plan a specific roadmap: in March 2015, they would strive for political framework; in the end of June, they would complete all technical details and draft the agreement.

The talks failed to reach the established goals due to political and technical differences. On November 20, the Director General of International Atomic Energy Agency reported at the board meeting that Iran had been still not to make any explanation and provide information to the Agency. The information was to clarify the doubts about Iran possible secret development of nuclear weapons. In Tehran in November, the Agency together with Iran held two technical talks, discussed the agreement. Iran did not give a satisfactory answer. According to Iran, in May 2014 with the International Atomic Energy Agency, Iran should take five measures before 25 August to provide relevant information in its nuclear program. Iran hadonly taken three other measures.

The Iranian nuclear negotiations were under two tracks: one was the International Atomic Energy Agency on Iranian nuclear facilities from the technological approaches to determine whether Iran had undeclared its nuclear material and nuclear activities, so as to determine whether Iranian nuclear program was for peaceful purpose. The other track was talks between Iran and six countries in the UN framework. Both track were independent and correlated.

Ⅲ. EU Cooperated Actively with Lifting Sanctions

1. The U. S. continued to improve relations with Iran, endeavored to sign a comprehensive agreement, which would limi tIranian nuclear ambitions. The Obama Administration has been adopted a dual – track strategy, that is to say, sanctions and negotiations on the Iranian nuclear issue. After organizing the largest international oil embargo union on Iran, the United States showed Iran an olive branch. In 2013, U. S. – Iran relations made breakthrough, the two heads of state has called directly for the first time since the Islamic revolution in Iran in 1979. On February 2, the U. S. Secretary of State Kerry and Iran Foreign Minister Zariff met at the 50th Munich Security Conference and started the negotiation on the follow – up problems of Iranian nuclear issues.

In October, Obama wrote to Iranian Supreme Leader, Khamenei, urging him to overcome mistrust, negotiate to restrict Tehran "nuclear ambitions" agreement. At the same time, the letter also said that the United States could strike IS with Iran. This was perhaps Obama's reconciliation with Iran, which changed the situation in the Middle East.

Although the United States has been actively promoting the Iranian nuclear issue to be solved, it did not forget to wave its big stick. On October 23, Deputy Secretary of State, Sherman said if unable to reach an agreement to limit Iranian nuclear program in return for lifting sanctions against Iran, the United States would increase its economic sanctions, and may even use military strike on Iranian nuclear facilities.

2. The U. S. and Europe have gradually reduced their sanctions. The United States: on January 20, the U. S. Department of States said in a statement, Secretary of State John Kerry had approved plan to ease sanctions, and would notify the Congress that day. The U. S. Department of State announced later about the guidline documents of lifting sanctions, including six documents which allowed Iranian existing customers to continue buying Iranian oil; Partners with the United States and Iran to establish the "financial channels" to Iran for trading humanitarian and medical funding, and transfer university tuition fees.

In addition, in the implementation of the Iranian nuclear issue agreement for a period of 6 months, the United States was to halt Iranian petrochemical products export, import and export of precious metals such as gold and sanctions to the goods and services in the automobile industry. At the same time, the government would allow Iranian aviation enterprise to importspare parts and purchase security maintenance and related services.

About $550 million oversea assets were unfrozen. This is the first phase of the Iranian nuclear issue since the agreement came into effect. According to the agreement, about $4. 2 billion of Iranian overseas assets would be unfrozen.

On October 24, the Boeing Company announced in the third quarter, according to the report for the first time, the company in 35 years sold its technical information to Iran, whichwas also a signal of U. S. – Iran relations "unfrozen" .

The European Union: in the related fields of oil trade, the EU would no longer be banned from Iranian oil transportation, no longer forbidden import, purchase and transport the Iranian petrochemical products and related services, in addition, also lifted the ban to Iran to provide the means of transportion. In the financial field, lifted the EU member states and financial institutions and between the Iranian government, central bank and the public sector of the precious metal trading ban.

Given the temporary nuclear agreement came into force, the European country's relations with Iran began their normalization.

UK – Iran relations: After the call of the two presidents last year, on September 24, British Prime Minister David Cameron and Iranian President met at the UN headquarters in New York City, this was the two leaders' first meeting in more than 30 years. Cameron believed that Iranian leaders could help fighting the threat posed by Islamic State. Iran could help ensure that Syria and Iraq, he thought, more stable and inclusive, and if Iran was willing to participate in the war, the western countries should be welcomed.

From analysis, it can be seen that in the context of counter – terrorism, the U. S. and the Europe countries wanted to strike IS through cooperation with Iran, and to maintain stability in the Middle East.

Ⅳ. China Participate Actively in Negotiations

As a member of the international nuclear non - proliferation treaty, China has been actively involved in the talks and played a constructive role. Among the negotiations, China was responsible for the relevant issues, specifically the coordination of talks, contributed Chinese wisdom in the talks. In 2011, China became the co - sponsors of the agreement. In 2013, Chinese President Xi Jinping had a phone call with Iranian President Rouhani and appreciated the Iranian government new measures. Chinese Foreign Minister Wang Yi attended the signing ceremony of historic agreement in Geneva.

2014, China continued to support a peaceful solution to the Iranian nuclear issue. In February, Chinese Vice Foreign Minister Li Baodong participated in the first round of the Iranian nuclear negotiations, and put forward five proposals: Looking for comprehensive, fair and reasonable long - term solutions; adhere to the path of dialogue and negotiation; adhering to the principle of reciprocity in stages; Creating favorable atmosphere of dialogue and negotiation; seek comprehensive treatment. The Chinese Foreign Ministry officials participated in the ten rounds of nuclear negotiations in 2014. China put forward many constructive proposals during the negotiations.

On July 14, Chinese President Xi Jinping had a meeting with the U. S. President Obama in Brazil. The two presidnets exchanged views on the Iranian nuclear issue. China had its important economic interests in Iran. China was ready to strengthen communication and coordination with the United States to promote the cooperation mutually, to strive for as soon as possible comprehensive and lasting solution to the Iranian nuclear issue.

V. Main Differences between Iran and P5 +1

The significance of the Iranian nuclear negotiations has gone way beyond the nuclear problem itself. It was not only about Iran to normalize relations with the west, it is of significant influence on geopolitics, terrorism, regional stability and international pattern. It can say the Iranian nuclear negotiations like a piece of hair, when it get rid of the head, it can hurt the body.

At present, there are two key differences hindering the comprehensive agreement to be reached: first, how to limit the scale and ability of Iranian uranium enrichment; second, how to make the schedules of lifting sanctions against Iran. Iranian appeal was a thorough lifting of sanctions quickly, while retaining a considerable amount of nuclear facilities and centrifuge. Iranian Supreme Leader Ali Khamenei argued that Iranian future would need a lot of centrifuge. At the same time, the United States and other western countries thought that Iran had installed 19000 centrifuges, at most allowed Iran to continue to run thousands of them, and the existing sanction could not be immediately lifted.

战术核武器
Tactical Nuclear Weapons

2014 年世界战术核力量发展

李文盛　张艳苹　刘　放

〔**内容提要**〕“战略核武器”和“战术核武器”的区分没有严格界限。战术核武器用于陆军、海军或空军攻击战役和战术纵深内的目标，以支援完成有限范围内的作战任务。战术核武器通常采用威力较低的核弹头，投射工具的射程较短。冷战后，虽然各国均倡导削减战术核武器数量，但同时又都在积极发展。2014 年，战术核武器在发展和使用方面呈现出了各自不同的特点。

主题词：世界　战术核武器　核力量　发展　综述

作者单位：中国国际问题研究院军控与国际安全研究中心

一、坚持各自主张，争取战略主动

对战术核武器的概念和定义涉及到未来军控谈判限制和削减的对象范围，因此在战术核武器的定义与内涵上，各国基本坚持自己的主张和认识。

美国的战术核武器还分为“战场”使用的和“战区”使用的核武器。战场核武器用于与敌方部队直接作战，在视距内使用，战区核武器要达到敌人后方地域，在视距外使用，因此，美军通常称为“战区核武器”或“非战略核武器”。美国防部的《军事和相关术语词典》（2010 年）是这样定义“非战略核力量”的：指配置于作战区域内的核能力部队，具有通过陆基、海基、空基核力量打击敌方部队的能力，还包含相关支援装备或设施。经授权，该部队有助于指挥官完成战区行动任务。在 2011 年美国防部发布的《核问题手册》中，阐明“非战略”与战略核三位一体的关系：“其他所有核武器都是非战略性的。”根据这一定义，非战略核武器包括双重能力飞机、原子爆破弹药、陆基巡航导弹、射程小于 5500 千米的陆基弹道导弹、火炮、防空武器和核深水炸弹。

俄罗斯也把战术核武器分为“战术”和“战役”两种，统称“战役战术核武器”。俄武装部队总参谋部军事研究院的定义为：“不属于战略核装备，但包括地面部队、海、空军部队中近程导弹核弹头，以及地面部队和海军使用的核炮弹与核地雷的核武器。”而法政府认为其任何一种核武器都是战略性的。而美国和俄罗斯认为法在飞机上装备的 ASMPA 近程巡航导弹是非战略性的，但巴基斯坦和印度射程较小的初级导弹核武器则是战略性的。

可见，美俄等国都从各自利益出发提出了有利于自己的概念和削减主张，

二、适当缩小规模，但保持对等关系

从美国和俄罗斯等国家对战术核武器的态度上看，目前均未有放弃此类武器的企图，但在拥有数量规模上出现了适当缩小规模的倾向。目前，美拥有的非战略核弹头估计有 760 枚，

可通过双重能力飞机和海基巡航导弹进行投送。这个数字不到1991 年的 1/10。这一削减完全消除了陆基核武器，并实现海军近似无核化。即使这样，2010 年的《核态势评估》还是指出，其他核能力已经足够用于支援北约完成延伸核威慑，现有非战略武器超出了需要。关于俄拥战役战术核武器规模有很大的不确定性，美国防部认为，俄拥有大约 2000—4000 枚战役战术核弹头，但外界普遍认为，这一数字大约为 2000 枚，甚至更少，但其储存有数千枚等待拆除的退役核弹头。俄官员在 2005 年和 2010 年两次宣称，非战略核武器的储备已经减少了 75%。即使没有新的削减武器协议，预计在未来 10 年随着老旧系统逐步淘汰，俄库存量还将进一步减少。

值得注意的是，美俄战术核武器的减少存在着关联性，双方基本保持了对等削减关系。美国会在 2010 年批准新的《削减战略武器条约》时提出，美需要能够达成“解决俄联邦与美国之间非战略（战术）核武器储备的差距，且以可验证的方式保护并减少战术核武器的协议”。同样，北约自 2010 年以来的战略构想和 2012 年出版的防御态势评估都声称，北约非战略核武器的任何削减必须充分考虑到俄更为庞大的库存。

三、调整力量构成，精简武器类别

为了适应国家安全环境的要求，加强对核力量的管理，并提高核武器部署安全性，美俄等国都开始精简战术核武器类别，并尽可能集中部署。2011 年底，俄罗斯海军攻击机（图 -22M3和苏 -24）及其携带的核武器全部移交空军，俄还计划将主要海军平台去除核打击任务。其中，“奥斯卡”级潜艇和“基洛夫”级巡洋舰将从携带 SS－N－19 核巡航导弹改为携带 SS－N－26 和 SS－N－27 非核巡航导弹。美国在 2010 年《核态势审议报告》中也明确将仅有的海军非战略核武器“战斧”对地攻击核巡航导弹（TLAM/N）列入退役计划，目前其使用的 W80－0型弹头已完成退役。这历史性地完成了持续数十年的美国单方面消除所有非战略核武器的行动。

四、探索新型作用，扩大威慑领域

近年来，美俄等国都在探索战术核武器的新作用，并积极扩大威慑领域。美国奥巴马政府上台后设想将合适的新型地区威慑框架与延伸核威慑、前沿存在、相应的常规能力（包括弹道导弹防御）相结合。这些地区性安全观和新型能力，使降低战略核武器在国家安全战略中的作用变得可能。此外，美军近年来突出了非战略性核武器的“独特性”，这是因为现在双重能力飞机几乎拥有所有战略轰炸机的优势，但其部署又可靠近战场，对敌人造成额外压力，从而提高了威慑能力。为此，美军还积极支持开发深钻地型战术核弹头，以降低核武器使用的门槛，提高威慑效能。而俄罗斯学者认为，非战略性核武器的使用将使区域核威慑成为可能。如果非战略性核武器无法有效发挥区域威慑作用，那么，它除了担负决定性打击敌人的任务外，还可用于阻止军事冲突的升级。“制止战争升级”（DE－FSCA-LATTON）是俄关于局部战争中核力量运用的一个术语，包括在战区内使用战略核力量和战术核武器。“制止战争升级”是为了显示决心而对核武器的实际运用，这一目的可通过部署非战略核武器实现，这可避免“核武器的运用急剧升级为战略核系统的相互大规模进攻”。

五、升级战术核武器，提高前沿威慑能力

对战术核武器进行技术升级与改造以提高前沿威慑能力，是美俄等国长期以来坚持的做法。目前，奥巴马政府正在对现有的非战略核武器库进行现代化升级。B61－4 是 B61 的三个非战略型号之一，目前美军正在对该型核弹进行“延寿”，并装备新型制导尾部组件以提高精度，达到与最大爆炸当量 36 万吨的 B61－7 战略核武器相同的风险控制水平。根据计划，要为这些 B61 核炸弹增加新的尾翼，使它成为可以由 F－35 隐形战斗轰炸机携载的制导武器。尽管 B61－4 已经是美国核武库中最安全的武器之一，其最新型号 B61－12 同时也配备了新的安全特性。B61－12 起初主要设计装备 F－15E、F－16 和“旋风”战机，但目前已经扩大到了具备隐身能力的新型 F－35“闪电”（联合打击战斗机）和 B－2 战略轰炸机。未来，只有 B61－12 同时执行非战略和战略任务。此外，俄罗斯和法国也在积极改进各自的战术核武器。2014 年 11 月，法国国防部透露，法已开启新型空射核导弹项目的研究，新一代空射核导弹将关注隐身与高超声速技术。新型武器代号为 ASN4G，其将是第四代 ASMP 巡航导弹项目，法将大胆地探索最前沿的隐身技术和高超声速技术，该项目与法国空军未来的形态紧密相关。

六、调整力量部署，应对国际现实威胁

近年来，美俄等国为应对同盟内部问题和国际现实问题，

不断调整战术核武器部署，以形成积极的威慑态势。目前，美国有近200枚部署在北约欧洲（比利时、德国、意大利、荷兰、土耳其）的6个基地中。储存在美的少量炸弹专用于太平洋地区，余下的弹头作为武器储备。在过去的10年中，美国战术核力量除了从德国的拉姆斯泰因和英国的莱肯希思空军基地撤除核弹外，美国空军还削减了其在本土的战术飞行中队。在上世纪90年代晚期及小布什总统的第一个任期，美国空军在本土保留了两个战术飞行中队作为在北约、中东和东北亚的核任务的备份。分别是位于北卡罗莱纳州约翰逊空军基地的第四飞行中队和位于新墨西哥州坎农空军基地的第27飞行中队。第四飞行中队的F－15E战机仍被认为是具备核运载能力的战机，但该中队不再主要担负核任务，第27飞行中队已经扩编，由不担负核任务的第27特种作战中队取代。这些战术核力量主要针对俄罗斯和朝鲜等的可能威胁。在欧洲战术核力量持续削减的大势下，近年来针对东北亚方向的本土核力量得到相对增强。

俄罗斯近年来也多次扩大了在其欧洲部分的战术核力量的部署，以此应对北约东扩，并慑止美国在东欧的导弹防御系统威胁。俄罗斯在靠近欧洲的西部加里宁格勒部署了SS－21和SS－26型导弹。最先部署这种导弹的是驻卢加的第26导弹旅，该旅驻地位于圣彼得堡以南130千米。该基地已经将保障SS－21导弹的设施根据SS－26型导弹的需求进行改造，这两种导弹据称按照俄前总统叶利钦签署的总统令，已经加装了核弹头。俄官员曾多次威胁使用战术核武器对抗美国在波兰部署导弹防御系统的计划。

目前，美俄双方的战术核武器部署已经成为遏制对方的重要手段。例如，美将保持欧洲战术核武器的部署规模，作为要求俄罗斯作出某种让步的重要手段。波兰和瑞典的外长强力支持美国推动提出令俄罗斯难以接受的要求：要求俄撤出在与新加入欧盟国家的接壤区（加里宁格勒和科拉半岛）部署的核武器。在此之前，北约领导人也向俄罗斯领导人提出过同样的要求，要求俄从与北约接壤的地区撤出战术核武器。

七、改进投送能力，提高威慑灵活性

由于战术核武器投送方式决定了其使用能力，因此各国都将改进战术核武器的投送能力，作为战术核力量发展的重要方式，以此来提高核威慑的灵活性。目前，俄罗斯正在对“逆火”（图 –22M3）轰炸机进行深度改造，重点是提高其核常兼容性，并加装了新型机载无线电电子系统，并在 2020 年前将 30 架图 –22M3升级为图 –22M3M，配备 Kh –32 巡航导弹。而正在论证的俄新一代轰炸机 PAK DA 将全面取代图 –160、图 –95MS和图 –22M3 轰炸机。此外，前线轰炸机苏 –24 也在进行现代化改造，但最终将被苏 –34 所取代，目前俄已开始在西部部署苏 –34。在海基战术核力量方面发展也很快。俄罗斯首艘“亚森”级攻击型核潜艇目前正进行服役前的海试，该艇配备有战役战术核武器，包括反潜火箭和 8 具巡航导弹垂直发射管。《2020 年前俄罗斯武器装备采购计划》显示，俄将建造 10 艘“亚森”级潜艇。美国在新《核态势审议报告》中也明确指出，将于 2017—2018 年装备部分具备核能力的 F –35 型联合攻击机，最终取代 F –15E 和 F –16 战机。北约的 3 个核打击任务国家——意大利、荷兰和土耳其计划在今后的 15 年中获得 F –35 联合攻击机。目前，美国已经开始对 F –35Block4 进行核能力改进。

八、改进调整核设施，提高生产与维护能力

为了维持较高的核武器战备水平和未来灵活的生产制造潜力，美俄等国近年来都十分重视保持和改进核设施对战术核武器的研发和维护能力。俄战术核武器通常认为存放在 12 个中央储存设施内。部分位于俄中部，另外一些位于远东、俄西部和科拉半岛等相对靠近投送系统基地的地方。由于弹头寿命有限，要保持核武库就需要持续不断地进行再生产。从 2002 年开始，俄原子能部开始按照“在 2002—2006 年改革核工业企业”辅助计划对原有 4 个核弹头生产联合体进行改革。当前，俄新型弹头制造集中在 4 家组装拆卸企业，其中，阿万卡德和“起点”制造联合体已终止弹头生产任务，核弹头裂变材料及零部件的生产任务基本集中在“玛雅克”制造联合体。目前新型核弹头的生产企业主要是位于列斯诺伊城的“电子化学仪器”联合体和位于特列赫戈尔内的仪器制造厂。为了确保 B－61 战术核弹的改进工作，美国从 2013—2014 年开始对战术核武器非核部件生产厂家（位于堪萨斯市）进行现代化改进。这些改进和调整将有效提高战术核武器的生产和维护能力。

A Review on Global Tactical Nuclear Weapons: 2014

*Li Wensheng, Zhang Yanping, and Liu Fang*①

There is no a clear – cut calarification between the "strategic nuclear weapons" and the "tactical nuclear weapons" . The tactical nuclear weapons are used for the targets within the campaign and tactical depthto support the completion of operational missions within limited scales. Nuclear warheads with relatively low yield are usually used among the tactical nuclear weapons, and the range of projection tools is relatively short. After the end of cold war, the nuclear weapons states all have initiated to reduce the number of tactical nuclear weapons, butthey have been developing new model of these weapon systems actively at the same time, especially in the aspect of utilities. Recently, different features have been showed.

I. Stick to Their Proposition

Concept and definition of tactical nuclear weapons are involved

① Li Wensheng, Zhan Yanping, and Liu Fang are researchers of the Centre of Arms Control and International Security Research at China Institute of International Studies.

in the restriction and reducing scopes in the negotiations of future arms control, so almost all countries stick to their own propositions and cognitions in the connotation of definitional domain of tactical nuclear weapons.

Tactical nuclear weapons in the United States are divided into those to be used in "battlefields" and in "war zones". Tactical nuclear weapons in battlefields are used to fight directly against the troops of enemy, and they should be used within the range of visibility; the tactical nuclear weapon in war zone should reach the area behind enemy line and to be used outside the range of visibility, so the U. S. Armed Forces usually call them "nuclear weapons in war zones" or "non – strategic nuclear weapons". In the *Military and Relative Term Dictionary* (2010) of the U. S. Department of Defense, the "non – strategic nuclear force" is defined as "troops set in the war zones with nuclear capabilities and have the ability to fight against troops of enemies though nuclear forces of continental rises, sea bases and air bases, and contain relative supporting equipments or facilities". Through authorization, those troops are helpful for commanders to complete the action assignement in war zones. The relationship between "non – strategic" and strategic nuclear trinity is clarified in the *Nuclear Issue Manual* published by the Department of Defense in 2011 that "all other weapons are non – strategic". Based on this definition, non – strategic weapon includes dual energy airplanes, atomic demolition munitions, ground – launched cruise missiles, and ground – launched ballistic missiles with the range of less than 5500 km, cannons, antiaircraft weapons and nuclear depth charges.

Russia also divides tactical nuclear weapons into "tactical" and "campaign", and they are called by a joint name of "campaign tactical nuclear weapon". The definition by Army Research Institute of the Headquarter of the General Staff in the Armed Forces is "not belonging to strategic nuclear weapons, but include the nuclear warheads of short – range missiles in ground, sea, and air forces, and nuclear weapons of nuclear projectiles and atomic mines used by ground forces and navies. While French government thinks that all nuclear weapons are strategic. The United States and Russia think that the ASMPA short – range cruise missiles equipped in the French airplanes are non – strategicones, while the primary missile nuclear weapons of Pakistan and India with relatively short ranges are thought to be strategic.

Thus, countries like The United States, Russia etc. have put forward the concepts and reduction in favor of themselves on the basis of their own benefits.

Ⅱ. Reduce the Scale Properly

Review onthe attitudes of The United States and Russia etc. towards tactical nuclear weapons, they have not any attempt to give up weapons of such kinds by now, but the trend of properly reduction of the scale has appeared in the quantities and scales that they own. At present, the non – strategic nuclear warheads owned by the United States are estimated about 760, and can be delivered by the dual – missioned airplanes and the sea base cruise missiles. The number is less than 1/10 of that in 1991. Their reduction has completely eliminated the ground – base nuclear weapons, and the two countries have realized the approximate denuclearization in their navies. Even so, it was also pointed out in the *Nuclear Situation Assessment* in 2010 that the other nuclear forces were enough to support the NATO to carry out their extended nuclear deterrence, and the existing non – strategic weapons were beyond their need. There is great uncertainty about the scale of campaign and tactical nuclear weapons owned by Russia, and the U. S. Department of Defense estimated that there would be about 2000 to 4000 tactical warheads owned by Russia, while it is widely believed that the number is about 2000 and even less, but there are thousands of retired warheads to be removed in the storage of Russia. Russian officials declared twice in 2005 and 2010 that the non – strategic nuclear weapon storage had reduced by 75%. Even though there is no new agreement on reducing the weapons, it was predicted that storage of Russia would be further reduced as the phase – out of old systems in the future 10 years.

Yet, it should be noticed that there is a correlation between the U. S. and Russian tactical nuclear weapon reduction. The two countries have kept a corresponding reduction tendency. The U. S. Congress ratified the *New Strategic Arms Reduction Treaty* in 2010, where they had claimed "the treaty we signed should be a treaty that can narrow the gap between Russian and the U. S. non – strategic (tactical) nuclear weapon storage. And the treaty was supposed to be verifiable and reduce tactical weapons". Meanwhile, NATO had stated in both its Strategic Concept in 2010 and *Defense Situation Assessment* published in 2012 that it is imperative for NATO to take full consideration of Russian weapon storage while reducing its non – strategic nuclear weapons.

Ⅲ. Adjust Force Structure

Countries such as the U. S. and Russia have been reducing their weapon categories and trying to centralize their weapon deployment so as to meet the needs of their own national security environment, enhance nuclear weapon management as well as improve the security of nuclear weapon deployment. By the end of 2011, TU – 22M3, SU – 24 of Russian Navy with thetactical nuclear weapons had been given to Russian Air Force. Russia also planned to remove nuclear attack mission from its main marine platforms. Particularly the Oscar – class submarine and Kirov class cruiser would be armed with SS – N – 26 and SS – N – 27 non – nuclear cruise missile instead of SS – N – 19 nuclear cruise missile. In the *Report of Nuclear Situation Review in 2010* , the United States listed its only marine non – strategic nuclear weapon named "Battleaxe" and Tomahawk land attack nuclear cruise missile, their W80 warheads were already retired. So far, the U. S. has historically accomplished its unilateral action of reducing non – strategic nuclear weapons, which have been lasting for several decades.

Ⅳ. Explore New Functions

The recent years have seen many countries such as the United

States and Russia managed to explore the new functions of their nuclear weapons and positively expanded their deterrent areas. The Obama Administration has envisaged an integral new regional deterrent framework, extension of the nuclear weapon deterrence, forward presence and conventional military capabilities (ballistic missile defense included) . Regional security, along with new capabilities, made it possible to lessen the influence of strategic nuclear weapons on national security strategy. Meanwhile, the U. S. military has recently highlighted the "uniqueness" of its non – strategic nuclear weapons. This was because the dual – missioned airplanes nearly had possed the advantages of all strategic bomber and their deployment would be near to the battlefield, which put additional pressure on enemies, thus would increase nuclear deterrent capability. Meanwhile, the U. S. has played an active role in supporting the invention of deep penetrating tactical nuclear warheads in order to lower the nuclear usage barrier and enhance its deterrent force. However, Russian scholars reckoned that using non – strategic nuclear weapons would probably lead to regional nuclear deterrence. If non – strategic nuclear weapons cannot perform its regional deterrent mission to the full extent, they could be used to give a decisive blow to the enemy as well as prevent the tension from going escalation. "DE – ESCALATION" is a term used in Russian nuclear power utilization of local war, which included the using of strategic nuclear power and tactical nuclear weapons within theaters. "DE – ESCALATION" is to show resolve through practical application of nuclear weapons. "DE – ESCALATION" can be accomplished through the deployment of non – strategic nuclear weapons, which can prevent nuclear weapon application from escalating into a mutual massive attack.

V. Upgrade Tactical Nuclear Weapons

The United States and Russia have insisted on upgrading and reforming the tactical nuclear weapons technology for a long time in order to improve the ability of frontier deterrence. Currently, Obama Administration has been modernizing the existing non – strategic nuclear arsenal. B61 – 4 is one of the three non – strategic types of B61, and the U. S. Armed Forces has been under its " extending life " of this type of nuclear bomb by equipping new type guidance tail units in order to improve the accuracy, thus achieve the same risk control level as B61 – 7 strategic nuclear weapon with maximum explosion of 360, 000 tons. According to the plan, they will add new wing for the B61 nuclear bombs, making it to be guided weapon that can be carried by the F – 35 stealth fighter. Although B61 – 4 has been one of the safest weapons, the latest type B61 – 12 is also equipped with new security features. The B61 – 12 designed primarily for F – 15E, F – 16 and "Tornado" fighters originally, but now has expended to new F – 35 "Lighting" (Joint Strike Fighter) and B – 2 strategic bomber. In the future, only B61 – 12 will carry out both non – strategic and strategic mission. In addition, Russia and France have been also actively improving their tactical nuclear weapons. In November 2014, according to French Defense Ministry, France has began research on the new type of air – launched nuclear missile project, and the new generation of air – launched nuclear missile will be focused on stealth and hyper - sonic technology. The code name of new weapon is ASN4G. It would be the fourth generation ASMP cruise missile project. France will explore the most cutting - edge stealthy technology and hyper - sonic technology, and the project is closely related to the future form of the French Air Force.

VI. Adjust Deployment of the Forces

In recent years, in order to respond to the internal issues of alliances and international issues, the U. S. , Russia and other countries have constantly adjusted the deployment of tactical nuclear weapons to format a positive deterrent posture. Currently, the U. S. has nearly 200 weapons deployed in six bases of NATO Europe (Belgium, Germany, Italy, the Netherlands and Turkey) . In the past ten years, the U. S. tactical nuclear weapons were removed from in Germany and UK; the U. S. Air Force also cut its tactical squadrons in Europe. In late 1990s and the first term of President George W. Bush, the U. S. Air Force retained two tactical nuclear weapon squadrons as the backup of nuclear task in NATO, the Middle East and Northeast Asia, one was the 4th squadron in North Carolina, and the other was the 27th squadron in New Mexico. The F - 15E fighter in the 4th squadron is still considered as aircraft with nuclear capability, but the squadron is no longer primarily responsible for the nuclear mission. The 27th Squadron has been expanded, and replaced by non - nuclear missions 27th Special Operations Squadron. These tactical nuclear troops were aimed at Russia and North Korea and other possible threats. In the situation of tactical nuclear forces in Europe continuously reducing, the local nuclear power against Northeast Asia has been relatively enhanced.

In recent years, Russia has repeatedly expanded the deployment of tactical nuclear troops in European in order to deal with NATO's eastward expansion and deter the U. S. from missile defense system in Eastern Europe. Russia deployed SS – 21 and SS – 26 missiles near Kaliningrad in the west of Europe. The 26th Missile Brigade was first deployed such missile in St Peterburg. The base has transformed the facilities that protect SS – 21 missile according to the needs of SS – 26 missiles, and the two types of missiles wer installed nuclear warheads according to Executive Order signed by Boris Yeltsin, the former President of Russia. Russian officials have repeatedly threatened to use of tactical nuclear weapons against the U. S. plan to deploy a missile defense system in Poland.

Currently, The U. S. and Russian tactical nuclear weapons deployment has become an important means to curb the other side. For example, the U. S. will maintain the size of the deployment of tactical nuclear weapons in Europe, which will be an important means to urge Russia to make some concessions. The foreign ministers of Poland and Sweden strongly support the U. S. to raise the unacceptable demands for Russia: require Russia to withdraw nuclear deployment in the place bordering the newly joined EU countries (Kaliningrad and the Kola Peninsula). NATO leaders also previously raised the same requirement to Russia leaders to withdraw tactical nuclear weapons in bordering places of NATO.

Ⅶ. Improve Delivery Capability

Since the nuclear weapon delivery decides the ability of use, every country will improve the delivery ability forits strategic nuclear weapon, it is the important way of strategic nuclear power development, so that to enhance the nuclear deterrent flexibility. Currently, Russia has been advancing the formation of the "Back – fire" (Tu – 22M3) bombers, the key point is to improve its nuclear compatibility, and install new airborne radio electronic systems, Russia will upgrade 30 Tu – 22M3 fighters to Tu – 22M3M with Kh – 32 cruise missile before 2020. The new generation bomber PAK DA in demonstration will wholly replace Tu – 160, Tu – 95MS and Tu – 22M3. Moreover, the front line bomber Su – 24 has been also taking modernization formation, but these planes will be replaced by Su – 34 finally. Till now, Russia has already begun to deploy Su – 34 in west. The development of sea – based strategic nuclear capability is also very fast. The first nuclear attack submarine is being tested before being put into service, the submarine is equipped with tactical nuclear weapons, including anti – submarine rockets and 8 vertical cruse missile launching tubes. *Purchase Plan of Russian Weapons and Equipment before 2020* shows that Russia will build 10 new submarines. The United States *Report of Nuclear Situation Review* clearly pointed out that The United States would deploy F – 35 joint strike fighters in 2017 – 2018, some of these will have nuclear operation ability, and they will replace F – 15E and F – 16 fighters at last. The

NATO's 3 nuclear mission countries – Italy, Holland and Turkey have planned to get F – 35 joint strike fighter in 15 years. Till now, The United States has begun to improve the nuclear capability of F – 35 Block4.

Ⅷ. Improve and Adjustment Nuclear Facilities

Inorder to keep a high operation readiness level and the potential manufacturing capability, in recent years, countries such as The United States and Russia have attached great importance to keep and improve nuclear facilities for the development and maintenance for nuclear weapons. It was thought that the Russian strategic nuclear weapons to be kept in 12 central storage facilities. Some of them are located in the middle of Russia, the others are located in the Far East, west part of Russia and Kola Peninsula, these locations are closer to the delivery system bases. Duc to the limited life of warhead, continuous production will be necessary. In 2002, Russia began to reform the original 4 nuclear warhead production facilities according to the assistance plan of "Reforming the Nuclear Industry Enterprises 2002 – 2006" . Currently, the production of new warheads is concentrated in 4 assembly and disassembly enterprises. The production enterprises of the new nuclear warheads are in Electronic Chemical Instrument Factory, which is located in Lesnoy City and the Instrument Manufacture Factory.

In order to ensure the improvement of B – 61 strategic nuclear warhead, from 2013 – 2014, The United Stateshas modernized the manufacture factory (located in Kansas City) of the non – nuclear parts of the nuclear weapon. Such improvement and adjustment would effectively improve the production and maintenance ability for the strategic nuclear weapon.